⟨ **W9-ADV-577**

## OTHER BOOKS BY JAIME O'NEILL

*What Do You Know?*

*What Do You Know?, Volume II*

*The Ultimate Test of TV Trivia*

# Jaime O'Neill

Illustrations by

Kelly O'Neill

# WE'RE HISTORY!

The 20th Century Survivor's
Final Exam

A FIRESIDE BOOK
Published by Simon & Schuster

FIRESIDE
Rockefeller Center
1230 Avenue of the Americas
New York, NY 10020

FIRESIDE and colophon are registered trademarks
of Simon & Schuster Inc.

Designed by Katy Riegel

Manufactured in the United States of America

1   3   5   7   9   10   8   6   4   2

Library of Congress Cataloging-in-Publication Data
O'Neill, Jaime.
We're history! : the 20th century survivor's final exam /
Jaime O'Neill ; illustrations by Kelly O'Neill.
        p.        cm.
"A Fireside book."
Includes index.
1. Twentieth century—Miscellanea.    I. Title.
CB425.053    1998
909.82—dc21       98-6512
CIP
ISBN 0-684-82922-3

All photographs courtesy of Corbis-Bettmann

# ACKNOWLEDGMENTS

With appreciation and love to Karen.
With gratitude to Mom and Dad.
With love to Sionann and Kelly.
With high hopes for Jim and Carolyn.
With thanks to Becky Cabaza, Dan Lane, and Sean Devlin.

This book is dedicated to Steve Scheinman.
Though I've searched and
researched the twentieth century,
I've yet to find a better friend.

# Contents

The poetry of history lies in the quasi-miraculous fact that once, on this earth, on this familiar spot of earth walked other men and women as actual as we are today, thinking their own thoughts, swayed by their own passions but now all gone, vanishing one after another, gone as utterly as we ourselves shall be gone, like ghosts at cockcrow.

G. M. Trevelyan, historian, 1991

# WE'RE HISTORY!

# Introduction: From Geronimo to Larry King Live

*A memory is what is left when something happens
and does not completely unhappen.*

—*EDWARD DE BONO*

A century ends, and with it, a millennium. The French phrase *fin de siècle* means "end of the century," but until lately the phrase has been most often associated with the end of the nineteenth century. Now the phrase applies to us. The Twentieth Century Limited is pulling into the station.

We're history. Whether we helped make it or just observed its passage, we're history. History is what we're made of, from the death of Queen Victoria to the death of Princess Diana. From the Wright Brothers at Kitty Hawk to the launch of the space station *Mir*, we're history. From the advent of aspirin in the century's first decade to the promiscuous use of Prozac in its last, we're history. From ragtime to reggae, from folk to fusion, from bebop to hip hop, from Caruso to Pavarotti, and from fox trots to mosh pits, we're history. From buggy whips to Beamers, from J. P. Morgan to Microsoft, from V-Mail to E-Mail, from party lines to cell phones, from Wonder Bread to Wonder Bras, and from Geronimo to *Larry King Live*, we're history.

Do you doubt it? Return, then, to the first decade of the twentieth century and follow the thread. Take a moment to visit some people and times that have not unhappened yet.

It is the first decade of the century. There are approximately 79 million people living in the United States. In 1907, Geronimo, the last Apache war leader, is granted permission to leave his reservation in the new state of Oklahoma to travel to Texas for a celebration with the Comanche chief known as Quanah Parker. While there, Geronimo gets drunk and takes off for Mexico. He is gone for several hours, making his way south on a government horse. When rounded up by soldiers from nearby Fort Sill, he tells them that his eighth wife has left him. According to the newspaper account of the incident, Geronimo complains that his domestic affairs have grown "irksome."

He is, in this year, seventy-eight years old. He will be dead in another sixteen months. Two years earlier, just five years into the new century, he had ridden down Pennsylvania Avenue in Theodore Roosevelt's inaugural parade. The year before that, in 1904, he rode a Ferris Wheel and sold autographs at the World's Fair in St. Louis.

Follow the thread forward through time to World War II. Theodore Roosevelt's niece, Eleanor Roosevelt, is the wife of the president of the United States. Paratroopers leap into battle from airplanes over European countrysides shouting Geronimo's name. On the other side of the globe, Geronimo's ancestral enemies, the Navajo, lend a hand in winning the war in the Pacific. Radioing vital information in the Navajo language, they provide a secure link in military communications. The year the war ends, the Chicago Cubs lose the World Series to the Detroit Tigers. The population of the United States has nearly doubled since the century began. Life expectancy has increased from forty-seven years to sixty-eight years. The number of states has grown from forty-five to forty-eight.

Follow the thread forward in time to 1962. Chuck Connors, former first baseman for the Chicago Cubs, portrays Geronimo

\* \* \*

In 1904, at the St. Louis World's Fair, Geronimo sold copies of his photograph to fairgoers for twenty-five cents each. He sold his autograph for a like amount.

As the century drew to a close, Geronimo's image was emblazoned on T-shirts available for purchase through a site on the World Wide Web for $18.95.

in a motion picture. This is not the first motion picture to bear Geronimo's name in its title. One such movie, made in 1936, featured a poster that read "ten thousand red raiders roar into battle." In reality, Geronimo never led more than a few hundred men. When he last surrendered, there were fewer than thirty in his band.

Follow the weave to Alcatraz in the late 1960s. The American Indian Movement has taken over the former federal prison in San Francisco Bay. "THIS IS INDIAN LAND" the banners read. The group of Indians occupy the prison for months before being forced off by federal marshals. Pictures of Geronimo can be seen in the background when the leaders hold televised press conferences. A few years later, in the early 1970s, a song called "Geronimo's Cadillac" is a minor hit for singer Michael Murphy.

Trace the thread another few years to the set of *Cheers*, television's most popular sitcom, where a portrait of Geronimo adorns the bar seen by tens of millions of viewers each week. In most quarters American Indians are known by now as Native Americans or Indigenous Peoples.

Come, then, to the final decade of the twentieth century. The U.S. population has tripled since Geronimo rode down Pennsylvania Avenue. Life expectancy has climbed to seventy-six years. Two movies about the Apache warrior are made and marketed, one to theaters, one for Turner Television. Geronimo is played by Native Americans in both of these productions, though neither actor is an Apache, nor does Geronimo

drink alcohol in these movies. Ted Turner, CEO of Turner Television, also owns the Atlanta Braves baseball team, which has been the target of criticism over the "tomahawk chop," a trademark cheer used by fans of that team. Native Americans insist that the cheer perpetuates negative stereotypes.

Fifty years after the death of Franklin D. Roosevelt, famed television interviewer Larry King, a Turner employee, interviews actor Marlon Brando before a huge international television audience broadcast to remote corners of the globe by satellites in space. To protest the depiction of American Indians in films, Brando had declined to accept his second Academy Award for best actor in 1972. Instead, he sent a woman, who called herself Sacheen Littlefeather, to read his statement refusing the award. Littlefeather claimed an Apache heritage. This later proves to be untrue.

As the century comes to an end, Geronimo moulders on the cyberspace reservation. Schoolchildren can call him back to life on CD-ROM. Those who seek him on the Internet find information for skydivers and advertisements for T-shirts bearing his likeness. He has not unhappened yet.

The fabric of the twentieth century is woven of many threads. Some threads are thin and indistinct; others are strong and easy to see. Together, these threads weave the tapestry that is our history over the last 100 years. These are the things that fired our imaginations, stirred our dreams, fueled our fears, occupied our minds, and directed our affairs.

You survived the century, but can you pass the test at the end of the century? How will you do on the fin de siècle final exam? The question-and-answer format of much of this book is a way of calling some of our shared history to mind, of coaxing the memory to yield back some of what we read, heard on the radio, saw on television, or experienced firsthand.

If you're an American old enough to read this book it's probable that you know the name of President Clinton's cat, President Roosevelt's dog, and Jerry Seinfeld's neighbor across the hall. You also might know Larry Melman's nickname, Harry Truman's middle initial, and what was missing from Barbara Eden's middle. Warren G. Harding was our twenty-ninth president; do you know what the G. stood for? More obscurely, do you know the silent screen siren whose name was said to be an anagram for "Arab Death"? If you don't know that, you probably do know young Bob Dylan's most famous girlfriend, and you might remember Lana Turner's murdered boyfriend. You know the name of Theodore Roosevelt's obstreperous daughter, don't you? And if you think about it a moment, you'll recall Dr. Kevorkian's press-bestowed nickname, and Leona Helmsley's, too.

You may remember what happened when Fibber McGee opened his closet, or what kind of car Jack Benny drove. You may also recall who was dubbed "the King of Jazz" and who was known as the "Vagabond Lover." Surely you remember who was referred to as "the Shiek," and you probably know that the Cord was a car and a blind pig was a place to get an illegal drink. The things we know, the ghosts that linger, are the things that haven't completely unhappened yet.

Do you remember Nullo? Spoolies? Dippity Doo? Does the name Ruby Begonia mean anything to you? What was Poof! During what decade did we first hear the phrase *cinema verité?* Do you know the difference between a wonk and a wanker? When were dashikis in vogue, and what were they? What did DMZ stand for, and when would most people have known that? What was a Stutz Bearcat? And what was the Lambeth Walk? How did a person gain admission to the Mile High Club? What was a fag hag? Did you ever hear of Ricky Ticky Stickies? Was strontium 90 a good thing or a bad thing? What about a Jarvik-7? Where was Checkpoint Charlie? What was a church key? What gargantuan engineering feat was nearly thwarted because of mosquitoes?

Remember paraquat? Plaster casters? Angel dust? Do you know the difference between a mood ring, an O-ring, and a cock ring? Ever hear of "kitchen sink" dramas? Cuisine Minceur? Tuck and roll? Dan Patch is still a piece of American folklore; who or what was Dan Patch?

Do you know what sampling was? Poodle skirts and fender skirts? Surely you know what "melts in your mouth, not in your hand." And you remember what a fuzz buster was, don't you?

What did Willis Carrier do in 1902 that would profoundly change the way people live? What president's wife served as a de facto president while her husband was gravely ill? And what president's wife hated Washington and the White House so much that she spent most of her husband's term in office at their home in Missouri?

Where was Stonewall, and what happened there? Is your memory long enough to recall whether Thalidomide was a good thing or a bad thing? What brand of cigarettes extolled its micronite filter? In what war would you have encountered puttees, and what were they, anyway? (If you didn't know the answer to all these questions, you can find them at the end of this introduction.)

Questions such as these (and the two thousand others you will find in this book) are meant to entice bits of our century back. They tease the past into making a visit to the present. In this way, we keep the past from unhappening.

We are the living history, those of us who have survived, who lived through it all to greet the dawn of a new century and a new millennium. When we are gone, some of what we have known will be gone with us. Before that happens, while we are here and the times of our lives are still fresh in our minds, I invite you to take a final exam, a look backward at the history we saw, the history we made, the history we are.

## ANSWERS TO QUESTIONS IN THE INTRODUCTION:

For those who wish to refresh their memories before beginning with the questions ahead, Clinton's cat was Socks, Roosevelt's dog was Falla, Seinfeld's neighbor was Kramer, Melman's nickname was Bud, Truman's middle initial was S, and Barbara Eden was missing a belly button due to network censors. Harding's middle name was Gamaliel, and it was Theda Bara who was said to have scrambled the words *Arab Death* to make her screen name. Dylan's most famous girlfriend was Joan Baez and Lana Turner's murdered boyfriend was named Johnny Stompanato. Teddy Roosevelt's obstreperous daughter was Alice, and Kevorkian's nickname, in the event you don't know, can be found in the questions to come. Leona Helmsley was dubbed "the Queen of Mean."

On radio, the contents of Fibber McGee's overstuffed closet always crashed down on him every time he opened the door. Benny drove a Maxwell. The "King of Jazz" and the "Vagabond Lover" can be found in chapter 11. "The Shiek" can also be found in the questions and answers ahead.

Nullo was a chlorophyll-based pill marketed in the 1940s as a deodorant. Poof! was an antiperspirant. The French gave us the phrase *cinema verité* in the 1950s. A wonk is a person who gets too minutely involved with policy matters and, in British slang, a wanker is one who is rather excessively involved with himself. Dashikis were blouse-like garments especially popular among African-Americans in the late '60s. DMZ stood for Demilitarized Zone during the Vietnam War. A Stutz Bearcat was a luxury car, introduced in 1914. The Lambeth Walk was the most popular dance of 1938. The Mile High Club was a term for people who engaged in sex while on commercial airline flights. *Fag hag* was a slang term for a woman who enjoyed the company of male homosexuals, and Ricky Ticky Stickies were those decorative appliques on baby bassinets and bathtubs during the Day-Glo '60s. Strontium 90 was a bad thing, present in radioactive fallout, and in our milk during the period of open-air nuclear testing. The Jarvik-7 was an early artificial heart, and Checkpoint Charlie was the border between East and West Berlin during the Cold War. A church key used to be street parlance for a beer-can opener. Work on the Panama Canal was nearly halted because mosquitoes were so thick, and so many workers were stricken with yellow fever.

Paraquat was a chemical defoliant sprayed on marijuana patches at home and abroad. Plaster casters can be found in chapter 9. Angel dust was also known as PCP, a drug that often incited violent behavior. Mood rings were supposed to change colors with your moods, and they were popular in the 1970s; defective O-rings led to the *Challenger* space shuttle explosion; and cock rings were marketed to men who were concerned about the duration of sexual activity.

Kitchen sink dramas were gritty proletarian plays by British Angry Young Men in the 1950s. Cuisine Minceur was a colorful cuisine of small portions and low calories that followed Nouvelle Cuisine as a food fad in the late 1970s. Tuck and roll was '50s customized auto upholstery, usually made of Naugahyde. In the first years of the century, Dan Patch was a record-setting horse in the history of harness racing. Sampling was the '80s and '90s practice of integrating snatches of old songs with new ones. Poodle skirts were a '50s fashion of round skirts with poodles on them (Laverne and Shirley both wore them). Fender skirts covered the wheel wells on customized '50s cars. M&Ms were the candy that "melts in your mouth, not in your hand." And a fuzz buster was a radar detection device first marketed in the '70s to outfox highway patrol officers.

Carrier invented air conditioning. It was Woodrow Wilson's wife, Edith, who took up his duties when he was very sick, and it was Truman's wife, Bess, who spent most of his administration back in Missouri with her mother.

The Stonewall Inn was a New York nightclub, the site of a spontaneous gay uprising in 1969. Thalidomide was a tranquilizer that caused birth defects in the early '60s. Kent cigarettes had a micronite filter and puttees were below-the-knee leg wrappings worn by soldiers in World War I.

I hope these questions and answers have whetted your appetite for those ahead.

# 1

# Educated Guesses

*My memory is the thing I forget with.*

—*A CHILD'S DEFINITION*

We are always proceeding with inadequate information. We peer ahead into the future apprehensively or optimistically; we look to the past and know only a fraction of what happened then. We look into the face of another and try to read the hidden heart. For that matter, our own hearts keep secrets from us. We invest in the stock market without access to volumes of information about things that might determine the success or failure of our stock picks. Past, present, and future, we are always groping around in semidarkness. What we know is a small boat in a vast ocean of ignorance.

We keep that boat from getting swamped by bailing, and that bailing takes the form of guessing. We put together the things we know with the things that seem logical or likely, and we keep our boats afloat in the choppy seas of ignorance. We guess. We surmise. We project. We extrapolate. We live by our wits, mixing what we know with what we don't know to keep our boats afloat.

And sometimes our ignorance sinks us. When Mira Sorvino won an Academy Award for best supporting actress in Woody Allen's film *Mighty Aphrodite*, a back-stage reporter asked her if it wasn't "difficult to play Aphrodite when you're not an African-American." Ms. Sorvino replied that it wasn't much of an issue since Aphrodite was a Greek goddess.

Now a reporter who confuses Aphrodite with Afro-Americans is bailing a pretty leaky boat, but we've all felt swamped by the inadequacy of our knowledge and the volumes of information it seems we are required to know.

College taught us to fake it with our best guesses. If you're a college grad, you took hundreds of multiple-choice tests, often surprising yourself with how well you did. We can get lucky with our guesses, and we can combine what we know with our common sense and make more knowledge out of that. Professors like multiple-choice tests because they can be graded by a machine in the blink of an eye, and the results often obscure how little students are learning. Students like the tests because they can hide some of what they don't know in those little boxes filled with the lead from a number-2 pencil.

This first chapter is a multiple-choice test. In each question, some of the choices are fairly absurd, and therefore easily eliminated. But in matters of the twentieth century, eliminating the absurd doesn't always work. There was much absurdity in the history we made and witnessed.

In college, we called tests like this one "multiple-guess" tests. But the process of sorting out the wrong answers helped us remember what we knew. So go ahead and guess. Since scores here don't count against our futures, since promotion isn't based on how well we do, the only objective in enter-

taining these questions is, in fact, being entertained by these questions.

Take your best guesses, and find out how much of the last 100 years is still a part of you.

## EDUCATED GUESSES

*Degree of difficulty: 5 (on a 10-point scale, with 10 being the highest degree of difficulty and 1 the lowest; throughout this book, you'll find similar scales of difficulty)*

1. In 1917, the AEF was:

a. the Antarctica Explorers Foundation

b. the Amazon Environmental Front

c. the American Expeditionary Force

d. the American Economist Federation

2. In 1990s slang, a Baldwin was:

a. a woman's breast (singular)

b. a computer hacker

c. a sexy man

d. a bureaucratic foul-up

3. In the 1940s, the Manhattan Project was:

a. the multibillion-dollar New York subway expansion

b. a group of jazz vocalists led by Peggy Lee

c. a study of police corruption

d. the effort to build the first nuclear weapons

## 4. A Mannlicher-Carrcano was:

a. a World War II–era fighter plane

b. the kind of rifle said to have killed President Kennedy

c. the make of car owned by Al Capone

## 5. Ganja is:

a. a river in India

b. the Rastafarian name for marijuana

c. slang for the interest paid to a loan shark

## 6. When Hell's Angels wear a patch with the number 13 on it, the number represents:

a. their bad luck with law enforcement officials

b. the letter M, for marijuana

c. the number of people in attendance at the Last Supper

## 7. "Kid" Ory was:

a. a legendary jazz pioneer

b. a notorious bank robber of the 1930s

c. one of the most popular child actors of the 1920s

d. the highest-paid tennis player of the 1940s

## 8. Be-Bop-a-Lula was:

a. a famous jazz groupie of the 1940s

b. a potent Prohibition cocktail made with bathtub gin

c. an early rock 'n' roll song by Gene Vincent

d. the nickname of the first A-bomb tested in New Mexico

## 9. Teapot Dome was:

a. a multimedia thrill ride at Disney's Epcot Center

b. a corruption scandal of the Harding administration

c. a campy '70s tea cozy marketed on television by Ronco

d. The Secret Service code name for First Lady Betty Ford

## 10. The Rainbow Coalition was:

a. a funk group of the 1970s

b. a political organization led by Jesse Jackson

c. the informal name for the First Marine Division in World War II

d. a Public Broadcasting System project to teach children to read

## 11. "The Man With a Thousand Faces" was:

a. Lon Chaney

b. Richard Nixon

c. Jim Carrey

d. Orson Welles

## 12. The precursor to the United Nations was:

a. the League of Nations

b. the Federation of Countries

c. One World Together

d. the Rainbow Coalition

## 13. In the '40s and '50s, it was called "the dozens." The 1990s variant was called "Snaps." It was:

a. a cookie-eating contest at midwestern state fairs

b. a military punishment involving beating with wet towels

c. a streetcorner exchange of clever insults

d. the fastenings on cowboy shirts

## 14. "The Saturday Night Massacre" occurred when:

a. Nixon fired his attorney general and deputy attorney general when they both refused to fire the Watergate special prosecutor

b. Hutus engaged in mass killings of Tutsis in Rwanda on Saturday, May 17, 1994

c. Al Capone's enemies struck back in retaliation for the St. Valentine's Day Massacre, 1929

## 15. The Schutzstaffel was:

a. a dessert torte popular in the 1950s

b. a dance popular with Swiss immigrants in the first decade of the century

c. a hybrid variant of the Dachshund

d. Hitler's SS

## 16. Ruby Ridge was:

a. a popular '70s song by Kenny Rogers

b. the site of a bungled U.S. government raid in the 1990s

c. a bloody battle of the Korean War

## 17. Yigal Amir was:

a. a virtuoso violinist in the 1920s

b. the sultan of Brunei

c. the assassin of Yitzhak Rabin

d. Kirk Douglas's real name

## 18. The DEW Line was:

a. a stalled World War II battlefront, known to the English as the "Dare England Win?" Line

b. established by a radical '60s environmental group: the "Die for Environmental Wellbeing Line"

c. a Cold War nuclear defense designation: the Distant Early Warning Line

d. talk show producers' jargon for the line they reserve for stupid callers: the Dimwits, Egomaniacs, and Weenies Line

## 19. a Kaiser-Frazier was:

a. a make of automobile

b. the kaiser's psychiatrist

c. a brand of tennis racket

d. a poppyseed pastry

## 20. "For Every Boy Who's on the Level/There's a Girl Who's on the Square" was:

a. the first published poem by Robert Frost

b. a song hit of 1920

c. a popular carpenter's bumper sticker of the 1950s

d. a secret code phrase in the 1940s French underground movement

## 21. The Pachanga was:

a. a Latin dance fad of the late '50s and early '60s

b. a species of carnivorous tropical fish banned from importation into the U.S.

c. a Mexican-American gang, based in Los Angeles

d. a Chevrolet customized for low riding

## 22. In the 1970s, SLA stood for:

a. Save Los Angeles, an antigrowth activist organization

b. Serve Lowenbrau Ale, an advertising campaign

c. Servants of Lhasa Apsos, a dog-breeding club

d. Symbionese Liberation Army, the group that kidnapped Patty Hearst

## 23. A pipe and a Pepsi are together associated with:

a. Chevy Chase

b. Gerald Ford

c. Hugh Hefner

d. Joan Crawford

## 24. "Squeeze Me," "Honeysuckle Rose," and "Ain't Misbehavin' " are all songs written by:

a. Sid Vicious

b. Willie Nelson

c. Cole Porter

d. Fats Waller

## 25. At John Kennedy's inaugural, he said "Ask not . . .

a. why we go to Vietnam"

b. what you can do for your country"

c. what your country can do for you"

d. why taxes are so high"

e. for whom the bell tolls"

## 26. Holly Golightly was:

a. the first chairperson of ACT-UP, the militant gay rights group

b. the first editor of *Cosmopolitan*

c. a character in a novel by Truman Capote

d. a solar system discovered by the Hubble Spacecraft in 1995

## 27. Dittoheads were:

a. office workers who ran copying machines

b. '60s people who got high on the solution used in mimeograph machines

c. what fans called the characters in *Archie* comic books

d. people who agreed with anything Rush Limbaugh said

## 28. The Dorothy Chandler Pavilion was:

a. where the Academy Awards presentation took place

b. where Howard Hughes is buried

c. in the Land of Oz

d. a building blown up in Oklahoma City

### 29. Josef Mengele was:

a. a Nazi monster

b. a celebrated conductor of the Leipzig Philharmonic

c. the man who found the cure for yellow fever

d. the most famous B-movie villain of the 1950s

### 30. In the 1980s, Mariel Harbor was famous as:

a. an ecdysiast

b. the place where presidential candidate Gary Hart got caught with a woman not his wife

c. the harbor in Key West, Florida, Ernest Hemingway named after his granddaughter

d. the place Cuban refugees departed from

e. World Wrestling Federation's top woman wrestler

### 31. Moms Mabley was:

a. the founder of Mothers Against Drunk Drivers (MADD)

b. a pioneering black stand-up comedienne

c. a legendary jazz vocalist

d. the first woman to swim the English Channel

### 32. In the 1970s, the Pentagon Papers were released to the press by Daniel Ellsberg. Those papers were about:

a. the U.S. military's development of nerve gas

b. waste in military procurement programs

c. the training of assassination squads

d. the failures of U.S. Indochina policy

### 33. In the 1980s, the Brat Pack was:

a. the media phrase for the century's second baby boom

b. a group of women lobbying for government-subsidized day-care centers

c. a group of young up-and-coming movie actors

d. slang term for disposable diapers

### 34. In the 1930s, the Brain Trust was:

a. a group of advisors who helped Roosevelt plan the New Deal

b. the name of the band that later became the Grateful Dead

c. the media name for Alan Greenspan and the Federal Reserve

d. the name producers used for contestants on *Jeopardy*

### 35. Of the following choices, Imelda Marcos is best remembered for:

a. her commitment to social justice

b. her exquisite sense of taste

c. her Saturday morning children's show on PBS

d. her three thousand pairs of shoes

### 36. The Pedernales River is associated with:

a. the Johnstown flood

b. the Los Angeles water system

c. Lyndon Johnson

d. the Tennessee Valley Authority

**37. Egon Schiele was:**

a. a painter

b. a poet

c. a pauper

d. a pawn

e. a king

**38. The guy who played Sam in the classic film *Casablanca* was:**

a. Woody Allen

b. Stepin Fetchit

c. Woody Strode

d. Dewey Redman

e. Dooley Wilson

**39. In South Africa, ANC stood for:**

a. the Apartheid Now Confederation

b. the All Negro Country party

c. the Afrikaaners Never Concede party

d. the African National Congress

**40. Of the following women, which one was not romantically linked with Woody Allen?**

a. Soon-Yi Previn

b. Louise Lasser

c. Glenn Close

d. Diane Keaton

**41. Of the following, which phrase is not attributable to Winston Churchill?**

a. "Iron Curtain"

b. "A fanatic is one who can't change his mind and won't change the subject"

c. "Blood, sweat, toil, and tears"

d. "Never have so many owed so much to so few"

e. "This royal throne of kings, this sceptred isle . . . This blessed plot, this earth, this realm, this England"

**42. Of the following, which is not a book by William Styron?**

a. *Prince of Tides*

b. *A Tidewater Memory*

c. *The Long March*

d. *The Confessions of Nat Turner*

**43. Of the following, which was not a hit song of the World War II era?**

a. "I'll Be Seeing You," by Jo Stafford

b. "K'K'K' Katy," by Geoffrey O'Hara

c. "You'd Be So Nice to Come Home To," by Dinah Shore

d. "The White Cliffs of Dover," by Vera Lynn

e. "It's Been a Long, Long Time," by Harry James with Kitty Kalen

**44.** Of the following, which two were not hits songs made popular by rock pioneers Bill Haley and the Comets?

a. "At the Hop"

b. "Shake, Rattle and Roll"

c. "Rock Around the Clock"

d. "Rock the Joint"

e. "Jailhouse Rock"

f. "Crazy Man Crazy"

**45.** "Desert Storm" was:

a. a classic Rudolph Valentino film

b. a Taco Bell ad campaign

c. T. E. Lawrence's campaign for Arab Unity

d. the operation to drive Iraq out of Kuwait

**46.** Of the following, which was not directed by John Ford?

a. John Wayne in *Stagecoach*

b. John Wayne in *The Searchers*

c. John Wayne in *The Quiet Man*

d. John Wayne in *She Wore a Yellow Ribbon*

e. John Wayne in *The Cowboys*

f. John Wayne in *The Man Who Shot Liberty Valance*

**47.** Of the following, which name is associated with George Bush's presidential campaign against Michael Dukakis?

a. Willie Loman

b. Willie Horton

c. Willie Nelson

d. Willie Shoemaker

e. Willie "the Lion" Smith

**48.** "Il Duce" was the Italian appellation for Mussolini. It means:

a. the deuce

b. the leader

c. the sweet

d. the duck

e. the great

f. the dominant

**49.** Anita Bryant became a controversial figure of the 1970s when she:

a. revealed that she had had a sex change operation

b. admitted that she was allergic to orange juice

c. spoke out against homosexuals

d. abandoned her children to run off with a fundamentalist preacher

**50.** World War I General John Pershing was known as "Black Jack" because:

a. he had a large birthmark on the side of his face

b. he had once commanded an all-black unit

c. as a cadet at West Point, he had once lost his horse in a legendary game of blackjack

d. he always wore a black armband out of respect to the men who died under his command

## 51. Reginald Denny was:

a. the founder of the Denny's chain of restaurants

b. the man who succeeded Churchill as British prime minister

c. the truck driver viciously beaten on videotape in the aftermath of the Rodney King verdict

d. David Niven's real name

## 52. Blues giant Muddy Waters's real name was:

a. Reginald Dwight

b. McKinley Morganfield

c. Chauncey Depew

d. Elmore James

e. Huddy Ledbetter

f. Sterling Wainwright III

## 53. The person who designed the special brassiere worn by Jane Russell in *The Outlaw* was:

a. Edith Head

b. Howard Hughes

c. Buckminster Fuller

d. Mae West

e. Hugh Hefner

f. Werner Von Braun

## 54. Cocaine was legal in the U.S. until:

a. the drug was massively overused in the 1970s

b. the surgeon general ruled it unhealthful in 1951

c. after its addictive properties became known, in 1914

. . . or . . .

d. cocaine was never legal in the U.S.

## 55. Kristallnacht was:

a. the pattern of White House china chosen by Nancy Reagan

b. What the press called the night in 1974 when Richard Nixon fired his attorney general

c. a biwinged German fighter plane of World War I

d. a night of violence against Jews in 1930s Germany

## 56. "My Sweet Little Alice Blue Gown" was a song written for:

a. Jackie Gleason's TV wife

b. Theodore Roosevelt's daughter

c. the film *Alice Doesn't Live Here Anymore*

d. Disney's version of *Alice in Wonderland*

e. Grace Kelly's wedding to Prince Rainier

## 57. When Richard Nixon invited Johnny Cash to sing at the White House in 1972, he specifically requested that Cash sing:

a. "Okie from Muskogee" and "Welfare Cadillac"

b. "I Walk the Line" and "A Boy Named Sue"

c. "Folsom Prison Blues" and "The Ballad of Ira Hayes"

## 58. When a Washington, D.C., columnist was critical of a musical performance given by Harry Truman's daughter, Truman threatened to:

a. have the writer fired

b. exclude the writer from White House press conferences

c. punch the writer

d. have the writer drafted

e. order an audit of the writer's taxes

## 59. Of the following artists, which did not record for Sun Records, in Memphis, Tennessee?

a. Carl Perkins

b. Elvis Presley

c. Johnny Cash

d. Jerry Lee Lewis

e. Buddy Holly

## 60. Mark Spitz was the focus of news in 1972 because:

a. he gave information to *Washington Post* reporters Woodward and Bernstein that cracked the Watergate story

b. he was the first openly gay Supreme Court nominee

c. he won seven gold medals in the '72 Olympic Games

d. he became the highest-paid male model in history

## 61. "Your mission, Jim, should you decide to accept it . . ." These were among the opening words of *Mission Impossible*. Jim's last name was:

a. Bush

b. Moriarity

c. Kelly

d. Phelps

e. Graves

## 62. The Macarena was a brief fad in the 1990s. It was:

a. a low-fat cookie

b. a youth-oriented hotel in the Bahamas

c. a Brazilian dance

d. a brand of cognac sipped with cigars

## 63. Of the following, which was not one of Franklin Roosevelt's vice-presidents?

a. Wendell Willkie

b. John Nance Garner

c. Henry Wallace

d. Harry S. Truman

## 64. The "Back to Africa" movement of the 1920s was led by:

a. the Ku Klux Klan

b. Booker T. Washington

c. Calvin Coolidge

d. Marcus Garvey

e. W. E. B. Du Bois

## 65. The most celebrated American war hero of World War I was:

a. Sergeant Bilko

b. Private Eddie Slovik

c. Sergeant Preston

d. Sergeant York

66. Gabriel Garcia Marquez was the foremost writer associated with the literary genre known as:

a. Dadaism

b. Surrealism

c. Minimalism

d. Industrial Realism

e. Revolutionary Idealism

f. Magic Realism

67. In the original *King Kong*, the heroine is played by:

a. Terry Moore

b. Fay Wray

c. Frances Farmer

d. Aldo Ray

e. Constance Bennett

68. The Senate Watergate hearings were chaired by:

a. Senator Sam Ervin

b. Senator Strom Thurmond

c. Senator Jessie Helms

d. Senator John Tower

e. Senator Richard Lugar

69. Nadine Gordimer, Alan Paton, and Athol Fugard were:

a. South African literary figures

b. better known as Peter, Paul, and Mary

c. the designers of the Vietnam War Memorial

d. members of the Manson family

70. The D in D-Day stands for:

a. demolition

b. demarcation

c. defenestration

e. day

71. The VE in VE Day stands for:

a. Vox Exultant

b. Victorious England

c. Victory in Europe

d. Vivisectionists Elated

72. The guy who founded Wal-Mart was:

a. Ray Kroc

b. Steve Jobs

c. Bill Walton

d. Walter Reuther

e. Sam Walton

f. Richard Walgreen

73. "Babe" Ruth's real name was:

a. Henry Hopkins Ruth

b. George Herman Ruth

c. Harold Arlen Ruth

d. Harcourt Brace Ruth

e. Baby Boy Ruth

74. The famous "Kitchen Debate":

a. took place in the '50s between Richard Nixon and Nikita Khrushchev

b. took place in the '70s between Bella Abzug and Phyllis Schlafly

c. took place in the '30s between Fred Allen and Jack Benny

d. took place in the '60s between Norman Mailer and his wife

## 75. Of the following, which was not a Paul Simon album?

a. *Graceland*

b. *One-Trick Pony*

c. *Hearts and Bones*

d. *Artless in Manhattan*

e. *Rhythm of the Saints*

## 76. Of the following, which two were not members of the Algonquin Round Table literary circle of the 1920s and '30s?

a. Langston Hughes

b. Dorothy Parker

c. Harpo Marx

d. Robert Benchley

e. Alexander Woollcott

f. Alice B. Toklas

## 77. The '60s musical group the Doors took their name from a book by Aldous Huxley called:

a. *The Doors of Heaven*

b. *The Doors to Doomsday*

c. *The Doors of Perception*

d. *The Doors to the Men's Room*

## 78. Trudeau, Larson, Schultz, Feiffer, and Crumb were:

a. artists collectively known as "the Ash Can school"

b. all indicted in the Savings and Loan scandal

c. cartoonists of the second half of the century

d. the law firm Teddy Roosevelt used to break monopolies

## 79. "Son of Sam" killer David Berkowitz said he killed because:

a. he was a disgruntled postal worker

b. his dog told him to

c. he got messages from a UFO

d. he ate too much junk food

e. the Mets couldn't seem to win a ballgame

## 80. The first black woman ever to be depicted on a U.S. postage stamp (in 1978) was:

a. Rosa Parks

b. Bessie Smith

c. Shirley Chisholm

d. Aretha Franklin

e. Harriet Tubman

f. Mahalia Jackson

## 81. Solidarnosc was:

a. a Greek resistance movement in World War II

b. a Polish labor union

c. a Dutch passenger ship sunk by U-boats in World War I

d. a cosmetic surgery procedure

e. a Russian automobile

## 82. The Great White Hope was:

a. Louisiana political aspirant David Duke

b. heavyweight boxer Jim Jeffries

c. an advertising slogan for Tide detergent

d. Ford Motor Company's decision to market its Model T line with an optional white paint job

## 83. The "Feel Like I'm Fixin' to Die Rag" was sung at Woodstock by:

a. the Lovin' Spoonful

b. Arlo Guthrie

c. Strawberry Alarm Clock

d. Country Joe and the Fish

e. Eric Burdon and the Animals

f. Hootie and the Blowfish

## 84. *Triumph of the Will* was:

a. political pundit George Will's autobiography

b. a best-selling book on negotiation by Henry Kissinger

c. a Nazi propaganda film by Leni Riefenstahl

d. the name of the first plane flown across the Atlantic

e. a book on business by Donald Trump

## 85. Olestra was:

a. a model of automobile, the Buick Olestra

b. an experimental opera by John Cage

c. an artificial fat

d. an Ethiopian fashion model

## 86. Kareem Abdul-Jabbar was a '70s basketball great whose original name was:

a. Leonard Abdul-Jabbar

b. Lew Alcindor

c. Lawrence Kareem

d. A. C. Cowlings

e. Mongo Santamaria

f. Cassius Clay

## 87. The '70s disco group the Village People featured all but which one of the following:

a. a policeman

b. an Indian chief

c. a cowboy

d. a Scout leader

e. a soldier

f. a construction worker

## 88. The Taft-Hartley Act of 1947 was landmark legislation in the field of:

a. labor

b. women's rights

c. environmental law

d. press restrictions

e. pornography

## 89. Of the following, which was not a notorious flop?

a. *Heaven's Gate*

b. *Hudson Hawk*

c. the Edsel

d. *Mousetrap*

e. *Cleopatra*

f. *The Last Action Hero*

## 90. Poet Sylvia Plath was married to poet:

a. Robert Bly

b. James Dickey

c. Rod McKuen

d. Ted Hughes

e. Allen Ginsberg

f. Edgar Plath

## 91. Which one of the following was not the last name of a recurring character on TV's *Seinfeld*?

a. Costanza

b. Benis

c. Kramer

d. Newman

e. Schindler

f. Seinfeld

## 92. The "chitlin' circuit" was a name for:

a. gourmet restaurants of New Orleans

b. southern honky-tonks that regularly employed blues musicians

c. digestive problems experienced after eating bad soul food

d. a stock car racetrack in North Carolina

## 93. In 1987, televangelist Oral Roberts told his viewers that God would claim him unless they:

a. were born again in Christ

b. prayed harder

c. sent him 8 million dollars

d. renounced Satan

e. reelected Richard Nixon

## 94. The rock group that launched Boy George was:

a. Culture Club

b. the Smiths

c. Club Nouveau

d. Spandau Ballet

e. Boyz R Us

f. Boy Howdy

## 95. Ivan Pavlov was:

a. a Russian premier

b. a Bolshevik leader of the communist revolution

c. a Nobel Prize–winning physiologist

d. the first dog to orbit the earth in a Soviet satellite

## 96. Most male adults of a certain age know that the word that transformed little Billy Batson into Captain Marvel was:

a. "Eureka"

b. "Excelsior"

c. "Alakalam"

d. "Shazam"

e. "Gloriosky"

f. "Potrezbie"

**97.** Of the following, which did not play one of the original Magnificent Seven?

a. Brad Dexter

b. Ernest Borgnine

c. Yul Brynner

d. Steve McQueen

e. James Coburn

f. Horst Buchholz

g. Robert Vaughn

h. Charles Bronson

**98.** In the language of Wall Street, IBM was familiarly known as:

a. "The Big I"

b. "Engulf and Devour"

c. "Big Blue"

d. "The Big Red One"

e. "Gravy"

f. "The Golden Parachute"

**99.** In the 1990s, Calvin Broadus was better known as:

a. Tupac Shakur

b. Ice Cube

c. Brad Pitt

d. Snoop Doggy Dogg

e. MC Hammer

**100.** The term "birth control":

a. predated the twentieth century

b. was coined by Margaret Sanger in 1914

c. was ruled obscene in a famous Tennessee abortion case in 1933

d. was coined by population biologist Paul Erlich in the 1960s

## ANSWERS

1. The AEF was c. the American Expeditionary Force.

2. In 1990s slang, a "Baldwin" was c. a sexy man.

3. In the 1940s, the Manhattan Project was d. the effort to build the first nuclear weapons.

4. A Mannlicher-Carrcano was b. the kind of rifle said to have killed President Kennedy.

5. Ganja is b. the Rastafarian name for marijuana.

6. When Hell's Angels wear a patch with the number 13 on it, the number represents b. the letter M.

7. "Kid" Ory was a. a legendary jazz pioneer.

8. Be-Bop-a-Lula was c. an early rock 'n' roll song by Gene Vincent.

9. Teapot Dome was b. a corruption scandal of the Harding administration.

10. The Rainbow Coalition was b. a political organization led by Jesse Jackson.

11. "The Man With a Thousand Faces" was a. Lon Chaney.

12. The precursor to the United Nations was a. The League of Nations.

13. In the '40s and '50s, it was called "the dozens." The 1990s variant was called "Snaps." It was c. a streetcorner exchange of clever insults (usually friendly) wherein the participants tried to top each other.

14. "The Saturday Night Massacre" occurred when a. Nixon fired his attorney general and deputy attorney general when they both refused to fire the Watergate special prosecutor.

15. The Schutzstaffel was d. Hitler's SS.

16. Ruby Ridge was b. the site of a bungled U.S. government raid in the 1990s.

17. Yigal Amir was c. the assassin of Yitzhak Rabin.

18. The DEW Line was c. a Cold War nuclear defense designation: the Distant Early Warning Line.

19. A Kaiser-Frazier was a. a make of automobile.

20. "For Every Boy Who's on the Level/ There's a Girl Who's on the Square" was b. a song hit of 1920.

21. The Pachanga was a. a Latin dance fad of the late '50s and early '60s.

22. In the 1970s, SLA stood for d. Symbionese Liberation Army, the group that kidnapped Patty Hearst.

23. A pipe and a Pepsi are together associated with c. Hugh Hefner.

24. "Squeeze Me," "Honeysuckle Rose," and "Ain't Misbehavin' " are all songs written by d. Fats Waller.

25. At his inaugural, John Kennedy said, "Ask not c. what your country can do for you."

26. Holly Golightly was c. a character in a novel by Truman Capote.

27. Dittoheads were d. people who agreed with anything Rush Limbaugh said.

28. The Dorothy Chandler Pavilion was a. where the Academy Awards presentation took place.

29. Josef Mengele was a. a Nazi monster.

Patricia Hearst (Tania)

I've been kidnapped, held prisoner, threatened, beaten, humiliated, raped, battered. I've been lied to and lied about and disbelieved. The only difference between what happened to me and what happens to other women is that mine was an extreme case.

—PATRICIA HEARST, 1978

30. In the 1980s, Mariel Harbor was famous as d. the place Cuban refugees departed from to come to the U.S.

31. Moms Mabley was b. a pioneering black stand-up comedienne.

32. The Pentagon Papers were about d. the failures of U.S. Indochina policy.

33. The Brat Pack was c. a group of young up-and-coming movie actors.

34. The Brain Trust was a. a group of advisors who helped Roosevelt plan the New Deal.

35. Imelda Marcos is best remembered for d. her three thousand pairs of shoes. (She angrily told the press, "I did not have three thousand pairs of shoes. I had 1,060.")

36. The Pedernales River is associated with c. Lyndon Johnson.

37. Egon Schiele was a. a painter.

38. The guy who played Sam in the classic film *Casablanca* was e. Dooley Wilson.

39. ANC stood for d. the African National Congress.

40. c. Glenn Close was not romantically linked with Woody Allen.

41. e. "This royal throne of kings, this sceptred isle . . . This blessed plot, this earth, this realm, this England" was penned by Shakespeare, not Winston Churchill.

42. Pat Conroy, not William Styron, wrote a. *Prince of Tides.*

43. b. "K'K'K' Katy" was a hit song of WW I, not World War II.

44. a. "At the Hop" was made popular by Danny and the Juniors; e. "Jailhouse Rock" was made popular by Elvis Presley.

45. "Desert Storm" was d. the operation to drive Iraq out of Kuwait.

46. Mark Rydell, not John Ford, directed e. John Wayne in *The Cowboys*.

47. b. Willie Horton's name is associated with George Bush's presidential campaign against Michael Dukakis.

48. "Il Duce" means b. the leader.

49. Anita Bryant became a controversial figure of the 1970s when she c. spoke out against homosexuals.

50. World War I General John Pershing was known as "Black Jack" because b. he had once commanded an all-black unit.

51. Reginald Denny was c. the truck driver viciously beaten on videotape in the aftermath of the Rodney King verdict.

52. Blues giant Muddy Waters's real name was b. McKinley Morganfield.

53. The person who designed the special brassiere worn by Jane Russell in *The Outlaw* was b. Howard Hughes

54. Cocaine was legal in the U.S. until c. after its addictive properties became known, in 1914.

55. Kristallnacht was d. a night of violence against Jews in 1930s Germany.

56. "My Sweet Little Alice Blue Gown" was a song written for b. Theodore Roosevelt's daughter.

57. Richard Nixon specifically requested that Johnny Cash sing a. "Okie from Muskogee" and "Welfare Cadillac."

58. Harry Truman threatened to c. punch the writer who criticized his daughter, Margaret.

59. e. Buddy Holly did not record for Sun Records.

60. Mark Spitz was the focus of news in 1972 because c. he won seven gold medals in the '72 Olympic Games.

61. Jim's last name was d. Phelps.

62. The Macarena was c. a Brazilian dance.

63. a. Wendell Willkie was not one of FDR's vice-presidents.

64. The "Back to Africa" movement was led by d. Marcus Garvey.

65. The most celebrated American war hero of World War I was d. Sergeant York.

66. Gabriel Garcia Marquez was the foremost writer associated with the literary genre known as f. Magic Realism.

67. In the original *King Kong*, the heroine is played by b. Fay Wray.

68. The Senate Watergate hearings were chaired by a. Senator Sam Ervin.

69. Nadine Gordimer, Alan Paton, and Athol Fugard were a. South African literary figures.

70. The D in D-Day stands for e. day.

71. The VE in VE Day stands for c. Victory in Europe.

72. The guy who founded WalMart was e. Sam Walton.

73. "Babe" Ruth's real name was b. George Herman Ruth.

74. The famous "Kitchen Debate" a. took place in the '50s between Richard Nixon and Nikita Khrushchev.

75. d. *Artless in Manhattan* was not a Paul Simon album.

76. Neither a. Langston Hughes nor f. Alice B. Toklas were members of the Algonquin Round Table.

77. '60s musical group the Doors took their name from a book by Aldous Huxley called c. *The Doors of Perception.*

78. Trudeau, Larson, Schultz, Feiffer, and Crumb were c. cartoonists of the second half of the century.

79. "Son of Sam" killer David Berkowitz said he killed because b. his dog told him to.

80. The first black woman ever to be depicted on a U.S. postage stamp was e. Harriet Tubman.

81. Solidarnosc was b. a Polish labor union.

82. The Great White Hope was b. heavyweight boxer Jim Jeffries.

83. The "Feel Like I'm Fixin' to Die Rag" was sung at Woodstock by d. Country Joe and the Fish.

84. *Triumph of the Will* was c. a Nazi propaganda film by Leni Riefenstahl.

85. Olestra was c. an artificial fat.

86. Kareem Abdul-Jabbar's real name was b. Lew Alcindor.

87. There was no d. Scout leader featured in The Village People.

88. The Taft-Hartley Act of 1947 was landmark legislation in the field of a. labor.

89. All were notorious flops but d. *Mousetrap*, an Agatha Christie play.

90. Poet Sylvia Plath was married to poet d. Ted Hughes.

91. All were recurring characters on TV's *Seinfeld* except e. Schindler.

92. The "chitlin' circuit" was a name for b. southern honky-tonks that regularly employed blues musicians.

93. Televangelist Oral Roberts told his viewers that God would claim him unless they c. sent him 8 million dollars.

94. The rock group that launched Boy George was a. Culture Club.

95. Ivan Pavlov was c. a Nobel Prize–winning physiologist.

96. The word that transformed little Billy Batson into Captain Marvel was d. "Shazam."

97. b. Ernest Borgnine was not one of the Magnificent Seven.

98. IBM was familiarly known as c. "Big Blue."

99. Calvin Broadus was better known as d. Snoop Doggy Dogg.

100. The term "birth control" was b. coined by Margaret Sanger (founder of Planned Parenthood) in 1914.

Scoring: This chapter is meant to ease you into a state of confidence to prepare you for the chapters that lie ahead. If you didn't know 70 or more of these, then you probably haven't gained any confidence at all. That means the questions failed in their purpose, and you're probably not too inclined to proceed. If, however, you scored 70 or more correct, then you're probably eager to try some of the more challenging questions ahead.

# THE MORE THINGS CHANGED . . .

Does Tobacco Kill Mouth Germs?
—Title of article in *The Literary Digest*, 1920

More doctors smoke Camels than any other cigarette.
—Camel ad, 1930

Personally, I think the relationship [between smoking and cancer of the lungs] is still undecided. I've smoked long enough to have incurred all the possible dangers and don't think I should stop now. . . . I don't think the evidence is great enough in this cigarette-versus-lung-cancer problem to warrant the A.M.A.'s advising people not to smoke.
—Dr. Walter B. Martin, president of the AMA, 1954

For the majority of people, smoking has a beneficial effect.
—Dr. Ian Macdonald, 1963

I'm not certain whether it's addictive.
—Presidential candidate Bob Dole on tobacco smoking, 1996

# 2

# First Things First

*Yesterday's avant garde experiment is today's chic and tomorrow's cliche.*

—*RICHARD HOFSTADER, 1963*

*Novelty is the new status quo.*

—*DOUGLAS RUSHKOFF, 1996*

Time travel to the year 1950. At mid-century you won't hear anyone labeled as dysfunctional. No one has PMS and there are no cases of attention deficit disorder. Though there are poor spellers, there are no dyslexics. Babies sometimes die in their sleep, but there is no such thing as sudden infant death syndrome.

In 1950, there are no such things because we have not invented words for them yet.

Teenagers are new. The word has only recently come into common usage. The first movie with the word "teenage" in its title is still seven years away—*I Was a Teenage Werewolf* will be along in 1957, helping to give cultural legitimacy to this word-created new period of human life.

No one has ever heard the expression "secondhand smoke," nor would anyone know what was meant by a phrase like "passive smoking." When you go to the movies, everyone in there is smoking; the light projected on the screen is paisleyed with swirls of smoke. People smoke in college classrooms, in restaurants, and on airplane flights. There are no "nonsmoking sections" in any of those places. And there are, of course, no commercial jet flights.

Though tampons have been around for fourteen years, no one has ever heard of toxic shock syndrome. That lies ahead, thirty years in the future, associated with Rely, a Procter and Gamble modification of the tampon idea.

There is no Super Bowl, and no unleaded gasoline. No one has a color television set, and the closest thing to a remote control device is to get the kids to change the channel for you. There's not much need to change channels anyway; there are only four networks. In most areas, viewers are lucky if they get one of them. Test patterns are the only thing on the screen for most of the hours of the day.

Children (and adults) routinely and even playfully x-ray their feet in shoe stores. Some people wear radium watches. Doctors bombard children's swollen glands with massive doses of radiation.

In 1950 AIDS is unknown; it will not visit itself upon humanity for another thirty-one years. Still, there is plenty of whispered fear about VD, an abbreviation for venereal disease, nearly as commonly heard in 1950 as HIV will be in the 1990s. In the '90s, VD itself will have been replaced by STD, an abbreviation for sexually transmitted disease.

No one is known as Ms. and no one has heard the phrase "spousal abuse." Child rearing is still governed by such ideas as "children should be seen and not heard" and "spare the rod and spoil the child," though Dr. Spock has begun to bring such attitudes into question.

The F-word (it will not come to be known as "the F-word" until the late 1980s) does not appear in print, and certainly not in the movies. In order to create an authentic sense of how World War II GIs talked and still remain within the bounds of contemporary standards of decency, Norman Mailer had had to invent the word "Fug" in his landmark 1948 novel *The Naked and the Dead*. Move ahead about twenty years and an iconoclastic New York rock group will call itself The Fugs.

It's not just "the F-word." In 1950, no moviegoer will hear an actor (let alone an actress) say "son of a bitch," "bastard," or "goddamn." Only ten years earlier, Clark Gable's immortal line "Frankly, my dear, I don't give a damn" had occasioned much handwringing at MGM. Forty years hence, movies featured every imaginable expletive, blasphemy, and obscenity as commonly as punctuation in a business letter.

There are, of course, no African-Americans in 1950. What there are in 1950 are Negroes and colored people. African-Americans will make their appearance in a dozen more years.

There are no WASPs, either. The acronym for White Anglo-Saxon Protestant will show up with the African-Americans in the late 1950s. There are "ofays," a pig-Latin phrase from the 1920s, meaning "foe." "Honkys" show up about this time, but most whites won't know this word until the mid-1960s.

There are no ATMs, but there are automats, remnants of the 1920s and '30s, places where you can buy sandwiches from a machine. There are no self-serve gas stations, no antilock brakes, no seatbelts in cars.

No one has ever heard the words "aerobicize," "environmentalist," "microchip," "carjacking," or "download." No one is reciting the Pledge of Allegiance to the flag with the phrase "under God" in it, but schoolchildren soon will.

In 1950, not even rich people can get a CAT scan. No one owns a microwave oven, and the idea of cooking without heat would seem like the looniest science fiction to all but a few people in laboratories. There are no compact disks, no VCRs, no lasers, no stereophonic sound. Though there will soon be ICBMs, there is no coronary ICU, no CPR, no RAM, no DOS, no IUD. No one puts money in an IRA, nor has anyone ridden in an LEM, eaten at an IHOP, or sought redress from the EEOC. If you speak of COBOL, CNN, COLAs, or dot com, no one will know what you are talking about.

If you want to buy the electronic gadgetry and appliances that do exist—a washing machine with a clothes wringer you crank by hand, for instance—you cannot do it with your VISA or MasterCard because there are no credit cards, though some large department stores will offer credit buying and layaway plans to preferred customers.

Now take another leap in time, back fifty more years to the beginning of the century. You will find no tanks, no safety razors, telephone booths, public opinion polls, radio stations, vacuum cleaners, foam rubber, policewomen, or windshield wipers. In fact,

you will not yet find windshields on the very few motorcars the world has thus far seen. You will not find a frozen food section in your supermarket because frozen foods will not make their first appearance for another thirty years. For that matter, supermarkets themselves are unknown. The first one of those is a dozen years off, appearing in Pomona, California, in 1912, but it looks nothing like the supermarkets we will know ninety years hence. There is no music known as jazz. Though there is a KKK, there is no NAACP. And there are no laundromats, motels, or fast-food restaurants. Beer will not be available in cans until 1935, the same year Alcoholics Anonymous is founded. No one has yet thought to train dogs to guide the blind; that won't happen until 1916. No one has, of yet, taken an IQ test because, though a man named Binet has been developing such a test, it has yet to be administered. In 1900, diabetics suffer without insulin, ice cream cones are unknown, and there are no Boy Scouts or Girl Scouts to eat them. The world has not yet seen a disk jockey, a dishwasher, or an electric dental drill. The world has not yet known a communist government. Instant coffee won't be tasted for nearly forty years, and it will take even longer for the public to accept the idea. There is no Defense Department (though there is a War Department), and the Pentagon will not be built for more than forty years. Paper clips are high-tech office equipment, introduced in 1900. No one has ever written with a ballpoint pen, and no one in the modern world has yet had a legal abortion. There are, of course, no movie stars, making the world of 1900 extremely difficult for us to imagine. And no one in that landmark year could conceive of splitting the atom. Such an idea is almost literally unthinkable, since the very word "atom" means something that cannot be divided.

Anthropologists characterize cultures by the material artifacts those cultures leave behind. By this standard, the culture of the late twentieth century is dramatically different from the culture at the beginning of the century. As we move through time, we note the changes.

It was a century of firsts, one hundred years of rapid change and innovation. Things came and went at a dizzying rate. It's no disgrace, then, if we have forgotten so much of what was once new. We have become easily diverted. It was a century in which the new displaced the new, and forgetting became a practical necessity.

In the following sets, your task is to determine which item was the first to appear. Guessing is not only allowed, it is encouraged. The answers to many of these can only be arrived at by deduction, by semieducated guessing. Few, if any, of us know the specific arrival dates of all the people and things to be found below, but a familiarity with our century should make it possible to figure out correct answers to over sixty of these.

Still, this first set of questions is as difficult as any in the book, so take encourage-ment from what you do remember to buoy yourself past the things you don't.

# FIRST THINGS FIRST

## (Degree of difficulty: 8)

1. Which personal computing landmark came first?

a. Apple II

b. IBM PC

c. Macintosh III

d. Windows 3

2. Which came first?

a. sliced bread

b. Pop Tarts

c. electric toaster

3. Which came first?

a. food stamps

b. social security

c. the Salvation Army

4. Which came first?

a. Art Deco

b. Art Nouveau

c. Pop Art

d. Art Brut

**5. Which TV western came first?**

a. *Gunsmoke*

b. *Bonanza*

c. *Rawhide*

**6. Which movie came first?**

a. *The Wolf Man*

b. *Frankenstein*

c. *King Kong*

**7. Which came first?**

a. the Fair Deal

b. the New Deal

c. the New Frontier

**8. Which came first?**

a. Pizza Hut

b. McDonald's

c. Wendy's

**9. Which came first?**

a. Life Savers

b. animal crackers

c. Hostess Twinkies

**10. Which came first?**

a. Ford Motor Co.

b. General Motors

c. Chrysler

**11. Which came first?**

a. Nike

b. Microsoft

c. Yahoo!

**12. Which came first?**

a. Tonys

b. Emmys

c. Oscars

d. Grammys

**13. Which did Hitler invade first?**

a. Finland

b. France

c. Sudetenland

d. Poland

**14. In Vietnam, which happened first?**

a. Dien Bien Phu

b. Gulf of Tonkin Incident

c. My Lai

**15. Which came first?**

a. the Rose Bowl

b. the Super Bowl

c. the Dust Bowl

**16. Which play came first?**

a. *Angels in America*

b. *Waiting for Godot*

c. *Death of a Salesman*

**17. Which magazine came first?**

a. *Reader's Digest*

b. *Sports Illustrated*

c. *Life*

**18. Which cult novel came first?**

a. *Catcher in the Rye*

b. *Catch-22*

c. *Lord of the Flies*

**19. Which of the following was the first American to win a Nobel Prize for Literature?**

a. William Faulkner

b. Theodore Dreiser

c. Sinclair Lewis

**20. Of the following, which battle was fought first?**

a. Corregidor

b. Iwo Jima

c. Tarawa

**21. Which trial came first?**

a. the Scopes trial

b. Harry K. Thaw/Stanford White trial

c. Sacco-Vanzetti trial

**22. Of the following, which Michael Jackson album came first?**

a. *Thriller*

b. *Bad*

c. *HIStory*

d. *Dangerous*

**23. Which of the following presidents was first to serve?**

a. Taft

b. Theodore Roosevelt

c. McKinley

**24. Which medical breakthrough occurred first?**

a. penicillin

b. the Salk polio vaccine

c. heart transplant

**25. Who was born first?**

a. Elvis Presley

b. James Dean

c. Marilyn Monroe

**26. Which was first into print?**

a. *Playboy*

b. *Esquire*

c. *Penthouse*

**27. Which group first topped the charts in the UK?**

a. the Rolling Stones

b. the Who

c. the Beatles

28. Of the following, who was the first man in space?

a. Yuri Gagarin

b. Alan Shepard

c. John Glenn

29. Which man was the first to be assassinated?

a. Martin Luther King, Jr.

b. Robert Kennedy

c. Malcolm X

30. Of the following, who was the first to become boxing's heavyweight champ?

a. Sonny Liston

b. Muhammad Ali

c. George Foreman

31. Which siege happened first?

a. Branch Davidians in Waco, Texas

b. MOVE in Philadelphia

c. the Weavers at Ruby Ridge, Idaho

d. Freemen Ranch in Jordan, Montana

32. Of the following, who was the first to coanchor the evening news?

a. Jane Pauley

b. Connie Chung

c. Barbara Walters

33. Which came first?

a. the Golden Gate Bridge

b. the Empire State Building

c. the Lincoln Highway

d. the World Trade Center

34. Which food product was first on the market?

a. Gerber Baby Food

b. Tang

c. Hamburger Helper

35. Which Beatles album came first?

a. *Rubber Soul*

b. *Hard Day's Night*

c. *Revolver*

36. Which of the following was the first to gain a following?

a. Cyndi Lauper

b. Rickie Lee Jones

c. Madonna

37. Which came first?

a. Bayer Aspirin

b. Alka-Seltzer

c. Kleenex

38. Which of the following writers was the first to gain a wide readership?

a. E. Annie Proulx

b. Anne Tyler

c. Amy Tan

**39. Which was the first credit card?**

a. VISA

b. Master Charge

c. Diner's Club

**40. Which came first?**

a. drive-in movies

b. hula hoops

c. Silly Putty

**41. Which toy was first on the market?**

a. Cabbage Patch doll

b. Kewpie doll

c. Raggedy Ann doll

**42. Which grownup toy was first on the market?**

a. Ford Mustang

b. Chevrolet Corvette

c. DeLorean

**43. Which fad came first?**

a. Rubik's Cube

b. Nintendo

c. Lava lamps

**44. Which book was first to sweep the country?**

a. *Everything I Needed to Know I Learned in Kindergarten*

b. *The Complete Book of Running*

c. *The Joy of Sex*

**45. Which flop flopped first?**

a. *Ishtar*

b. *Heaven's Gate*

c. *Hudson Hawk*

d. *The Last Action Hero*

**46. Which children's show came first?**

a. *Captain Kangaroo*

b. *Mister Roger's Neighborhood*

c. *Sesame Street*

d. *Howdy Doody*

**47. Which came first?**

a. Velcro

b. Spandex

c. polyester

**48. Which was the first feature-length Disney animated film?**

a. *Pinocchio*

b. *Cinderella*

c. *Snow White*

**49. Which came first?**

a. Valium

b. LSD

c. Prozac

d. crack cocaine

50. Which game came first?

a. Scrabble

b. Trivial Pursuit

c. Monopoly

51. Which candy came first?

a. M&Ms

b. Baby Ruth

c. Almond Joy

52. Which innovation came first?

a. UPC (Universal Product Codes, aka "bar codes")

b. ZIP Codes (Zone Improvement codes)

c. PIN (Personal Identification Numbers)

53. Of the following, which president was the first to appear on television?

a. Hoover

b. Franklin D. Roosevelt

c. Truman

d. Eisenhower

54. Which singing sensation was the first to be sensational?

a. Bing Crosby

b. Dean Martin

c. Frank Sinatra

d. Rudy Vallee

55. The first black actress to win an Academy Award was:

a. Butterfly McQueen in *Gone With the Wind*

b. Lena Horne in *Stormy Weather*

c. Hattie McDaniel in *Gone With the Wind*

56. Who was the first African-American athlete to win an Olympic gold medal?

a. Cassius Clay

b. Carl Lewis

c. Jesse Owens

d. Arthur Ashe

57. The expedition that first landed men on the moon was:

a. Apollo 8

b. Apollo 10

c. Apollo 11

d. Apollo 13

58. The first Seattle-based "grunge" band to gain major national attention was:

a. Pearl Jam

b. Nirvana

c. Hole

d. Mudhoney

59. The man credited with being the first to reach the North Pole was

a. Roald Amundsen

b. Robert Peary

c. Robert Falcon Scott

## 60. Which came first?

a. Kool-Aid

b. Cool Whip

c. Frosty-Os

d. Eskimo Pies

## 61. The first president to throw out the first ball of the baseball season was:

a. Teddy Roosevelt

b. William Taft

c. Woodrow Wilson

## 62. In what year was Mother's Day first celebrated nationally?

a. 1902

b. 1913

c. 1933

d. 1955

## 63. Which came first?

a. HBO

b. CNN

c. MTV

## 64. The first American president born in a hospital was:

a. Kennedy

b. Nixon

c. Hoover

d. Ford

e. Carter

## 65. Of the following, which was first on television?

a. *M*A*S*H*

b. *All in the Family*

c. *Sanford and Son*

## 66. Which fragrance was the first on the market?

a. Chanel No. 5

b. My Sin

c. Shalimar

## 67. Which disposable diaper was the first on the market?

a. Luvs

b. Huggies

c. Pampers

## 68. Which brand of cigarettes was marketed first?

a. Lucky Strikes

b. Marlboros

c. Virginia Slims

d. Kools

## 69. Which was the first laundry detergent?

a. Tide

b. Surf

c. Rinso

d. Fab

70. Which country did the U.S. invade first?

a. Grenada

b. Dominican Republic

c. Nicaragua

71. Of the following horses, which was the first to win racing's Triple Crown?

a. Whirlaway

b. Gallant Fox

c. Secretariat

d. Sir Barton

72. Of the following, who was the first born?

a. Newt Gingrich

b. Bill Clinton

c. Dan Quayle

73. Of the following, which was the first to have his own talk show?

a. Jack Paar

b. Steve Allen

c. Johnny Carson

d. Merv Griffin

74. James Dean starred in only three films. Which was first?

a. *Giant*

b. *Rebel Without a Cause*

c. *East of Eden*

75. Of the following, which was the first to win a Super Bowl?

a. Green Bay Packers

b. San Francisco 49ers

c. Denver Broncos

d. New York Jets

76. Of the following Stephen King novels, which was the first to become a best seller?

a. *Carrie*

b. *The Shining*

c. *Cujo*

77. Of the following, who was first appointed to the U.S. Supreme Court?

a. Sandra Day O'Connor

b. Antonin Scalia

c. Clarence Thomas

d. Ruth Bader-Ginsburg

78. The first man to fly faster than the speed of sound was:

a. Howard Hughes

b. John Glenn

c. Chuck Yeager

d. Wiley Post

79. Of the following songs, which was the first to win a Grammy for best record?

a. "Graceland," by Paul Simon

b. "Just the Way You Are," by Billy Joel

c. "Bette Davis Eyes," by Kim Carnes

d. "We Are the World," by USA for Africa

## 80. Of the following, which country was the first to legalize abortion?

a. U.S.

b. France

c. the Soviet Union

d. Cuba

## 81. The first nuclear-powered aircraft carrier was:

a. the USS *Snark*

b. the USS *Missouri*

c. the USS *Enterprise*

## 82. In 1972, it was the first hardcore porno film to gain acceptance with a national mixed-sex audience. That film was:

a. *Behind the Green Door*

b. *Deep Throat*

c. *Long Dong Silver*

## 83. Which advice column came first?

a. *Ann Landers Says*

b. *Dear Abby*

c. *Ask Beth*

## 84. The first woman admitted to the Citadel, an all-male military academy, was:

a. Shannon Hoon

b. Shannon Faulkner

c. Shannen Doherty

d. Shannon Tweed

## 85. The first Madonna album was called

a. *Like a Virgin*

b. *Like a Prayer*

c. *Erotica*

d. *Madonna*

## 86. Of the following early films, which was first?

a. *The Great Train Robbery*, Edward Porter, director

b. *Voyage to the Moon*, George Melies, director

**The First Western**
*The Great Train Robbery.* The film was only ten minutes long. It was filmed in the wilds of New Jersey, and it ended with this buckaroo discharging his pistol directly at the audience—a fitting preview of attractions to come throughout the century.

c. *Tillie's Punctured Romance*, Mack Sennett, director

## 87. Which came first?

a. the Watergate hearings

b. the Army-McCarthy hearings

c. the Warren Commission

d. the Kefauver hearings

## 88. Which environmental disaster happened first?

a. *Exxon Valdez* oil spill

b. evacuation of Love Canal, New York

c. Union Carbide's toxic gas leak in Bhopal, India

d. Cuyahoga River catches fire

## 89. Which came first?

a. New Kids on the Block

b. Kid 'n Play

c. Kids in the Hall

d. Dead End Kids

## 90. Of the following, which medical procedure came first?

a. kidney transplant

b. heart transplant

c. brain transplant

## 91. Of the following, which came first?

a. birth control pill

b. Heimlich maneuver

c. coronary bypass operation

## 92. Which has been around the longest?

a. Tupperware

b. Polaroid camera

c. electric toothbrush

d. aerosol spray cans

## 93. Which came first?

a. Soviet invasion of Afghanistan

b. Iraqi invasion of Kuwait

c. Soviet invasion of Hungary

## 94. Of the following U.S. companies, which is the oldest?

a. Standard Oil

b. Archer-Daniels-Midland

c. General Mills

d. Philip Morris

## 95. Which dance did we dance first?

a. the Twist

b. the Swim

c. the Stroll

d. the Pony

## 96. Of the following pitchers, whose career came first?

a. Jim "Catfish" Hunter

b. Bob Feller

c. Sandy Koufax

d. Nolan Ryan

**97. Which Christmas song came first?**

a. "Rudolph the Red-Nosed Reindeer"

b. "I Saw Mommy Kissing Santa Claus"

c. "White Christmas"

d. "Jingle Bell Rock"

**98. Of the following films, which was the first to be directed by Steven Speilberg?**

a. *Sugarland Express*

b. *The Color Purple*

c. *Jaws*

d. *Close Encounters of the Third Kind*

**99. Which disaster came first?**

a. the Loma Prieta earthquake

b. the eruption of Mount St. Helens in Washington State

c. Chernobyl

**100. Which was the first to go out of business?**

a. Eastern Airlines

b. Pan Am

c. Braniff Airlines

## ANSWERS

Those were surely difficult questions, but then it was a pretty tough century. What you didn't remember, or never knew, you now can learn.

1. a. Apple II came first, in 1977. The IBM PC came out in 1981, the Mac in 1984, and Windows 3 in 1990.

2. c. The electric toaster, oddly enough, predated sliced bread. The toaster turned up in 1918, sliced bread came along a decade later, and Pop Tarts were introduced in 1964.

3. c. The Salvation Army predates the twentieth century, beginning in 1878. Social security was enacted in 1935, food stamps were first issued in 1939, but widespread issuance began in 1963.

4. b. Art Nouveau was first, in the years preceding World War I. Art Deco followed in the '20s; Pop Art in the '60s; Art Brut in the '70s.

5. a. *Gunsmoke* came first. It premiered in 1955. *Rawhide* and *Bonanza* premiered in '59.

6. b. *Frankenstein* came first, in 1931. *King Kong* was released in 1933, and *The Wolf Man* followed in 1940.

7. b. The New Deal was first, followed by Truman's Fair Deal and Kennedy's New Frontier.

8. b. McDonald's was first franchised in 1948, followed by Pizza Hut ('58), and Wendy's ('69).

9. b. Animal crackers, 1902; Life Savers, 1913; Twinkies, 1930.

10. a. Ford Motor Co., 1903, followed by GM, then Chrysler.

11. a. Nike came first in '73, Microsoft was establishing itself in '81, and Yahoo! went public in '96.

12. c. Oscars were first awarded in 1929, though they weren't known by that name until the mid-'30s; Tonys (after Antoinette Perry) were first awarded in '47; Emmys in '49; and Grammys in '58.

13. c. Sudetenland was invaded first (1938), followed by Poland (1939), and France (1940). Finland was not invaded by the Germans; it was a reluctant ally.

14. a. Dien Bien Phu happened first. The French were defeated there in 1954. The Gulf of Tonkin Incident did (or, more precisely, did not) take place in 1964, and the My Lai massacre took place in 1968.

15. a. The Rose Bowl was first in 1902. The Dust Bowl was a midwestern drought in 1934–35, and the Super Bowl was first played in '67.

16. c. *Death of a Salesman* came first, in 1949; *Godot* in '52, and *Angels* in '92.

17. a. *Reader's Digest* came first, in 1922, then *Life* in 1936, and *Sports Illustrated* in 1954.

18. a. *Catcher in the Rye* was first, in 1951, followed by *Lord of the Flies* in 1954, and *Catch-22* in 1961.

19. c. Sinclair Lewis won a Nobel Prize in 1930, Faulkner in '49. Dreiser never won a Nobel Prize.

20. a. Corregidor was fought (and lost) first, in 1942. Tarawa was fought (and won) in 1943, and Iwo Jima was won in 1945.

21. b. Harry K. Thaw/Stanford White trial was in 1906, Sacco-Vanzetti in 1921, and Scopes in 1925.

22. a. *Thriller* was the first of these Jackson albums, in 1982, followed by *Bad* in 1987, *Dangerous* in 1991, and *HIStory* in 1995.

23. c. McKinley was first to serve (1897–1901). VP Roosevelt took office when McKinley was assassinated. Taft took office in 1909.

24. a. Penicillin was first in 1929, the Salk vaccine followed in '53, and the first heart was transplanted in '67.

25. c. Marilyn Monroe (1926) was the first-born of these '50s icons. Dean was born in 1931; Presley in 1935.

26. b. *Esquire* bowed in 1933. Hefner worked there briefly before launching *Playboy* in '53. *Penthouse* started in '69.

27. c. The Beatles charted in 1962, the Stones in 1964, and the Who in 1965.

28. a. Yuri Gagarin was the first man in space in 1961; Shepard followed about three weeks later. Glenn orbited the Earth in 1962.

29. c. Malcolm X was killed in '65; King and Kennedy in 1968.

30. a. Sonny Liston lost his title to Muhammad Ali (Cassius Clay) in 1964. Foreman became champ in 1973.

31. b. The Move siege ended in 1985 when city police bombed the building the group was holed up in, killing eleven and leaving over two hundred homeless. The other sieges were mid-'90s episodes that took place in the following sequence: Ruby Ridge, Waco, Freemen.

32. c. Barbara Walters was the first woman coanchor in 1976.

33. c. The Lincoln Highway, a coast-to-coast highway, came first, in 1913. After that came the Empire State Building in 1931, the Golden Gate Bridge in 1937, and the World Trade Center in 1970.

34. a. Gerber Baby Food was first, in 1927. Tang turned up in 1966, and Hamburger Helper in 1970.

35. b. *Hard Day's Night* was first, in 1964, followed by *Rubber Soul* in '65, and *Revolver* in '66.

36. b. Rickie Lee Jones was first, with her hit "Chuck E's in Love" in 1979.

37. a. Bayer Aspirin came first in 1905, Kleenex in 1924, and Alka-Seltzer in 1931.

38. b. Anne Tyler was the first of these to become popular. She published her first novel in 1963.

39. c. DINER'S CLUB was the first plastic cash, 1950.

40. a. Drive-in movies came first in 1933, then Silly Putty in '49, and Hula Hoops in '58.

41. b. Kewpie doll was first in 1913, followed by Raggedy Ann in '18, and then it's a big jump to the Cabbage Patch hysteria of '83.

42. b. Chevrolet Corvette came first in '53; the Mustang was introduced in '64, and the DeLorean was first marketed in 1980.

43. c. Lava lamps were first (in '65), Rubik's Cube was second in 1980, and Nintendo followed in '85.

44. c. *The Joy of Sex* was popular in '72, *Running* in '78, and *Kindergarten* in '89.

45. b. *Heaven's Gate* flopped hugely in 1980, *Ishtar* in '87, *Hudson Hawk* in '91, and *The Last Action Hero* in '93.

46. d. *Howdy Doody* was first in 1947; *Captain Kangaroo* next in 1955. *Mister Rogers* arrived in 1967, and *Sesame Street* in '69.

47. a. Velcro turned up in 1948, polyester came along in the '60s, and Spandex in the '70s.

48. c. *Snow White* was the first feature-length Disney animated feature, in 1938, followed by *Pinocchio* in 1940, and *Cinderella* in 1950.

49. b. LSD was developed in 1943, Valium in '63, crack in the early '80s, and Prozac in 1988.

50. c. Monopoly was introduced during the Depression, in 1935. Scrabble was first marketed in 1952, and Trivial Pursuit in 1984.

51. b. Baby Ruth came first in 1921. M&Ms were introduced in 1940, and Almond Joy bars were first marketed in 1947.

52. b. ZIP Codes were introduced in 1963. PINs accompanied ATMs when they were first seen in New York in 1969 (though most of us wouldn't see one for another decade). Bar codes came along in 1973.

53. b. Roosevelt was the first president to appear on television, at the World's Fair in 1939.

54. d. Rudy Vallee was a sensation in the 1920s, Crosby followed in the '30s, Sinatra in the '40s, and Martin in the late '40s.

55. c. Hattie McDaniel was the first black actress to win an Academy Award in 1939. Neither Horne nor McQueen were so honored.

56. c. Jesse Owens was the first African-American to win an Olympic gold medal, in Berlin in 1936. Clay won gold in 1960, Lewis in 1983. Ashe was not an Olympic competitor.

57. c. Apollo 11 was the mission that first landed men on the moon, on June 20, 1969.

58. b. Nirvana was the first of the Seattle-based "grunge" bands.

59. b. Admiral Robert Peary is generally credited with being the first to the North Pole in 1909, though some controversy remains.

60. d. Eskimo Pies came first in 1921. Kool-Aid came out in 1927, Frosty-Os in 1959, and Cool Whip in 1965.

61. b. William Taft was the first president to throw out the first ball of the baseball season in 1911.

First Ball, W. H. Taft, 1911

62. b. 1913 was the year Mother's Day was first celebrated.

63. a. HBO came first in '72. CNN started in 1980, MTV in 1981.

64. e. Carter was the first American president to be born in a hospital. (That surprised me. Did it you?)

65. b. *All in the Family* came first, in 1971, *Sanford and Son* in January of '72, and *M*A*S*H* in September of '72.

66. a. Chanel No. 5 was first in 1921. My Sin and Shalimar were first marketed in 1925.

67. c. Pampers were first on the market in 1966, followed by Huggies in 1978, and Luvs in 1980.

68. a. Lucky Strikes was the first of these brands, marketed in the 1920s with such ad testimonials as this one from actress Constance Talmadge: "Light a Lucky and you'll never miss sweets that make you fat." Kools were first marketed in the early

'50s, and Marlboros were introduced to compete with Winstons in the late '50s. Virginia Slims went on the market in 1968, targeting women with an ad campaign ("You've Come a Long Way, Baby") and the old reminder that cigarettes suppress appetite, as in "Slims."

69. c. Rinso was first out in 1918. Tide joined the market in 1946. Fab and Surf rounded out the field in 1949.

70. c. Nicaragua. The U.S. sent troops to Nicaragua in 1912, to the Dominican Republic in 1916 and again in 1965, and to Grenada in 1983.

71. d. Sir Barton was the very first horse to win the Triple Crown, in 1919.

72. a. Newt Gingrich was the first of these, arriving in 1943. Bill Clinton was born in 1946. Dan Quayle was born in 1947.

73. b. Steve Allen hosted the *Tonight Show* beginning in 1954, Paar took the show in 1957, and Johnny Carson in 1962, the same year Merv Griffin began his own talk show.

74. c. *East of Eden* was Dean's first, in 1955, followed by *Rebel Without a Cause*, the same year, and *Giant* was released after his death, in 1956.

75. a. The Green Bay Packers were the first team to ever win a Superbowl in 1967.

76. a. *Carrie* was King's first best seller in 1974. *The Shining* followed in 1977, and *Cujo* was a best seller in 1981.

77. a. Sandra Day O'Connor was first appointed to the U.S. Supreme Court in 1981. Scalia was appointed in 1986, Thomas in 1990, and Bader-Ginsburg in 1994.

78. c. Chuck Yeager was the first to fly faster than the speed of sound in 1947.

79. b. "Just the Way You Are" won a Grammy for Billy Joel in 1978, "Bette Davis Eyes" won in '81, "We Are the World" in '85, and "Graceland" in '87.

80. c. The Soviet Union was the first to make abortion legal in 1920, but that decree was rescinded in 1935 when Stalin said the nation needed more men. In 1973, *Roe* v. *Wade* made abortion legal in the U.S.

81. c. The USS *Enterprise* was the first nuclear-powered aircraft carrier, launched in 1960.

82. b. *Deep Throat* was the first widely accepted porno film.

83. a. *Ann Landers Says* was first, in 1955.

84. b. Shannon Faulkner was the first woman admitted to the Citadel, in 1995.

85. d. *Madonna* was the first Madonna album, in 1983

86. b. *Voyage to the Moon* was first, in 1902. *The Great Train Robbery* was a western filmed in New Jersey in 1903. *Tillie's Punctured Romance* wasn't made until 1914.

87. d. The Kefauver hearings came first in 1950–51. The Army-McCarthy hearings were in 1954. The Warren Commission followed the Kennedy assassination, in 1964, and the Watergate hearings were conducted in 1973.

88. d. The Cuyahoga River caught fire in 1969, Love Canal was evacuated in '78–'79, Union Carbide's leak killed over two thousand people in '84, and the *Exxon Valdez* polluted Prince William Sound in '89.

89. d. The Dead End Kids were first seen in 1937. New Kids on the Block were a flavor-of-the-week rock group in 1986. Kids in the Hall were a Canadian improv comedy group first seen on HBO in 1988, and Kid 'n Play first gained attention in the 1989 film *House Party*.

90. a. A kidney transplant was first done in 1950. The first heart transplant was in 1967. To date, there has been no brain transplant.

91. a. The birth control pill came first, in 1960. The first coronary bypass was done in 1967, and the Heimlich maneuver was developed in 1974.

92. d. Aerosol spray cans made their appearance in 1941. Tupperware has been around since 1945. The Polaroid Land Camera was introduced in 1948. The first electric toothbrushes were manufactured in 1961.

93. c. The Soviets invaded Hungary to put down a revolt in 1956. The Soviets invaded Afghanistan in 1979. Iraq invaded Kuwait in 1989.

94. a. Standard Oil goes back to 1882, though the monopoly has been broken up and reorganized several times. Philip Morris was formed in 1991. Archer-Daniels-Midland (the massive political campaign contributor) was incorporated in 1923, General Mills in 1928.

95. c. The Stroll was a '50s dance. The others were from the '60s.

96. b. Bob Feller was first (and one of the fastest) in the early 1950s.

97. c. "White Christmas," by Bing Crosby, swept the world in 1942. "Rudolph the Red-Nosed Reindeer" was a postwar hit, and the other two were '50s phenomena.

98. a. *Sugarland Express* was Speilberg's first feature for movie theaters. He

directed it in 1974. *Jaws* was '75, *Close Encounters* '77, and *The Color Purple* '85.

99. b. Mount St. Helens erupted in 1980, blasting half a mountain into the sky. Chernobyl was blighted in 1986. The Loma Prieta quake shook the San Francisco Bay Area in 1989.

100. c. Braniff failed in 1982, Eastern and Pan Am in 1991.

Scoring: 100–86 correct: Extraordinary. You're first among firsts. 85–61 correct: Still quite good. Chronologically gifted. 60–40 correct: About average. Fewer than 40 correct: You're either very young or very forgetful, or you just didn't pay much attention to things happening around you.

If you scored above 60, you'll want to press on. If you scored below 60, you may want to seek out friendlier questions. In either case, the century lies ahead.

# 3

# The Best Thing Since Sliced Bread

*We grew up founding our dreams on the
infinite promises of American advertising.*

—ZELDA FITZGERALD, 1920S

*The world is getting too high-tech
to spend time looking at cows.*

—DARREN GUTENBERG, AGE ELEVEN, AT
THE MARIN COUNTY FAIR, 1996

If we could take a time machine back to the dawn of this century, one of the things sure to prove most disorienting would be the absence of nearly everything familiar to us. Our lives are grounded in inventions and innovations that became commonplace and unremarkable almost the instant they arrived in our lives.

Time travel, then, to the year 1901.

There are no Oreos, no refrigerators, no air-conditioning or washing machines, no M&Ms. MSG has not yet been discovered. There are Chinese restaurants, nonetheless.

There are no Hershey bars, no Reese's Peanut Butter Cups, no Milk Duds, and no movie theaters to eat them in.

No one has yet found a cost-effective way to can tuna fish, and there is no mayonnaise sold in jars, which makes it very difficult to get a tuna fish sandwich.

There is no Pepsi, and there are no Popsicles. There are no TV dinners, of course, and no TVs to watch while we eat them. Unless they have traveled in Italy, most Americans have never even heard of broccoli, let alone tasted the stuff.

Were he alive, TV talk phenom David Letterman would not be able to give canned hams to his studio audience; there are no canned hams, and of course, the phrase "studio audience" is meaningless to anyone you might talk to in 1901.

Though there is food for babies, there is no such thing as baby food, or at least nothing marketed as such. There is also no income tax, no social security or unemployment insurance. There is no novocaine and no penicillin.

Though these are the Old Days, there are no "Oldies" stations because there are no records, no radio, and most assuredly, no rock 'n' roll.

You won't find panty hose, or Barbie dolls, or supermarket shopping carts. Or supermarkets. Don't cut yourself; there are no Band-Aids. Nor will you find Kotex, aspirin tablets, or Hallmark cards.

If you're a small-town businessman, you'll have to find another way to spend the lunch hour: There are no Rotary clubs. If you're a kid, rainy afternoons are a little longer because there are no Crayolas. And no Cheerios, either.

In fact, the familiar things missing in our visit to 1901 are the very things that make the end of the century so different from its beginning. Difference is in the details.

The number of new things this century has spawned is astonishing. No comparable period in human history has been so swept by technological change, by the marketing of new products, and by endless innovations. We think of ourselves now as consumers, something no one would have done in the nineteenth century, and the human mind is everywhere busy conceiving new things for us to consume.

Survey the appliances in your home. We are so used to the digital clock, the computer, the electric coffee maker, the CD player, and the VCR that it is hard to imagine a time when we didn't have them.

Then look at the things outside your home—the jet plane overhead, the seat belts in your car, the traffic lights, the ATM, the cellular phone, and the Golden Arches of McDonald's. These and a thousand other things have come to seem fundamental, but all of them are new, many of them new in the last decade of this century. And every new thing is heralded as "the best thing since sliced bread," and, indeed, packaged sliced bread is an innovation of our century.

We take these innovations for granted almost as soon as they show up. In the first sequence of questions following, your task is to pick out the things that are not of our time, the things that came before our century. Don't feel badly if you don't know. What you don't know, you might deduce.

In the following clusters, all but one of the items have their origins in the twentieth century. Imagine a time when these things did not exist, then find the one that predates our century.

## SLICED BREAD

### *Sequence 1: Our Century, or the One Before?*

1. The one that became an official holiday before 1900 is:

a. Veteran's Day

b. Thanksgiving Day

c. Father's Day

2. The one invented before 1900 is:

a. hula hoop

b. teddy bear

c. bicycle

3. The one introduced before 1900 is:

a. Band-Aids

b. adhesive postage stamps

c. Scotch tape

4. The one that predates our century is:

a. rubber bands

b. Dixie cups

c. Kleenex

5. The one introduced before 1900 is:

a. rubber ice tray

b. carbon paper

c. paper clips

6. The one that predates the turn of the century is:

a. lipstick

b. brassiere

c. platform shoes

7. The one our nineteenth-century forebears knew was:

a. Hershey bars

b. M&Ms

c. Three Musketeers bars

d. Schrafft's gum drops

8. The one that originated before 1900 is:

a. Spam

b. Morton salt

c. Ritz crackers

9. The one known before 1900 is:

a. Graham crackers

b. Popsicles

c. Milky Way bars

10. The one that came before 1900 is:

a. beer in cans

b. potato chips

c. commercial baby food

11. The one that came into being before 1900 was:

a. National Association for the Advancement of Colored People

b. Ku Klux Klan

c. Alcoholics Anonymous

**12. Which of these magazines began publication before 1900?**

a. *Harper's*

b. *Reader's Digest*

c. *Time*

**13. All but one of these nation states came into being in the twentieth century. Which name precedes the century?**

a. Israel

b. Union of Soviet Socialist Republics

c. Iraq

d. Persia

e. Bangladesh

f. Pakistan

**14. Which game was known before the twentieth century began?**

a. mah-jongg

b. Scrabble

c. Monopoly

**15. Which preceded the twentieth century?**

a. Campbell's soup

b. Bumble Bee tuna

c. Heinz catsup

**16. Which of these football milestones began before 1900?**

a. Army–Navy game

b. National Football League Championship

c. forward pass introduced

**17. Only one originated before the twentieth century. Which one?**

a. Yo-yo

b. Silly Putty

c. birthday cakes

d. Barbie dolls

**18. Which one was seen before the twentieth century?**

a. tennis shoes

b. button-down collar

c. nylon stockings

**19. In Europe and the U.S., which one established its popularity before the twentieth century dawned?**

a. pajamas

b. Levis

c. saddle shoes

**20. Which presidential cabinet post preceded the twentieth century?**

a. secretary of commerce

b. secretary of labor

c. secretary of health, education, and welfare

d. secretary of state

Check how well you did, or move directly on to the next series, a multiple-choice sequence that may prove a bit easier.

## CULTURE SHOCK MEETS FUTURE SHOCK: A BRIEF NOTE BEFORE PROCEEDING

When the first McDonald's opened in Tokyo in 1971, the Japanese proprietor told reporters: "The reason Japanese people are so short and have yellow skins is that they have eaten nothing but fish and rice for two thousand years. If we eat McDonald hamburgers and potatoes for one thousand years, we will become taller, our skin will become white, and our hair will become blond."

## SLICED BREAD

*Sequence 2: What's New?*

21. Skateboards are now seen everywhere, but they haven't always been around. Skateboards were first marketed in:

a. the 1920s

b. the 1940s

c. the 1960s

d. the 1980s

22. "Put a tiger in your tank" was an advertising catchphrase from the 1960s. The slogan promoted:

a. STP

b. Exxon gasoline

c. Kellogg's Corn Flakes

d. Texaco gasoline

e. Barry Goldwater's presidential campaign

23. "Machinery is the new Messiah." The man who said this is also remembered for having said "History is more or less bunk." That was in 1916. He was:

a. Henry Ford

b. Thomas Edison

c. Willis Carrier

d. Theodore Roosevelt

e. J. D. Rockefeller

24. Soyuz 7 was:

a. a high-energy protein made from soybeans

b. a Soviet spacecraft

c. a hair product, marketed by Brylcreem

d. a mid-'80s punk rock band from Poland

e. a high-yield fertilizer that helped create the "Green Revolution"

**25.** Rinso White and Rinso Blue. If you're old enough, you'll remember them as:

a. early models of Harley-Davidson motorcycles

b. hair colorings

c. laundry soaps

d. toothpastes

**26.** The word "newscast" was coined by *Time* magazine. *Time* gave us the word during the:

a. 1920s

b. 1940s

c. 1950s

d. 1960s

**27.** The "Breakfast of Champions" made its first appearance in 1924. In the 1970s, Kurt Vonnegut would take the slogan as the title of one of his novels. It's unlikely that you'll have forgotten that the "Breakfast of Champions" is:

a. Cheerios

b. Kellogg's Corn Flakes

c. Cap'n Crunch

d. Wheaties

e. Raisin Bran

f. Quaker Oats

**28.** "It's not nice to fool Mother Nature" was a ubiquitous advertising slogan on 1970s television. The product it advertised was:

a. unleaded gasoline

b. margarine

c. detergent

d. hair coloring

e. tooth polish

f. perfume

**29.** Though Willis H. Carrier's name is little remembered, his 1902 invention fundamentally changed the way we lived. By 1944, most Americans had:

a. a radio

b. a refrigerator

c. a record player

d. a windshield

e. sheetrock

f. a camcorder

**30.** The entrepreneur who started CNN in 1980 was:

a. Rupert Murdoch

b. Ted Baxter

c. Ted Turner

d. Henry Luce

e. Ben Bradlee

f. David Sarnoff

**31.** Of the following, which was not a model or make of automobile?

a. Hispano-Suiza

b. Pierce Arrow

c. Ford Edsel

d. Stanley Steamer

e. Studebaker Avanti

f. Ryan NYP

**32.** Which bathing suit came first?

a. the thong

b. the bikini

c. the topless

**33.** DDT was introduced in 1939. It would be banned by the EPA thirty-two years later. DDT was:

a. an insecticide

b. a hairspray ingredient

c. an abortion pill

d. a house paint additive

e. a petroleum by-product

f. a food dye

**34.** "This is the greatest week in the history of the world since the creation." Maybe hyperbolic, maybe not. The words are Richard Nixon's. The occasion was:

a. the first heart transplant in 1967

b. the landing of men on the moon in 1969

c. the first "Earth Day" observance in 1972

d. the opening of the World Trade Center in 1970

e. the opening of Walt Disney World in 1971

**35.** It was new in '62. Translated from the Portuguese, it means "new beat." It was:

a. the bossa nova

b. the pachanga

c. the rumba

d. the samba

e. the lambada

f. the merengue

**36.** Aspartame was first marketed in 1981, but we know it better under its commercial name, which is:

a. Velveeta

b. WD-40

c. NutraSweet

d. Cool Whip

e. Miracle Whip

f. Cheez Whiz

**37.** The movie was a harbinger of change. In it, Marlon Brando was asked what he was rebelling against. His reply? "Whaddya got?" The movie was:

a. *On the Waterfront*

b. *One-Eyed Jacks*

c. *Rebel Without a Cause*

d. *The Wild One*

e. *The Fugitive Kind*

**38.** Few of us had heard the word antioxidants in the 1980s, but it got our attention in the 1990s as:

a. a motor engine lubricant

b. disease-preventing vitamin supplements

c. a rust preventative

d. hair restoration enzymes

**39.** The "New" Coke was a marketing disaster in 1985, and Coca Cola was forced to bring back the "old" Coke under the name:

a. the Real Thing

b. Coke Classic

c. the Original Coke

d. Coke Basic

e. the True Coke

f. Coke

**40.** Do you remember a world without Hamburger Helper? If you do, that world changed in:

a. 1950

b. 1960

c. 1970

d. 1980

## SLICED BREAD

*Sequence 3: Creators and Creations*

Match the creators to the character they created.

41. R. Crumb _____          a. Nurse Ratchet

42. Dana Carvey _____       b. Woody Woodpecker

43. W. C. Fields _____       c. Hercule Poirot

44. Mickey Spillane _____    d. The Church Lady

45. Ken Kesey _____          e. Dick Tracy

46. Walter Lantz _____       f. Nancy Drew

47. Jonathan Winters _____   g. Egbert Souse

48. Lily Tomlin _____        h. Aram Yossarian

49. Agatha Christie _____    i. Miniver Cheevy

50. Chic Young _____         j. Oswald the Rabbit

51. Mike Myers _____          k. the Wizard of Oz

52. Carolyn Keene _____       l. Bigger Thomas

53. Chester Gould _____       m. Maude Frickert

54. Edgar Rice
Burroughs _____              n. E.T.

55. Joseph Heller _____       o. Fat Albert

56. Walt Disney _____         p. Wayne
                             (of *Wayne's World*)

57. L. Frank Baum _____       q. James Bond

58. Steven Spielberg _____    r. Mike Hammer

59. Langston Hughes _____     s. Tarzan

60. Edgar Lee
Masters _____                t. Edith Ann

61. P. G. Wodehouse _____     u. Mr. Natural

62. Richard Wright _____      v. Bart Simpson

63. Matt Groening _____       w. Dagwood

64. Ian Fleming _____         x. Jeeves

65. Bill Cosby _____          y. Simple

## SLICED BREAD

### Sequence 4: Decades of Change

This one is fairly easy. The following sequence is a list of innovations, changes, novelties, and nicknames. All you have to do is supply the decade when these things appeared, these laws were enacted, or these words gained currency.

66. social security _____

67. Rock 'n' roll _____

68. Pong _____

69. ATMs _____

70. the Internet _____

71. Pillsbury bakeoff _____

72. Prozac _____

73. Cinemascope _____

74. Chanel No. 5 _____

75. Popeye the Sailor _____

76. *Roe* v. *Wade* _____

77. the Gideons put Bibles in hotel rooms _____

78. Apple computers _____

79. Betamax _____

80. Affirmative action _____

81. Automatic transmissions _____

82. Food stamps _____

83. Disposable diapers _____

84. Girl Scouts of America _____

85. Eight-track tapes _____

## SLICED BREAD

*Sequence 5: The Last Dance*

We danced down the decades. Each decade seemed to require a new dance, a generational stomp and stamp of identity. The following dances each characterized one decade of the century. Choreograph the dances by naming the decade in which they were the new thing.

86. The twist _____

87. The jerk _____

88. The Charleston _____

89. Disco dancing _____

90. Slam dancing _____

91. The stroll _____

92. Moshing _____

\* \* \*

Dance 'til you drop: The dance marathon craze went on for nearly ten years, beginning in 1923. After the Depression struck, the fad grew more desperate. In 1935, Horace McCoy described it this way: "The way to beat a marathon dance was to perfect a system for those ten-minute rest periods: learning to eat your sandwich while you shaved, learning to eat when you went to the john, when you had your feet fixed, learning to read newspapers while you danced, learning to sleep on your partner's shoulder while you were dancing" (*They Shoot Horses, Don't They?*).

93. The cha cha _____

94. The black bottom _____

95. The Castle walk _____

96. Big Apple _____

97. Hustle _____

98. Break dancing _____

99. Vogueing _____

100. Bunny hug _____

## ANSWERS

**SLICED BREAD**

*Sequence 1: Our Century, or the One Before?*

1. b. Thanksgiving Day was officially established by President Abraham Lincoln in 1863. Veteran's Day began as Armistice Day, after World War I: Father's Day came a bit earlier, first observed in 1910.

2. c. The bicycle predates the twentieth century: In various forms, it turned up in Scotland in 1849, and in England in 1885. The teddy bear was marketed in 1903, named for Teddy Roosevelt after it was reported that he declined to shoot a mother bear while on a hunt. Hula hoops were, of course, a '50s hit for Whammo.

3. b. The adhesive postage stamp was first patented in England in the 1840s. Band-Aids were introduced by Johnson and Johnson in 1920. Scotch tape showed up in the late '30s.

4. a. Rubber bands predate the century, first patented in 1845. The precursor to Kleenex (known as Celluwipes) turned up in 1924. The first paper cups were marketed in 1908.

5. b. Carbon paper turned up in England in 1806. Rubber ice trays had to wait for the refrigerator to be marketed in 1913, and even then the ice tray didn't arrive until 1932. The paper clip came in with the century, in 1900.

6. c. Platform shoes (called "chopines") turned up as early as 1510 in Venice. The brassiere was introduced in 1902, but it didn't become popular until elastic was added to the product in 1914. Lipstick was first marketed in 1915.

7. d. Schrafft's gum drops were enjoyed by Union soldiers in the Civil War. Hershey bars came in with the century,

in 1900. The Three Musketeers bar was first sold in 1932. M&Ms were concocted as a nonmessy treat for soldiers in 1941.

8. b. Morton salt was established in 1885. Ritz crackers appeared in 1933, and Spam soon followed, in 1937.

9. a. Graham crackers appeared around 1830. Popsicles were first marketed in 1924, and Milky Way bars in 1923.

10. b. Potato chips were developed in the 1850s. The first beer in cans was sold during the Depression. Gerber began marketing baby food in 1927, though an earlier commercial baby food was marketed in 1922.

11. b. The Ku Klux Klan was founded during Reconstruction in 1866. The National Association for the Advancement of Colored People was established in 1910, and AA was founded in 1935.

12. a. *Harper's* was founded in 1850. *Reader's Digest* and *Time* were both founded in the 1920s.

13. d. Persia is the only one on that list to predate the century.

14. a. Mah-jongg. Though playing the game was a huge fad in the 1920s, the game can be traced far back into Chinese history. Monopoly, ironically, was first marketed during the Depression, and Scrabble was first marketed in 1952.

15. c. Heinz catsup was first marketed in 1876. It's likely that Sitting Bull tasted it, and certain that Wyatt Earp did. Campbell's soup turned up in the 1920s, and Bumble Bee tuna in the 1930s.

16. a. The Army–Navy game was first played in 1890. The forward pass was introduced in 1906. The NFL championship was won for the first time in 1933 (by the Chicago Bears).

17. c. The birthday cake is a centuries-old tradition. Yo-yos were introduced in 1929, Silly Putty in 1949, and Barbie dolls in 1958.

18. b. The button-down collar was introduced in 1890, but it was the big thing in men's fashion again in the 1950s. Keds marketed the first tennis shoes in 1917, and nylon replaced silk for stockings in 1940.

19. b. Levis was a popular brand of jeans throughout the last third of the nineteenth century. Pajamas became popular in 1910, and saddle shoes replaced spats in the late 1920s, then were popular again in the 1950s.

20. d. Secretary of state was a cabinet post during George Washinton's time. Thomas Jefferson was the first to hold that post. Secretaries of commerce and labor were posts created in 1913. HEW was founded in 1953.

*Apollo–Soyuz* linkup

## SLICED BREAD

### Sequence 2: What's New?

21. Skateboards were first marketed in c. the 1960s.

22. "Put a tiger in your tank" was a slogan promoting b. Exxon gasoline.

23. a. Henry Ford said "Machinery is the new Messiah."

24. *Soyuz 7* was b. a Soviet spacecraft.

25. Rinso White and Rinso Blue were c. laundry soaps (the world's first, introduced in 1918).

26. The word "newscast" was coined in the a. 1920s.

27. The "Breakfast of Champions" is: d. Wheaties.

28. "It's not nice to fool Mother Nature" advertised b. margarine.

29. b. A refrigerator was what Willis H. Carrier made possible.

30. c. Ted Turner started CNN in 1980.

31. The f. Ryan NYP was not an automobile. It was the plane Lindbergh flew to Paris in 1927.

32. b. The bikini came first, in 1946.

33. DDT was a. an insecticide.

34. "The greatest week," according to Nixon, was the week that saw: b. the landing of men on the moon in 1969.

35. a. The bossa nova was new in '62.

36. Aspartame was marketed under the name c. NutraSweet.

37. Marlon Brando rebelled against everything in d. *The Wild One.*

38. Antioxidants were b. disease-preventing vitamin supplements.

39. The "old" Coke came back under the name b. Coke Classic.

40. Hamburger Helper joined the array of choices in c. 1970.

## SLICED BREAD

### Sequence 3: Creators and Creations

41. R. Crumb created: u. Mr. Natural

42. Dana Carvey created: d. The Church Lady

43. W. C. Fields created: g. Egbert Souse

44. Mickey Spillane created: r. Mike Hammer

45. Ken Kesey created: a. Nurse Ratchet

46. Walter Lantz created: b. Woody Woodpecker

47. Jonathan Winters created m. Maude Frickert

48. Lily Tomlin created t. Edith Ann

49. Agatha Christie created: c. Hercule Poirot

50. Chic Young created w. Dagwood

51. Mike Myers created: p. Wayne

52. Carolyn Keene created: f. Nancy Drew

53. Chester Gould created: e. Dick Tracy

54. Edgar Rice Burroughs created: s. Tarzan

55. Joseph Heller created: h. Yossarian

56. Walt Disney created: j. Oswald the Rabbit

57. L. Frank Baum created: k. the Wizard of Oz

58. Steven Spielberg created: n. E.T.

59. Langston Hughes created: y. Simple

60. Edgar Lee Masters created: i. Miniver Cheevy

61. P. G. Wodehouse created: x. Jeeves

62. Richard Wright created: l. Bigger Thomas

63. Matt Groening created: v. Bart Simpson

64. Ian Fleming created: q. James Bond

65. Bill Cosby created: o. Fat Albert

**SLICED BREAD**

*Sequence 4: Decades of Change*

66. Social Security: 1935

67. Rock 'n' roll: 1950s

68. Pong: 1970s

69. ATMs: 1980s

70. the Internet: 1990s

71. Pillsbury bakeoff: 1940s

72. Prozac: introduced in 1988; became widely known in the 1990s

73. Cinemascope: 1953

74. Chanel No. 5: 1921

75. Popeye: debuts in 1929, hits popularity peak in the 1930s

76. *Roe* v. *Wade*: 1973

77. The Gideons: traveling salesmen founded the group in 1899, but the placement of Bibles began in the first decade of the twentieth century.

78. Apple computers: 1970s

79. Betamax: 1970s (By the mid-'80s, this superior home video format had lost the war for market share.)

80. Affirmative action: 1970s

81. Automatic transmissions: 1930s

82. Food stamps: first issued on a limited scale in 1939. The program ends in 1943, then is reactivated widely in the 1960s.

83. Disposable diapers: 1960s

84. Girl Scouts of America: 1913

85. Eight-track tapes: 1970s

## SLICED BREAD

### Sequence 5: The Last Dance

86. The twist: 1960s

87. The jerk: 1960s

88. The Charleston: 1920s

89. Disco dancing: 1970s

90. Slam dancing: 1980s

91. The stroll: 1950s

92. Moshing: 1990s

93. The cha cha: 1950s

94. The black bottom: 1920s

95. The Castle walk: 1910–20

96. Big Apple: 1930s

97. Hustle: 1970s

98. Break dancing: 1980s

99. Vogueing: 1990s

100. Bunny hug: 1900–10

Scoring: Since few of us know when many of our most ubiquitous consumer products were launched, these questions called for a fair amount of guessing. And guessing can lead to error. If you had over 65 of these correct, you did very well, indeed.

Benito Mussolini

# MUSSOLINI: ROLE MODEL

It makes no difference how we regard Benito Mussolini, whether as a heaven-sent leader as do many, or as a more or less benevolent tyrant, as do some of the more thoughtful of his countrymen, we must admit he has a positive genius for advertising and selling. . . .

[He understands] the essence of modern sales management: A firm hand, an ear open for news from the field, an eye on competition, a jealous guarding of the faith stream, flexibility of mind and plans, respect for the strength and energy of the young men of his force, and a determination not to let it be killed by the cynical sophistication of the old timers.

This is the sales management of today—and of tomorrow: firm, clean cut, open minded, intelligently arbitrary, back turned on yesterday.

—*The Magazine of Business*, June 1929
(from an article entitled "Benito Mussolini, Master Sales Manager")

# 4

# Hairy Times

*The temptation to condescend to the past
through nostalgia . . . is irresistible.*

—GREIL MARCUS, 1978

This chapter is intended as a diversion. Ostensibly, its subject is hair. There are fewer questions than you'll find in other chapters, and many of the questions are about show business.

Albert Camus said of modern man: "He fornicated and read the papers." The definition is incomplete. Modern man (and woman) also spent lots of time making mischief and trouble, and we spent a nearly equivalent amount of time and energy seeking entertainment and fretting about our appearance.

In the late 1960s, Crosby, Stills, and Nash had a song called "I Almost Cut My Hair." The significance of this little aural artifact is bound to be lost on anyone who didn't live through the hair hysteria of the 1960s, when a decision to cut one's hair was freighted with political, social, and existential weight. To cut one's hair was to lose one's soul, to sell out, to give up one's identity. In the '60s, you were what you ate, and you also were what your hair proclaimed you to be.

Though, for all that, hair has been prominent among our concerns in every decade. The '60s may have been unusually preoccupied with hair, but so was the first decade of the century, exemplified by the "big" hair styles of the Gibson girl, an iconic image of that time. The early years of this century saw the Marcel wave gain wide popularity, followed by the permanent wave and the home permanent, which had become common by the 1920s. "Hairdo" was a new word in that decade. Bobbed hair characterized the flapper, just as the flapper characterized the Jazz Age. Though times were tight in the 1930s, the decade did come up with a loose feather-cut style that would reappear in slightly different form during the 1970s on the head of Farrah Fawcett-Majors (and nearly every young woman who ever beheld her image in that decade). Women's hairstyles continued to grow longer in the early World War II years, especially in the over-one-eye look inspired by Veronica Lake (who would cut her hair, and therewith her career, in service to the war effort). During the '50s, the line between crew cuts and ducktails was a central cultural division. The '60s brought us a hit musical called *Hair*, which seemed to call for the worship of hair, and the late '70s and early '80s saw people moussing, coloring, and spiking their hair in yet another hirsute statement of outrage, disaffection, or identification with one or another group, attitude, or social posture. The '80s also gave us the phrase "bad hair day," which became a cliché in nearly record time. By the early '90s, people were shaving their heads in intricate patterns, or affecting "the Rachel cut" in emulation of a character on a popular sitcom.

Through flood, famine, war, and pestilence, we fussed over our hair. From the high and the mighty, to the low and meek, we colored it, teased it, feathered it, razor-cut it, bobbed it, blew it dry, moussed it, sprayed it, rinsed it, dyed it, and forced it into shapes it didn't want to make. We made it stand up and lay down, and we made it stand for ideas, positions, and class origins. When our hair abandoned us, we transplanted it to our heads from other parts of our bodies, or we sprayed bald patches to make them look as though the hair was still there. It was a century that asked a lot of our hair, occupying the attention of nearly everyone, including First Lady Hillary Clinton, who said:

> Hair to me has always been the one part of my body that I had control over. I could not grow any taller, I could not lengthen my legs, I could not make my eyes have perfect vision—there was nothing else I could really do . . . I've cut it, permed it, highlighted it, worn it short, worn it long. I was always having fun with it, and I never realized it would be such a serious subject.

During the same decade Ms. Clinton was talking about her hair, Stanford University was offering a course called "Black Hair as Culture and History." Among the topics covered were the role hair played in the evolution of black society. Among the lectures: "The Rise of the Afro" and "Fade-O-Rama, Braiding, and Dreadlocks." The course could be taken toward fulfillment of the university's multiculturalism requirements.

If a First Lady and a major university aren't credible proof of our preoccupation with hair, then check out Kato Kaelin on the subject. In *Details* magazine, the world's most famous houseguest wrote:

When I was going through the trial, clumps of my hair were coming out from stress. Now I lose more hair taking my sunglasses out of it after I've pushed them up than from anything else. The hair gets caught on the lip of the glasses where you have the little nose things, and I need those kind of glasses for my eyes. But that's eye care, and a whole nother story.

That hair loss theme runs through men's obsession with hair, though we did manage ways of dealing with it. TV and movie star Ted Danson handled his bald spot thus: "My hair is not a problem. I look in the mirror, and I look fantastic. When I turn my back to you, then you've got a problem, but I don't. This is my cosmic mooning to the rest of the world."

And, if that comment wasn't cosmic enough, here are a few words from *Interview* magazine about a fashionable hairdresser:

[He] is to hair in the 1990s what Betsy Ross was to the American flag in 1776. . . . Like our old friend Betsy, he encourages everyone to . . . share in what this look signifies—that all life is about going through all kinds of patches, that nothing and no one is perfect, and that acts of mending and piecing things together are acts of healing, humanity, and grace.

So, it seems we put a great deal of weight on our hair, and not just when our heads hit the pillow.

The questions that follow are pretty hairy. Some you'll know; some you won't.

## HAIRY TIMES

1. Name the popular country singer whose hair nearly reached the floor. Her biggest hit was in 1979 with "Don't It Make My Brown Eyes Blue?" _____

2. Name that long-haired singer's sister. _____

3. "Does she, or doesn't she?" That was an innuendo-packed '50s advertising slogan for what product? _____

4. Who would you have seen if you'd gone to a concert on the "Blonde Ambition" tour of the 1990s? _____

5. "I'm Gonna Wash That Man Right Out of My Hair" was a song from a hit Broadway musical of 1949. Name it. _____

6. That Broadway hit was based on a 1947 best seller written by one of the century's most popular writers. Name him. _____

7. "I'd love to kiss you, but I just washed my hair." It's a famous line from a less-remembered '30s film. Who said it? _____

8. *The Hairy Ape* was a 1922 play by _____

9. The "Rachel cut" was named after a character on the '90s sitcom *Friends*. The actress who played Rachel was _____

10. "Angel-headed hipsters" were found in a revolutionary 1950s Allen Ginsberg poem called _____

11. He was the ex-con boxing promoter with the trademark fright wig hair. _____

12. On '70s TV, he was the character who endured bald jokes from the "Happy Homemaker." _____

13. Writer Kingsley Amis said this national leader lacked "compassionate hair." He was talking about the longest-serving British prime minister of the twentieth century. That was _____

14. "If truth is beauty, how come no one has their hair done in the library?" This question was posed by the same comedian whose characters included

Ernestine and Edith Ann. She

was _____

15. Dreadlocks. The fashion came from Jamaica, along with the music known as reggae, in the late 1960s. The dreadlocks were part of a religious stance taken by people who called themselves _____

16. In the first Beatles film, a journalist asks George Harrison what he calls his haircut. "Arthur," is Harrison's reply. What was the name of that film? _____

17. Johnny Carson once described this pioneer TV talk show host as looking as if he had a dead cat on his head. Who was Carson talking about? _____

18. In his autobiography (as told to Alex Haley), he told of having his hair "conked" in Harlem barber shops. That was in the late '40s, when he was still Little, before he became _____

19. What does "conked" mean, anyway? _____

20. His most famous short story was "Haircut," published in 1926. _____

A brief digression before pressing on. Peruse the cultural artifact below for a glimpse of the kind of blatant racism once found on display in our most respected newspapers. The "news" item, quoted in its entirety, is a 1905 *New York Times* article about a threatened strike of black barbers.

\* \* \*

## NEGRO BARBERS REVOLT

*No Sunday Work, They Say, as the Picnic Season Draws Nigh*

With the opening season for watermelons about due, the negro barbers of Brooklyn are in revolt against Sunday shaving. The journeymen barbers have informed their bosses that if they don't yield to the demand for Sunday closing a general strike will go into effect on June 10.

An outbreak of religion among the barbers is said to be responsible for the Sunday closing movement. But the boss barbers laughed derisively yesterday when the religious feature of the trouble was suggested.

"Ah guess Ah knows what's at de bottom od dis heah Sunday closin' business, all right," said one who has a shop in Hudson Avenue. "Dis am de season of do year, son, when de black man's fancy turns to thought ob dodgin' work. Just about now de Sunday picnics begins, and dey ain't no joy for a coon to be working wid a razzer in a shop when he might be adoin' more artistic work wid de blade out where de band am playin'. Dat coon what dey say got converted is Chairman of sebenteen picnic committees, and Ah guess it's de prospect of leadin' de gran' march 'stead of religion what's set him agin Sunday shavin'."

We return you now to the questions, already in progress.

* * *

21. Three Flowers, Excellente, Dixie Peach, and Black & White were all _____.

22. *Gentlemen Prefer Blondes* was a 1925 novel by Anita Loos, and a 1953 movie starring Jane Russell and _____.

NOTE: A headline in a California paper of 1900 read, "BLONDE BRIDE SEEKS A DIVORCE." It was common through much of the century to identify women in news stories by hair color. Seventies feminists ended this practice by pointing out, quite reasonably, that no headline about males ever read "RAVEN-HAIRED CEO," or "BRUNETTE CONGRESSMAN."

23. "Handkerchief heads" was a term of derision among blacks during the 1960s. Why? _____.

24. "Spoolies" turned up in the 1950s. What were they? _____.

25. The cartoon character with the big blue beehive hairdo was _____.

26. "And a ponytail hangin' down . . . Oh baby you know what I like . . . " These words are from a song by '50s rocker the Big Bopper. Do you remember the title? _____.

27. Do you recall this jingle from the early years of television? If so, fill in the blank: "Use Wildroot Hair Oil, _____."

28. He was a featured vocalist with the Ted Weems orchestra in the 1930s, but before that he was a barber from

Pennsylvania. He had forty-two top-ten hits between 1944 and 1958, and he was one of the most loved TV entertainers of the 1950s. He was _____.

29. Stephen Sondheim wrote a musical based on an old melodrama about a barber who murdered his customers. The show opened on Broadway in 1979. The show and the barber were _____.

30. "A little dab'll do ya," was ad copy used to sell _____.

31. On *The Andy Griffith Show*, the name of Mayberry's barber was _____.

32. "It may cost a little more, but you're worth it" was an ad slogan used to sell what line of hair products? _____

33. Born in 1902, he was first elected to public office in 1933, and he was still running as an incumbent senator from South Carolina in the late '90s. When he was on television, it was hard not to notice his orange-tinted hair transplants. Name? _____

34. There was a decade when women took to pressing their hair on the ironing board. What decade? _____

35. What were "cornrows," and when were they in fashion? _____

36. Main Street America may have seen its first Afro haircut on the '60s television show *The Mod Squad*. Name the actor who sported that sizeable Afro, or the character he played. _____

37. This Spanish surrealist painter was known for his 1931 painting *The Persistence of Memory*, for his relentless self-promotion, and for his elaborately waxed mustache. He was _____.

38. Warren Beatty played a hairdresser in a 1975 film. That film was entitled _____.

39. This TV newsman wore an obvious hairpiece, took an annual government subsidy of ninety-seven thousand dollars for his sheep ranch, and coanchored the show called *Prime Time Live*. He was _____.

40. The decade when the comic strip character Blondie first showed up was _____.

41. Name the early rock 'n' roll pioneer who wore a spit curl on his forehead. _____

42. The actor with the shaved head who played Kojak was _____.

43. "I think the most important thing a woman can have—next to talent of course—is her hairdresser." The actress and Pepsi executive who made that observation in 1957 was also the subject of the book and movie called *Mommie Dearest*. Her name? _____

44. In his first year in office, he was criticized for getting a haircut on Air Force One and backing up air traffic in the process. That president was _____.

45. He was the basketball player with the orange hair (depending on what day of the week it was). He was also as "Bad as [he wanted] to be." _____

46. "Kookie, Kookie, lend me your comb" was a novelty record of the 1950s. Can you name the actor who played Kookie? _____

47. Marlon Brando said of him: "He's the kind of guy that when he dies, he gives

God a bad time for making him bald." The guy in question wore a hairpiece since the times when his career was reborn with the role of Maggio in *From Here to Eternity*. He is _____.

48. Loose talk about "a pubic hair on a can of Coke" nearly brought this nominee down on allegations of sexual harassment. Though 31 percent of Americans couldn't identify him in 1995, you probably remember that his name was _____.

49. Latin-American literary lion Jorge Luis Borges said this 1982 war was "a fight between two bald men over a comb." What war was fought in 1982? _____

50. The country singer whose career started with Porter Wagoner was once asked how long it took to do her hair. She said she didn't know; she wasn't there when it happened. That wig wearer was _____.

## ANSWERS

1. "Don't It Make My Brown Eyes Blue?" singer: Crystal Gayle

2. Crystal Gayle's sister: Loretta Lynn

3. "Does she, or doesn't she?" advertised: Clairol

4. The "Blonde Ambition" tour: Madonna

5. The hit Broadway musical of 1949: *South Pacific*

6. The man who wrote the 1947 best seller: James Michener

7. " . . . but I just washed my hair" was dialogue for: Bette Davis. The movie was *Cabin in the Cotton*, 1932. She later said it was her favorite line.

8. *The Hairy Ape*: Eugene O'Neill

9. The actress who played Rachel: Jennifer Aniston

10. "Angel-headed hipsters" was a line from: *Howl*

11. Ex-con boxing promoter: Don King

12. TV character who endured bald jokes: Murray Slaughter, played by Darren McGavin on *The Mary Tyler Moore Show*.

13. The leader who lacked "compassionate hair": Margaret Thatcher

14. Ernestine and Edith Ann creator: Lily Tomlin

15. Dreadlocks were worn by: Rastafarians

16. The first Beatles film: *A Hard Day's Night*

17. Carson was talking about? Phil Donahue

18. After he was (Malcolm) Little, he became: Malcolm X

19. "Conking" hair was: A chemical process of hair straightening, considered hip among black men until it came to be considered politically incorrect.

20. "Haircut" writer: Ring Lardner

21. Three Flowers et al.: hair pomades, such as Bud's Butch Wax

22. *Gentlemen Prefer Blondes* star: Marilyn Monroe

23. "Handkerchief heads" was a term of derision: because blacks who had their hair straightened kept it straight by wearing a handkerchief on their heads. Hair straightening was considered a failure to show proper ethnic pride.

24. "Spoolies": rubber spools used to curl hair

25. The cartoon character with the blue beehive: Marge Simpson

26. Song by the Big Bopper: "Chantilly Lace"

27. "Use Wildroot Hair Oil, Charley."

28. Ted Weems featured vocalist: Perry Como

29. Stephen Sondheim show: *Sweeney Todd*

30. "A little dab'll do ya," ad copy for: Brylcreem

31. Mayberry's barber: Floyd Lawson

32. "It may cost a little . . ." was an ad for: L'Oreal

33. Senator with orange-tinted hair transplants: Strom Thurmond

34. Hair-pressing decade: 1960s

35. "Cornrows": rows of tight braids separated by narrow parts, worn by roots-seeking (not a pun) black folk of the 1970s.

36. *The Mod Squad* actor/character: Clarence Williams III played Linc Hayes

37. Spanish surrealist painter: Salvador Dali

38. 1975 Warren Beatty film: *Shampoo*

39. Coanchor of *Prime Time Live*: Sam Donaldson

40. Blondie first showed up: 1930

41. Rock 'n' roll pioneer: Bill Haley

42. The actor who played Kojak: Telly Savalas

43. The subject of *Mommie Dearest*: Joan Crawford

44. Air Force One haircut given to: Bill Clinton

45. "Bad as [he wanted] to be" basketball player: Dennis Rodman

46. The actor who played Kookie: Edd Byrnes

47. Maggio in *From Here to Eternity*: Frank Sinatra

48. "Pubic hair on a can of Coke" nominee: Clarence Thomas

49. War fought in 1982: the Falklands War (between Great Britain and Argentina)

50. The country singer/wig wearer: Dolly Parton

Scoring: 50–41 correct: two heads up. 25–40 correct: You're receding. Fewer than 25: a bad hair day.

# 5

# Anachronisms—
# The Challenge of
# the Century

*Time is what prevents everything from happening all at once.*

—MARVIN COHEN

Have you ever played "Spot the Anachronism," where you go to bad movies and try to catch the historically inaccurate detail, the most glaring visual anachronisms? The sword-and-sandal epics used to yield the best results, with Roman gladiators wearing watches and extras wearing sunglasses. B westerns sometimes offered up people wearing pants with zippers long before zippers were invented, or shooting guns that had yet to be seen in the periods depicted.

"Out of time"—that's what an anachronism is. In the following brief sets, it's your job to pick out the anachronism, to spot the mistake, to toss out the one that doesn't belong with the others.

No one, of course, could be expected to remember or know all of the things included in the upcoming list of over four hundred events of the century. Much of this is time out of mind—things you may have once known but have since forgotten. As in other challenges in this book, the hope is that what you know will allow you to make deductions that lead you to right answers, even when you may not know every item in each set.

This is a series you can think your way through. If you

know some things with certainty, you can deduce others. I have made no sequence difficult for the sake of difficulty. On the contrary, some of the anachronisms are, perhaps, too easy to spot. And what you may have forgotten (or may not have known) can disclose itself to you as you go through the deductive process of sorting out what happened when, and what never happened at all.

All that said, this is not an easy series (degree of difficulty: 8). We all know the surprise of being reminded that a particular event took place a dozen years ago when our memories seemed convinced that it had happened much more recently. As Willie Nelson had it in his song, "Ain't it funny how time slips away." See how much has slipped away, and see how much you can piece back together.

This is, after all, the challenge of the century. Year by year, what is out of place?

## THE FIRST DECADE

The problem of the twentieth century is the problem of the color line.

—W. E. B. Du Bois, 1900

### 1900

a. Boer War rages in South Africa.

b. McKinley/Roosevelt elected president/vice-president.

c. Israeli troops skirmish with Egyptians.

d. Boxer Rebellion sweeps China.

### 1901

a. Termed "unsinkable," *Titanic* sinks in North Atlantic.

b. Queen Victoria dead at eighty-two.

c. President McKinley falls to an assassin.

d. First Nobel Prizes awarded.

### 1902

a. Aswan Dam completed in Egypt.

b. Serbs and Croats fight each other in Slavic capital of Agram.

c. Sinclair Lewis's novel *Main Street* stirs controversy.

d. French filmmaker Georges Melies makes first sci-fi film, called *A Trip to the Moon*.

### 1903

a. Ford sells its first car.

b. First World Series played in Boston.

c. First multivehicle accident ties up San Francisco's Golden Gate Bridge.

d. Wrights achieve heavier-than-air flight at Kitty Hawk.

## 1904

a. Ivan Pavlov wins Nobel Prize for studies in "conditioned responses," the salivating dog cliché of all psych courses to follow.

b. Tom Mix is top western film star.

c. New York City subway system opened.

d. A woman is arrested for smoking in public on Fifth Avenue in New York City.

## 1905

a. President Roosevelt plays key role in ending Russo-Japanese war.

b. Massacre at Wounded Knee quells Sioux Ghost Dance uprising.

c. IQ tests make their first appearance.

d. Belmont Park Race Track opens in Long Island, New York.

## 1906

a. Over one thousand people perish in San Francisco earthquake/fire.

b. British prime minister Winston Churchill presides over one-fifth of the globe, the peak of Britain's imperial empire.

c. Booker T. Washington says race relations improved after an Atlanta riot left over a dozen blacks dead in the streets.

d. Upton Sinclair publishes The Jungle, exposing conditions in the meat-packing industry.

## 1907

a. "The Gibson Girl" sets the style for women.

b. Picasso and others develop the school of painting known as Cubism.

c. The Boy Scouts initiated by Englishman Sir Robert Baden-Powell.

d. Charlie Chaplin introduces his "Little Tramp" character to motion picture audiences.

## 1908

a. "Great White Hope" Jim Jeffries defeated by Jack Johnson in Reno, Nevada.

b. The phrase "young Turks" enters the English-speaking lexicon after the Young Turk Movement rebels in futile hopes of saving the Ottoman Empire.

c. Boy Scouts founded in Great Britain.

d. Marlon Brando born in Nebraska.

## 1909

a. Theodore Roosevelt dead at age fifty-one.

b. One hundredth anniversary of Abraham Lincoln's birth celebrated in New York. Speakers include Booker T. Washington and Civil War general George McClellan's son, who is the mayor of New York.

c. National Association for the Advancement of Colored People (NAACP) founded in New York.

d. William Howard Taft is inaugurated president of the U.S.

e. Robert E. Peary makes it to the North Pole.

# 1910–19

The cinema is little more than a fad. . . .
What audiences really want to see is flesh
and blood on the stage.

—Charlie Chaplin, 1916

You will be home before the leaves have
fallen from the trees.

—Kaiser Wilhelm of Germany,
seeing his troops off in August 1914

## 1910

a. President William Howard Taft, America's
heftiest president, enters his second year in office.

b. U.S. population reaches nearly 92 million
people, a 20 percent increase in a twenty-year
period.

c. Mark Twain dead at age seventy four.

d. Crooner Rudy Vallee sweeps the nation in
popularity.

e. Stravinsky introduces *The Firebird* ballet.

## 1911

a. Lucille Ball and Ronald Reagan enter the world.

b. War breaks out in Europe after Archduke
Ferdinand is assassinated in Sarajevo.

c. Roald Amundsen leads a successful expedition
to the South Pole.

d. Harriet Quimby, first licensed U.S. woman pilot,
dies in aviation accident.

## 1912

a. Native American athlete Jim Thorpe wins the
Olympic decathlon in Sweden.

b. U.S. troops dispatched to Nicaragua to prop up
U.S. puppet, President Adolfo Diaz. Troops will
remain for nearly twenty years.

c. Czar Nicholas II and his family assassinated by
Bolsheviks.

d. Explorer Robert Scott and companions perish
in Antarctica.

## 1913

a. The Armory Show in New York introduces
modernism in art to Americans. Artists shown
include Picasso, Duchamp, and Brancusi.

b. Richard Nixon, Gerald Ford, and Rosa Parks all
born this year.

c. Stravinsky's *Rite of Spring* premieres this year,
another milestone of modernism.

d. Amos 'n' Andy debut on radio.

## 1914

a. The fox-trot fad sweeps America's dance floors.

b. *Tarzan of the Apes,* first Tarzan book, published.

c. Work begins on the Panama Canal.

d. Trench warfare begins in Europe.

## 1915

a. D. W. Griffith's controversial film *Birth of a
Nation* opens in New York.

b. One hundred twenty-four Americans perish as British liner *Lusitania* is sunk by German submarine.

c. Scott Joplin, Eubie Blake, and others introduce the music known as ragtime.

d. Frank Sinatra and Edith Piaf both born this year.

## 1916

a. "Black Jack" Pershing is chasing Pancho Villa all over Mexico after Villa stages a raid on a town in New Mexico.

b. "Shell shock" first diagnosed as a war-caused affliction.

c. Lucky Strike cigarettes taken off the market as being too high in nicotine, and therefore too addictive.

d. T. E. Lawrence (Lawrence of Arabia) begins to build his legend in the Middle East.

## 1917

a. U.S. enters World War I.

b. World War I ends in German defeat.

c. Piggly Wiggly launches first supermarket chain.

d. George M. Cohan writes "Over There," virtually the anthem of the First World War.

## 1918

a. Nelson Mandela, Mike Wallace, Ella Fitzgerald, and Ted Williams are born.

b. On the eleventh hour of the eleventh day of the eleventh month, World War I ends in German defeat.

c. Czar Nicholas and family killed by Bolsheviks in the Ural Mountains.

d. Gary Cooper and Humphrey Bogart both make their film debuts.

## 1919

a. In the U.S., it is the year of the "Red Scare," and the year the American Communist party is founded.

b. Senator-to-be Joseph McCarthy is eleven years old.

c. The pogo stick makes its first appearance and becomes instantly popular.

d. Jimmie Rodgers, the father of country music, has one of his first hits with the song "In the Jailhouse Now."

# THE 1920s

If Jesus were alive today, He would be a Shriner.

> —Reverend Whitcomb Brougher,
> Los Angeles, 1926

The Episcopal Church provides churches for Negroes. Several of these churches are within easy reach of this locality. Therefore, the rector of this parish discourages attendance or membership in this church of members of that race.

> —Reverend John Blackshear,
> Brooklyn, New York, 1927

## 1920

a. Woodrow Wilson is president, though he is recovering from a stroke. Many of his presidential duties have been assumed by his wife.

b. Women turn out in large numbers to cast their votes in favor of the nineteenth amendment to the constitution.

c. Eight Chicago White Sox players are indicted for fixing the World Series.

## 1921

a. Republican Calvin Coolidge becomes thirtieth president of the United States.

b. Heart disease surpasses tuberculosis as leading cause of death in the U.S.

c. Ad agency dreams up "Betty Crocker" as a symbol of Gold Medal flour.

d. Sacco and Vanzetti trial commands international attention.

## 1922

a. Diabetics get insulin for the first time in history.

b. Hitler assumes power in Germany.

c. T. S. Eliot publishes "The Waste Land."

d. Charles Atlas, a former "ninety-seven-pound weakling," and soon-to-be inspiration to millions of skinny adolescents, is named the "world's most perfectly developed man" by *Physical Culture* magazine.

## 1923

a. Billie Holiday joins the ranks of jazz giants with the release of the songs "Gimme a Pigfoot" and "Downhearted Blues."

b. Vice-President Calvin Coolidge assumes the presidency after the death of Warren Harding.

c. Mah-jongg fad reaches its peak with 10 million American women playing the game on a regular basis.

d. The word "Frigidaire" enters the language as GM markets its refrigerator under that name.

## 1924

a. Calvin Coolidge is reelected.

b. Elvis Presley is born in Tupelo, Mississippi.

c. Ford Motor Company produces its 10 millionth automobile.

d. After a takeover, CTR (Computing Tabulating Recording Company) is renamed IBM (International Business Machines).

## 1925

a. Surrealist painters hold first collective show in Paris.

b. The Charleston is hottest dance craze.

c. Mark Twain decries decline in morality.

d. Hitler publishes *Mein Kampf.*

e. "Monkey trial" ends with Scopes's conviction.

f. F. Scott Fitzgerald's *The Jazz Age* is a popular chronicle of the times.

## 1926

a. Ernest Hemingway's *The Sun Also Rises* is published, defining a generation and influencing prose styles for the rest of the century.

b. Marilyn Monroe, Miles Davis, Chuck Berry, and Hugh Hefner enter the world, as does the first Winnie-the-Pooh book.

Adolf Hitler, 1889–1945

The broad masses of people will more easily fall victim to a big lie than to a small one.

—ADOLF HITLER,
*MEIN KAMPF*, 1924

We want peace and understanding, nothing else.

—ADOLF HITLER,
SPEECH, BERLIN, 1933

* * *

c. U.S. Marines chase the original "Sandinistas" around Nicaragua.

d. Edward G. Robinson makes screen debut in *Little Caesar.*

e. Harry Houdini, master illusionist, dies on Halloween night.

## 1927

a. King Edward VIII abdicates the throne of England in order to marry a divorced commoner.

b. *The Jazz Singer,* generally regarded as the first talking motion picture, has its premiere in New York.

c. Wonder Bread is first marketed to a nation hungry for soft white bread of questionable nutritional value.

d. The Heisenberg Uncertainty Principle is introduced, shaking ideas of "objective truth" and scientific objectivity.

## 1928

a. The world gets its first taste of Peter Pan peanut butter and Fleer's Dubble Bubble bubble gum.

b. The world gets its first look at Mickey Mouse.

c. The world first hears the voices of Amos 'n' Andy on radio.

d. The U.S. sees the first automobile maps issued by Gulf Oil.

## 1929

a. St. Valentine's Day Massacre results in death of seven gangsters in Chicago mob wars.

b. Tennessee Williams premieres *The Glass Menagerie* on Broadway.

c. Stock market crashes on "Black Tuesday."

d. *All Quiet on the Western Front,* a novel of World War I, is a best seller.

# THE 1930s

B.O. is no respecter of persons.

—Lifebuoy soap ad, 1936

Are we going to sit here and think, or are we going to do something.

—Line of dialogue,
*The Mark of the Vampire,* 1935

\* \* \*

## 1930

a. John Steinbeck's *The Grapes of Wrath* makes a literary protest against the plight of migrant workers.

b. The planet Pluto is discovered by astronomers in Arizona.

c. Herbert Hoover assures the nation that "the Depression is over."

d. Bobby Jones becomes the first to win golf's "Grand Slam."

## 1931

a. Stalin firmly in control of the Soviet Communist party.

b. Baseball great Willie Mays is a rookie with the San Francisco Giants.

c. Boris Karloff stars in the original *Frankenstein*.

d. In Alabama, the nine young black men known to history as the "Scottsboro Boys" are convicted of rape in the first of a succession of trials.

## 1932

a. Elizabeth Taylor and Edward Kennedy enter the world, but "Baby Lindy" leaves it, dead at the hands of his kidnapper.

b. Army Chief of Staff Douglas MacArthur drives the Bonus Army (depression-weary WWI vets petitioning the government for emergency payments of promised bonus benefits) out of Washington. Two are killed, and dozens are injured.

c. The game of Monopoly is first marketed. It had been turned down by several toy companies before finally being marketed in this Depression year. Through the end of the Cold War, the game will be outlawed in the Soviet Union.

d. Richard Nixon elected to the California State Assembly, his first political post.

## 1933

a. Hitler is at the reins of power in Germany; Roosevelt is inaugurated as president of the U.S.

b. Nazis begin book burnings.

c. Prohibition ends in the U.S.

d. Jessie James dies in a Columbia, Missouri, nursing home.

## 1934

a. John Lennon born in Liverpool, England.

b. New Deal is fully underway to fight the Depression.

c. Bonnie and Clyde die in Texas Ranger ambush.

d. Bank robber John Dillinger gunned down by FBI agents outside a Chicago movie theater.

## 1935

a. Social Security system enacted into law by President Roosevelt.

b. Depression audiences cheered by Jimmy Stewart's performance in Frank Capra's film *It's a Wonderful Life*.

c. Dust storms devastate the American heartland.

d. Italy invades Ethiopia.

## 1936

a. Mussolini declares victory in Ethiopia.

b. Nazi troops overrun Paris; occupation of France begins.

c. Civil War erupts in Spain.

d. Jesse Owens spurned by Hitler after winning 100- and 200-meter events at Berlin Olympic games.

## 1937

a. Kirk Douglas makes his screen debut in *The Strange Love of Martha Ivers*.

b. Roosevelt begins his second term with the speech that includes the line: "I see one-third of a nation ill-housed, ill-clad, ill-nourished."

c. Ernest Hemingway reports on the Civil War in Spain, and George Orwell fights there on the side of the Republicans.

d. German dirigible *Hindenburg* explodes at mooring site in New Jersey.

## 1938

a. Nazis take Austria.

b. Orson Welles scares America with radio broadcast of *War of the Worlds*.

c. It will henceforth be produced by thousands of high-school drama departments, but Thornton Wilder's *Our Town* makes its debut on Broadway in this year.

d. "Twelfth of Never" is a hit song for Johnny Mathis.

e. Superman makes his first comic book appearance.

## 1939

a. John Wayne achieves major stardom in the role of Johnny Ringo in *Stagecoach*.

b. Norman Mailer publishes his first novel, *The Naked and the Dead*.

c. Germany seizes Czechoslovakia, then Poland.

d. Americans hear Judy Garland sing "Over the Rainbow" for the first time in *Wizard of Oz*.

## THE 1940s

The motel is the new home of disease, bribery, corruption, crookedness, rape, white slavery, thievery, and murder.

—J. Edgar Hoover, on motels, 1941

Nuts.

—General A. C. McAuliffe's press-laundered reply to a German demand that he surrender Bastogne, 1944

## 1940

a. Joe Louis is boxing's heavyweight champ.

b. Battle of Britain prompts Churchill's famous line: "Never was so much owed by so many to so few."

c. Mickey Rooney is top box-office star.

d. American troops begin invasion of North Africa.

## 1941

a. This is the year that contains the day "that will live in infamy."

b. This is the year that *Citizen Kane* is released, and the year that no Hearst paper will carry ads for it.

c. This is the year the Nazis invade the Soviet Union.

d. This is the year the United Nations is formed in San Francisco.

## 1942

a. MacArthur commands U.S. forces in Korea.

b. The Philippines falls to the Japanese.

c. Huge naval battle at Midway

d. On orders from their Nazi occupiers, French police arrest thirteen thousand Jews and herd them into the Velodrome in Paris.

## 1943

a. MGM Studios opens MGM Grand Casino in Las Vegas, the first major casino built in the desert town.

b. "The Desert Fox," Field Marshal Rommel, defeated in North Africa.

c. *Casablanca,* starring Humphrey Bogart and Ingrid Bergman, is released to theaters.

d. Warsaw ghetto uprising crushed. Storm troopers kill all remaining Jewish inhabitants.

## 1944

a. U.S. troops fight in Italy at Anzio and Monte Cassino.

b. D-Day invasion in Normandy

c. Amelia Earhart lost and feared dead in Pacific flight

d. Anne Frank and her family are taken by the Gestapo in Amsterdam.

## 1945

a. Atomic weapons are dropped on Hiroshima and Nagasaki.

b. VE and VJ days are celebrated.

c. Frankie Laine has number I hit record: "Rawhide."

d. After Eva Braun and Adolph Hitler are married, they take their own lives in a Berlin bunker.

## 1946

a. Truman assumes the office of president after Roosevelt dies in Georgia of a cerebral hemorrhage.

b. Dr. Benjamin Spock publishes *The Common Sense Book of Baby and Child Care,* as influential (and sometimes as controversial) as any book of the century.

c. GI Bill swells college enrollments.

d. Tide detergent turns up in this year, though it will soon seem as though we were never without it.

## 1947

a. The first Barbie dolls are marketed, rumored to be modeled after dolls used to advertise wares in an Amsterdam brothel.

b. India and Pakistan become independent nations.

c. Being newborns, O. J. Simpson, David Letterman, Dan Quayle, and Arnold Schwarzenegger have yet to master toilet training.

d. Jackie Robinson breaks major league baseball's color barrier as the first black man to play for Brooklyn Dodgers.

## 1948

a. Israel becomes a nation state.

b. Alger Hiss case launches Nixon's career nationally.

c. Truman beats Dewey.

d. James Dean appears in *East of Eden*.

## 1949

a. Hank Williams is the ascendant star of country music with songs like "Lovesick Blues."

b. Arthur Miller's *Death of a Salesman* opens on Broadway.

c. First Super Bowl game played in Los Angeles.

d. Orwell's *1984* published.

## THE 1950s

Have you no sense of decency, sir, at long last? Have you left no sense of decency?
　　—Joseph Welch to Joseph McCarthy, 1954

M-I-C—see you real soon. K-E-Y. Why? Because we like you.
　　　　　　　—Mouseketeers song, 1955

## 1950

a. California Governor Richard Nixon signs nation's first civil rights legislation into law.

b. Joseph McCarthy launches witch hunt by saying, "I have here in my hand a list of 205 members of the Communist party still working and shaping policy in the State Department."

c. John Wayne is top box-office star.

d. Jane Russell announces herself a "born-again Christian," calls God "a livin' doll."

## 1951

a. Elvis Presley explodes onto the scene with "Hound Dog" and "Heartbreak Hotel."

b. *Peanuts* comic strip begins to gain wide attention.

c. The Rosenberg spy trial ends in a double conviction.

d. Rock 'n' roll is given its name by disk jockey Alan Freed.

## 1952

a. Eisenhower/Nixon ticket prevails at the polls.

b. 3-D movies reach out to touch big American movie audiences.

c. The first hydrogen bombs are tested in the Pacific.

d. Babe Ruth leaves coaching, retires from baseball.

## 1953

a. Mass innoculations of Salk vaccine against polio (infantile paralysis) begin.

b. *Bonanza* debuts on NBC.

c. Test pilot Chuck Yaeger exceeds sixteen hundred miles per hour in X-1A jet.

d. Burt Lancaster stars in *From Here to Eternity*.

e. The coronation of Queen Elizabeth II takes place in London.

f. Patti Page sings "How Much Is That Doggie in the Window?"

## 1954

a. Ernest Hemingway commits suicide in Ketchum, Idaho.

b. The *Nautilus,* history's first nuclear-powered submarine, is launched at New London, Connecticut.

c. J. R. R. Tolkien's *The Fellowship of the Ring* is published, but it won't become popular for another dozen years, when it will become very popular indeed.

d. Army–McCarthy hearings break McCarthy's power.

e. Battle of Dien Bien Phu drives the French from Vietnam.

## 1955

a. Rosa Parks sets off a bus boycott after refusing to give up her seat in the whites-only section of a Montgomery, Alabama, bus.

b. The "coonskin cap" fad hits high gear in response to Disney's Davy Crocket series, and Disneyland is opened in Anaheim, California.

c. Fighting continues in Korea. Chinese communists make gains.

d. Emerging film star and cultural icon James Dean dies in auto accident.

## 1956

a. Football legend-to-be Joe Montana and tennis champ-to-be Bjorn Borg enter the world.

b. The novel *Peyton Place* is a big best seller. High-school kids share the racy parts.

c. Harry Belafonte and calypso ("Day-O") gain fad status.

d. Betty Friedan's *The Feminine Mystique* is published, and it begins to change the way women think of their roles.

## 1957

a. "Freedom Riders" Schwerner, Goodman, and Cheney are killed in Mississippi.

b. *American Bandstand* bows as a nationally televised celebration of rock music.

c. Jack Kerouac publishes *On the Road,* a '50s landmark.

d. Tennis star Althea Gibson becomes the first black player to win at Wimbledon.

## 1958

a. Carrie Fisher's dad, Eddie Fisher, leaves Debbie Reynolds to join the list of Liz Taylor's husbands.

b. Madonna and Michael Jackson are set loose upon the world, each born in this year.

c. Seat belts are made mandatory in all American automobiles.

d. Transatlantic passenger jet service begins.

## 1959

a. Landmark Miles Davis album *Kind of Blue* released.

b. Ray Charles scales the pop charts with "What'd I Say?"

c. Pat Boone publishes *'Twixt Twelve and Twenty,* a book of advice for teens.

d. Johnny Carson becomes host of the *Tonight* show.

e. Cuba falls to Castro.

# THE 1960s

The torch has been passed to a new generation of Americans.

—John F. Kennedy, inaugural, 1961

It's alright, ma, I'm only bleedin'.

—Bob Dylan, 1965

## 1960

a. Kennedy and Nixon conduct first televised presidential debates.

b. *Brown* v. *Board of Education* case rules that separate facilities are inherently unequal.

c. U-2 spy plane shot down over the Soviet Union. Pilot Francis Gary Powers convicted of espionage. (After his release from a Soviet prison, Powers would die in a helicopter crash in 1977 while working as an "eye in the sky" traffic reporter in southern California.)

d. Hitchcock's *Psycho* hits movie screens this year.

## 1961

a. Roger Maris breaks Babe Ruth's 1927 record of sixty home runs by hitting sixty-one.

b. Kennedy inaugurates the Peace Corps.

c. Bay of Pig fiasco dampens Kennedy's first year in office.

d. J. D. Salinger's *Catcher in the Rye* is published.

e. Ernest Hemingway a suicide in Ketchum, Idaho.

## 1962

a. Cuban Missile Crisis brings the world to the brink of nuclear war.

b. Best-selling books include *Happiness Is a Warm Puppy* and *One Flew Over the Cuckoo's Nest.*

c. Whites riot as James Meredith integrates the University of Mississippi.

d. Marilyn Monroe dead at thirty-six.

e. Rolling Stones' "I Can't Get No (Satisfaction)" tops record charts.

## 1963

a. President Kennedy assassinated in Dallas.

b. Betty Friedan's *The Feminine Mystique* is published.

c. Martin Luther King delivers "I Have a Dream" speech.

d. Elvis Presley is drafted; pundits predict it will kill his career.

## 1964

a. "Extremism in the defense of liberty is no vice" is a line uttered by Barry Goldwater at the GOP convention. Some think it costs him the election.

b. Barbra Streisand has a hit record with "People."

c. *All in the Family* debuts to disappointing early reaction.

d. *Goldfinger,* the third James Bond film, is released to great popularity.

## 1965

a. Bob Dylan offends traditional folkies and is booed after he goes electric at the Newport Folk Festival.

b. Watts riots leave thirty dead in LA after five days of violence.

c. Cassius Clay KOs Sonny Liston in forty-eight seconds of the first round to claim the heavyweight crown.

d. General Norman Schwarzkopf approves "free fire zones" in Vietnam wherein troops are authorized to fire at anything that moves.

## 1966

a. Mao's "Cultural Revolution" launched in China.

b. U.S. invades tiny island nation of Grenada.

c. Richard Speck murders eight nurses in Chicago.

d. Texas Tower sniper Charles Whitman kills twelve, wounds thirty-three at the University of Texas.

## 1967

a. American astronauts Grissom, White, and Chaffee die in flames at Cape Kennedy.

b. First Super Bowl game pits Packers against the Chiefs.

c. Salk vaccine introduced to conquer polio, dreaded scourge of childhood.

d. Muhammad Ali refuses military induction and is stripped of his heavyweight crown.

e. It is the "Summer of Love" in San Francisco

## 1968

a. Martin Luther King assassinated in Memphis.

b. Robert Kennedy assassinated in Los Angeles.

c. Viet Cong and North Vietnamese attack over one hundred Vietnamese cities and villages in Tet Offensive.

d. President Nixon announces increased bombing of North Vietnam.

e. Olympics held in Mexico City. Two American medalists suspended for giving the black power salute.

f. Beatles release *Magical Mystery Tour* album.

## 1969

a. Disney releases *Fantasia,* the first full-length animated feature film to use classical music as a score.

b. It's a bloody year that includes the My Lai massacre and Manson murders.

c. In a move seen by many as censorship, CBS cancels *The Smothers Brothers Comedy Hour.*

d. "One giant leap for mankind" taken by Neil Armstrong as man lands on the moon.

e. Mary Jo Kopechne drowns in mishap at Chappaquiddick.

# THE 1970s

You hear so much these days from the younger generation about relating to people. The fact is they do not know the first goddamned thing about love. They are so unhappy with themselves they are unfit for relationships.

—Nathaniel Branden, psychologist, 1970

Conservation is not a Republican ethic.

—John Erlichman, 1971

If the president does it, that means that it is not illegal.

—Richard Nixon, lawyer, 1977

## 1970

a. The Beatles break up.

b. Environmental movement institutionalized with observance of the nation's first Earth Day celebration.

c. National Guardsmen kill four at Kent State.

d. Harrison Ford stars in the first Indiana Jones adventure.

e. O. J. Simpson and A. C. Cowlings, formerly of Galileo High in San Francisco, are Buffalo Bills teammates.

## 1971

a. American dead in Vietnam exceed forty-five thousand.

b. *Ms.* magazine publishes first issue.

c. Attica prison riot in New York; forty-nine people die.

d. *The Graduate* introduces film audiences to Dustin Hoffman.

e. The *Pearl* album is released, a posthumous Janis Joplin collection.

## 1972

a. Anne Frank's diary found in Amsterdam.

b. Nixon orders mining of North Vietnamese harbors.

c. Nixon goes to China.

d. Francis Ford Coppola's *The Godfather* revives Brando's sagging career.

## 1973

a. *Roe* v. *Wade* case establishes a woman's right to an abortion during the first two trimesters of pregnancy.

b. Vice-president Agnew forced to resign after pleading "no contest" to tax evasion charges.

c. Bar codes for pricing are first seen in supermarkets. Many consumers fear the codes will be used to obscure prices.

d. Chevrolet introduces the Corvette.

## 1974

a. Thalidomide produces thousands of deformed children worldwide.

b. Lines lengthen at gas pumps at the height of the oil embargo.

c. Nixon resigns.

d. Ford pardons Nixon.

Anne Frank, 1929–45

By warding off the Jews, I am fighting for the Lord's work.

—ADOLF HITLER, 1938

We all live with the objective of being happy; our lives are all different and yet the same.

—ANNE FRANK, DIARY, 1944

\* \* \*

## 1975

a. Saigon falls to the North Vietnamese and Viet Cong.

b. Margaret Thatcher elected as first female British prime minister.

c. *Jaws* is movie hit of the year.

d. "Thrilla in Manila" fought between Muhammad Ali and Joe Frazier.

e. Ghost of Elvis makes first recorded appearance in New Jersey K-Mart.

## 1976

a. Barbara Walters becomes first woman in broadcasting to command a million-dollar-per-year salary.

b. America celebrates its tricentennial year.

c. *Rocky* makes Sylvester Stallone a star.

d. Jimmy Carter beats Ford in bid for the presidency.

## 1977

a. Love it or hate it, disco dancing is a national fad.

b. Gary Gilmore's execution breaks a ten-year ban on capital punishment in the United States.

c. *Roseanne* debuts on television to disappointing early ratings.

d. *Star Wars* is a bonanza at the box office.

e. Elvis is dead at forty-two.

## 1978

a. "We committed an act of revolutionary suicide protesting the conditions of an inhumane world." These were the last words of cult leader Jim Jones, who led 911 of his People's Temple followers to their deaths in Guyana.

b. *Dallas* debuts as the first of the prime-time TV soaps.

c. Lee Iacocca chosen to head ailing Chrysler Corp.

d. Air bags become standard equipment in American cars.

## 1979

a. *The Brady Bunch* appears on television for the first time.

b. Iran takes over U.S. embassy in Tehran, beginning the "hostage crisis."

c. John Wayne is dead of cancer at seventy-two.

d. Three Mile Island accident in Pennsylvania undermines confidence in nuclear power plants.

# THE 1980s

We have a different regard for human life than those monsters do.
—Ronald Reagan on the Soviets, 1980

We love your adherence to democratic principles—and to the democratic process.
—George Bush toast to Ferdinand Marcos, 1981

Cocaine is God's way of telling you you're making too much money.
—Robin Williams, 1984

## 1980

a. U.S. boycotts Moscow Olympic Games to protest Soviet military action in Afghanistan.

b. Attica prison riot: Twenty-eight inmates and nine guards die.

c. John Lennon killed in New York.

d. Mount St. Helens explodes in Washington state.

## 1981

a. Fifty-two American hostages released after 444 days of Iranian captivity.

b. Ronald Reagan shot; tells Nancy, "Honey, I forgot to duck."

c. Pope John Paul II shot, later forgives his would-be assassin.

d. *Saturday Night Fever* is box-office hit for John Travolta.

## 1982

a. Eight-track tapes introduced as home entertainment innovation.

b. Falkland Islands War pits Argentina against Great Britain.

c. Tylenol recalled after eight people die from poisoning in the first of many product-tampering incidents.

d. *Rambo* is a major hit movie.

e. *Real Men Don't Eat Quiche* is a best-selling sign of the times.

## 1983

a. "Crack"—the word and the substance—begins to be widely known in American society.

b. Opposition leader Benigno Aquino assassinated on his return to Manila.

c. Lorena Bobbitt severs her husband's penis.

d. Compact disk players are new on the market.

## 1984

a. The Los Angeles Raiders win Super Bowl XVIII in Tampa, Florida.

b. Jack Nicholson and Shirley MacLaine win Oscars for *Terms of Endearment.*

c. Geraldine Ferraro is the first woman to be a major party candidate for vice-president.

d. John Lennon and wife Yoko release *Double Fantasy,* their last album together.

## 1985

a. British scientists warn of a growing hole in the ozone layer.

b. Soviet Premier Gorbachev ushers in the period of perestroika.

c. Yuppies. Cocaine. Bret Easton Ellis's *Less Than Zero.* A decade gains definition.

d. Muhammad Ali loses his last fight, defeated by Leon Spinks.

## 1986

a. Space shuttle *Challenger* explodes over Florida, crew lost.

b. "The Chunnel" begins rail service between England and France.

c. Corazon Aquino, wife of slain Philippine reformer Benigno Aquino, takes over power in that country.

d. Chernobyl, the world's worst nuclear accident, contaminates a vast area near Kiev.

## 1987

a. First Dog "Millie" produces a best seller with *Millie's Book.*

b. Robert Bork nominated to the Supreme Court, but he is denied confirmation.

c. *The Cosby Show* is most watched television show of the decade.

d. Oliver North lies to congressional committee about Iran-Contra.

e. Stock market drops 508 points in one day.

## 1988

a. Jay Leno takes over as host of *The Tonight Show.*

b. Pan Am flight 103 explodes over Lockerbie, Scotland.

c. Bobby McFerrin's advice, "Don't Worry, Be Happy," is taken to heart. It sells 10 million copies.

d. VP debater Lloyd Bentsen tells Dan Quayle he's "no Jack Kennedy."

## 1989

a. Oliver North found guilty of obstructing congressional investigation.

b. Oil tanker *Exxon Valdez* spills two hundred forty thousand barrels of oil into Alaska's Prince William Sound.

c. Berlin Wall comes tumblin' down.

d. Vice-president Dan Quayle praises Samoans as "happy campers."

e. Murderer Gary Gilmore executed by Utah firing squad.

# THE 1990s

Life has a funny way of sneaking up on you.
—Alanis Morrisette, 1995

It's the economy, stupid.
—Clinton campaign slogan, 1992

## 1990

a. South African black nationalist leader Nelson Mandela freed after twenty-seven years in prison.

b. D.C. mayor Marion Barry arrested for and later convicted of smoking crack cocaine.

c. Germany reunified after forty-five years.

d. Iraq annexes Kuwait by force of arms.

e. Steve Martin's "King Tut" is a major novelty record hit.

## 1991

a. Desert Storm, the hundred-hour war, drives Iraq out of Kuwait.

b. The Navy's Tailhook scandal begins after a female officer files a complaint of rampant sexual harassment.

c. Coca Cola introduces the "New" Coke.

d. Anita Hill alleges that Supreme Court nominee Clarence Thomas sexually harassed her, but the charges do not block his confirmation.

## 1992

a. Ross Perot enters, leaves, then reenters presidential race.

b. Anwar Sadat assassinated in Egypt.

c. Culture wars begin with Dan Quayle assailing Murphy Brown for bearing a child out of wedlock and Pat Buchanan calling Hillary Clinton a radical feminist.

d. Serbs engage in "ethnic cleansing" in Bosnia; rape and murder of noncombatants is standard policy.

## 1993

a. Clinton appoints the first female attorney general, Janet Reno.

b. Muslim terrorists bomb the World Trade Center in New York.

c. The North American Free Trade Agreement is ratified despite opposition from people as various as Ross Perot, Ralph Nader, and Pat Buchanan.

d. Oil tanker *Exxon Valdez* spills 11 million gallons of oil into Alaska's Prince William Sound.

## 1994

a. Kurt Cobain, lead singer of rock group Nirvana, commits suicide.

b. Oprah Winfrey debuts her hugely successful TV talk show.

c. U.S. troops on a peacekeeping mission to Haiti.

d. O. J. Simpson in low-speed chase with LA police in pursuit.

e. *The Mask*, with Jim Carrey, is a major movie hit.

## 1995

a. Bomb blast rips government building in Oklahoma City.

b. American space shuttle *Atlantis* links with Russian space station *Mir;* crew members exchanged.

c. O. J. Simpson trial concludes after nine months.

d. House Speaker Tip O'Neill lends support to Republican's "Contract With America."

e. *Bridges of Madison County* hits movie screens after years as a best-selling novel.

## 1996

a. Israelis shell Lebanon in retaliation against Hezbollah. Scores die, including women and children. Hopes for peace dim again.

b. Dole emerges as Republican standard-bearer after beating Buchanan, Gramm, and Alexander in the primaries.

c. Seven-year-old Jessica Dubroff dies in plane crash while attempting to fly coast-to-coast in light aircraft.

d. Jerry Garcia's ashes strewn on the Ganges River.

e. Menendez trial ends in two hung juries.

## 1997

a. India celebrates fifty years of independence.

b. Clinton begins second term.

c. China regains sovereignty over Hong Kong.

d. After development delays, Microsoft introduces Windows '95.

e. Princess Diana killed in Paris auto accident.

## 1998

a. Mickey Mouse is seventy.

b. "The Boss," Bruce Springsteen, turns fifty.

c. Bill Clinton turns fifty, too.

d. Superman is sixty.

## 1999

a. U.S. relinquishes control over Panama Canal Zone.

b. The Macy's Thanksgiving Day Parade celebrates its seventy-fifth year.

c. The fiftieth annual Emmy Awards are observed.

d. Paul Newman turns seventy.

## 2000

a. Scholastic Aptitude Tests are one hundred years old.

b. Microsoft's Bill Gates turns fifty-five.

c. Mick Jagger is fifty-seven.

d. Had he lived, James Dean would be sixty-nine, and had she lived, Marilyn Monroe would be seventy-four.

\* \* \*

. . . the dying twentieth century . . . possibly the rottenest of all centuries.

—Cynthia Ozick, 1995

Wrap up the twentieth century; Fred Astaire is gone.

—Jack Kroll, 1987

## ANSWERS

The following things did not happen during the years in question.

### THE FIRST DECADE

1900: c.  Israeli troops did not skirmish with Egyptians. There was no state of Israel.

1901: a.  The "unsinkable" *Titanic* won't be launched or sunk for eleven more years.

1902: c.  Sinclair Lewis's novel *Main Street* will not stir controversy until it is published, in the 1920s.

1903: c.  A multivehicle accident couldn't tie up San Francisco's Golden Gate Bridge because the bridge is more than three decades from being built.

1904: b.  Tom Mix is not a top western film star, and he won't be for a half-dozen years or more. The very concept of a film star has yet to engulf the planet.

1905: b.  The massacre at Wounded Knee took place fifteen years earlier.

1906: b.  Winston Churchill does not preside over one-fifth of the globe. In 1906, he is thirty-two, serving as undersecretary for the colonies.

1907: d.  Charlie Chaplin is eighteen years old in 1907. His "Little Tramp" won't appear until 1915.

1908: d.  Marlon Brando was not born this year. If he had been, he would have been forty-something when he starred in *The Wild One*.

1909: a.  Theodore Roosevelt has ten years more of life left to him.

### 1910–19

1910: d.  Crooner Rudy Vallee is nine years old in 1910. He will not be popular until the 1920s.

1911: b.  War does not breaks out in Europe until after Archduke Ferdinand is assassinated in Sarajevo in 1914.

1912: c.  Czar Nicholas II and his family will have to wait six more years before being assassinated by Bolsheviks.

1913: d.  Amos 'n' Andy won't turn up on radio for another fifteen years. In 1913, there is no commercial radio for them to turn up on.

1914: c.  Work didn't begin on the Panama Canal this year; it was completed and 1914 saw its opening. Construction had begun ten years earlier, in 1904.

1915: c.  Ragtime originated in the nineteenth century, around 1890.

1916: c.  Lucky Strike cigarettes weren't taken off the market in 1916. This is the year they were first on the market.

1917: b.  World War I ends in 1918.

1918: d.  Neither Gary Cooper nor Humphrey Bogart make a film debut in 1918. Cooper is seventeen. Bogart is nineteen and in the Navy.

1919: d.  Jimmie Rodgers won't father country music until after he makes his first recordings in 1927.

## THE 1920s

1920: b.  Women couldn't cast their votes in favor of the nineteenth amendment since that was the amendment that gave women the right to vote. Besides, amendments to the constitution are not made by popular vote.

1921: a.  Coolidge will have to wait until Harding dies in 1923 before he becomes thirtieth president of the U.S.

1922: b.  Hitler does not assume power in Germany until 1933.

1923: a.  Billie Holiday is eight years old in 1923. Her first recordings are ten years in the future.

1924: b.  Elvis Presley won't be born in Tupelo, Mississippi, until 1935.

1925: c.  Mark Twain cannot decry anything because rumors of his death are no longer even slightly exaggerated. Twain died in 1910.

1926: d.  Edward G. Robinson won't make *Little Caesar* until 1931.

1927: a.  King Edward VIII won't abdicate the throne until after ascending to it in 1936.

1928: d.  The first automobile maps turned up in 1914. Did you think drivers just rode around lost for all those years?

1929: b.  *The Glass Menagerie* premiere is sixteen years in the future for Tennessee Williams. He's eighteen in 1929.

## THE 1930s

1930: a.  Steinbeck's *The Grapes of Wrath* is nine years off, to be published in 1939.

1931: b.  Willie Mays is not a rookie with the San Francisco Giants. The color line in baseball won't be broken for another generation, and Willie Mays is busy being born in 1931, and the Giants are still in New York City.

1932: d.  Richard Nixon is not elected to the California State Assembly. He is a mere lad of nineteen.

1933: d. Jessie James has been dead for over fifty years.

1934: a. John Lennon won't be born in Liverpool for another six years.

1935: b. If you've seen *It's a Wonderful Life*, you know that the story ends after World War II.

1936: b. Nazi occupation of France is four years off, beginning in 1940.

1937: a. Kirk Douglas won't make his screen debut until after the war, in 1946.

1938: d. Sure "Twelfth of Never" is a hit song for Johnny Mathis, but not just yet. Mathis is only three years old in 1938.

1939: b. Norman Mailer's great novel of World War II will not be published until the war is over.

## THE 1940s

1940: d. American troops don't begin invasion of North Africa. U.S. is not yet in the war.

1941: d. The United Nations must wait until after the war is over.

1942: a. MacArthur does not command U.S. forces in Korea. That'll be the next fracas, in about eight years.

1943: a. Las Vegas is a postwar phenomenon, pioneered by Bugsy Siegel. MGM won't open a casino in Nevada until the 1970s.

1944: c. Amelia Earhart has been lost and feared dead in the Pacific since 1937.

1945: c. Frankie Laine's "Rawhide" won't be heard for another fourteen years.

1946: a. Truman assumed the office of president in 1945.

1947: a. Barbie dolls won't be marketed until 1959, but a rumor will arise that the dolls were modeled after dolls in an Amsterdam brothel.

1948: d. James Dean, that quintessential '50s icon, won't show up in *East of Eden* until 1955. In 1948, he is seventeen.

1949: c. The first Super Bowl game won't be played until 1967, and it won't be dubbed the Super Bowl until 1969.

## THE 1950s

1950: a. Nixon is never to be governor of California. When he loses his bid for that post in 1962, he prematurely tells the press they "won't have Nixon to kick around anymore."

1951: a. Elvis Presley is sixteen in 1951. "Hound Dog" and "Heartbreak Hotel" will have to wait until his talent matures at age twenty-one.

1952: d.  Babe Ruth retired in 1935, died in 1948.

1953: b.  *Bonanza* won't debut on NBC until fall of 1959.

1954: a.  Hemingway commits suicide in Ketchum, Idaho, in 1961.

1955: c.  Fighting halted in Korea in 1953.

1956: d.  *The Feminine Mystique* is a '60s phenomenon, and won't be published until 1963.

1957: a.  "Freedom Riders" Schwerner, Goodman, and Cheney will die in Mississippi in the summer of 1964, but their deaths give impetus to the passage of the Civil Rights Act of that year.

1958: c.  The first mandatory seat belt law won't be enacted (in New York state) until 1984. In 1958, seat belts are not even optional equipment on most cars.

1959: d.  Johnny Carson will not become host of the *Tonight* show until 1962.

## THE 1960s

1960: b.  The *Brown* v. *Board of Education* decision was handed down in 1954.

1961: d.  *Catcher in the Rye* was published a decade earlier, in 1951.

1962: e.  "I Can't Get No (Satisfaction)" is definitely post–Kennedy assassination, hitting the charts in 1965.

1963: d.  Elvis Presley was drafted in 1957.

1964: c.  *All in the Family* debuts to disappointing early reaction in 1971.

1965: d.  Though Schwarzkopf fights and is twice wounded in Vietnam, he is not yet a general. Free-fire zones are a fact of the war.

1966: b.  The U.S. won't invade Grenada until 1983, under the command of General Schwarzkopf.

1967: c.  The Salk vaccine was introduced in 1953.

1968: d.  Nixon doesn't announce increased bombing because he is not yet president.

1969: a.  Fantasia was released in 1940. It does have revival popularity in 1969 among hippies who like to trip on the film with LSD.

## THE 1970s

1970: d.  *Raiders of the Lost Ark*, the first Indiana Jones adventure, hits theaters in 1981.

1971: d. We met Hoffman when *The Graduate* came out in 1967.

1972: a. Anne Frank's diary was recovered in 1946, and 1947 saw its publication.

1973: d. This was a freebie. Chevy introduced the Corvette in 1953.

1974: a. The sleeping pill known as thalidomide caused over twelve thousand birth defects in 1962.

1975: e. Sightings of Elvis's ghost don't begin until after his death in 1977.

1976: b. America celebrated its bicentennial year. The tricentennial won't be until 2076.

1977: c. For those who don't like her, it only seems as though *Roseanne* has been on since 1977. Actually, the show began in 1988.

1978: d. Air bags won't become standard equipment in American cars until the 1990s.

1979: a. *The Brady Bunch,* the Gen-Xer's formative cultural experience, first appeared on television in 1969.

## THE 1980s

1980: b. The big Attica riot happened in 1971.

1981: d. *Saturday Night Fever* was a piece of the disco fad in 1977.

1982: a. Eight-track tapes were nearly obsolete by 1982.

1983: c. John Wayne Bobbitt's penis will remain intact for another decade.

1984: d. John Lennon and wife Yoko released *Double Fantasy* just before Lennon's death in 1980.

1985: d. Muhammad Ali fought his last fight in 1980. He fought Spinks in 1978.

1986: b. "The Chunnel" begins rail service between England and France in 1994.

1987: a. "Millie" doesn't become First Dog until 1989, and the Barbara Bush best seller is later than that.

1988: a. Jay Leno won't take over *The Tonight Show* until 1992.

1989: e. Gary Gilmore was executed in 1977.

## THE 1990s

1990: e. Steve Martin's "King Tut" was a '70s hit.

1991: c. In a major marketing fiasco, Coca Cola introduced the "New" Coke in 1985.

1992: b. Anwar Sadat was assassinated in Egypt in 1981.

1993: d. The *Exxon Valdez* spill took place in 1989.

1994: b. Oprah was first nationally syndicated in 1986.

1995: d. Tip O'Neill is dead. Newt Gingrich lends support to Republicans' "Contract With America."

1996: e. The first Menendez trial ended in two hung juries in 1993. They were convicted in 1996.

1997: d. Windows '95 was really introduced in '95.

1998: c. Bill Clinton turned fifty in 1996.

1999: d. Newman turned seventy in 1995.

2000: b. Multibillionaire and Microsoft master Bill Gates will only be forty-five when the new century dawns.

Scoring: The level of difficulty here is 8. If you're between thirty and forty, any score over your age is a good score. If you're over fifty, you should expect a bit more of yourself since you were here for more of these events. Any score 10 points over your age is a good score. Whatever your age, any score under 30 fails the challenge of the century.

# THE MORE THINGS CHANGED . . .

## 1947

In a War Department survey taken shortly after World War II, 51 percent of American GIs still stationed in Europe thought Hitler had done Germany "a lot of good before the war."

## 1996

Marge Schott, owner of the Cincinnati Reds baseball team, created yet another media storm of criticism for suggesting the same thing.

# 6

# "But I Don't Remember Where or When"

*The modern world lacks not only hiding places,
but certainties.*

—SALMAN RUSHDIE

History unfolds where it pleases. None could have predicted that the First World War would be touched off in an
obscure little village in the Balkans, or that U.S. presidents
would issue into the world from such unlikely places as
Plains, Georgia, and Tampico, Illinois. Remote islands in the
Pacific became the sites of pivotally contested battles in
World War II. Celebrated figures found their deaths in un-
expected places. If you chose to hide from history, you
wouldn't have known where to go (though those of us who
had the foresight to be born in the U.S. did manage to hide
from some of the century's nastier dustups).

Just as people do, places make their claim on our memories. In the upcoming series of questions, see if the names of
the places combine with the dates to trigger a memory of
the event or events that took place there. If memory
serves, you'll then know the what by triangulating it with
the where and when.

The questions get a bit tougher as the series proceeds.
There are 102 questions. The degree of difficulty is 6 (on a
10-point scale). If you know where or when, you should be
able to deduce the correct answer to about 80 of these. Any

score above that suggests a keen awareness of where history placed a great many significant events.

## WHERE OR WHEN

1. It is November 22, 1963. The place is Dealy Plaza. What's going on here?

2. It is a night in late October 1993. The place is the Viper Room on the Sunset Strip in Hollywood. What's going on here?

3. It is the night of July 18, 1969. The place is Chappaquiddick. What's going on here?

4. The date is June 12, 1994. The place is Bundy Drive. What's going on here?

5. It is June 8, 1968. The place is the Ambassador Hotel in Los Angeles. What's going on here?

6. The date is June 28, 1919. The place is the Hall of Mirrors at Versailles. What is going on here?

7. It is July 20, 1969. The place is the Sea of Tranquility. What's going on here?

8. It is October 1935. The place is Ethiopia. What's going on here?

9. It is July 1925. The place is Dayton, Tennessee. What's going on here?

10. The date is April 19, 1906. The place is San Francisco, California. What's going on here?

11. The date is July 16, 1945. The place is Los Alamos, New Mexico. What's going on here?

12. It is December 1969. The place is Altamont Pass in California. What's going on here?

13. It is July 1955. The place is Anaheim, California. What's going on here?

14. The date is August 16, 1936. The place is Berlin. What is going on here?

15. The date is September 6, 1901. The place is the Temple of Music at the Pan-American Exposition in Buffalo, New York. What's going on here?

16. It is any year since the late 1970s. The place is Silicon Valley. What goes on here?

17. The year is 1936. The place is Cooperstown, New York. What's going on here?

18. It is July 1996. The place is East Moriches, New York. What's going on here?

19. It is April 5, 1968. The place is the Lorraine Motel in Memphis, Tennessee. What's going on here?

20. The date is March 5, 1982. The place is Chateau Marmont in Hollywood. What's going on here?

21. The date is August 8, 1974. The place is 1600 Pennsylvania Avenue. What's going on here?

22. The date is April 12, 1945. The place is Warm Springs, Georgia. What's going on here?

23. The date is September 8, 1935. The place is the Louisiana House of Representatives in Baton Rouge. What's going on here?

24. It is October 1, 1964. The place is Sproul Plaza, University of California Berkeley. What's going on here?

25. The date is May 6, 1937. The place is Lakehurst, New Jersey. What's going on here?

26. The date is January 31, 1986. The place is ten miles above Cape Canaveral. What's going on here?

27. It is August 1969. The place is Max Yasgur's farm. What's happening?

28. The year is 1964. The place is the Gulf of Tonkin off the coast of North Vietnam. What's going on here?

29. The date is July 22, 1934. The place is outside the Biograph movie theater in Chicago. What's going on here?

30. The year is 1951. The place is Eniwetok atoll. What's going on here?

31. The date is November 19, 1978. The place is Jonestown, Guyana. What is going on here?

32. The date is July 3, 1976. The place is Entebbe Airport. What's going on here?

33. The date is December 3, 1984. The place is Bhopal, India. What is going on here?

34. The years are 1978 and 1979. The place is Love Canal, New York. What's going on here?

35. It is Thursday, October 24, 1929. The place is Wall Street. What's going on here?

36. The year is 1961. The place is New York's Peppermint Lounge. What's shakin'?

37. It is May 8, 1915. The place is at sea in the North Atlantic, ten miles off the coast of Ireland. What's going on here?

38. The years are 1942–45. The places are Manzanar, California, Heart Mountain, Wyoming, and Tule Lake, California. What's going on here?

39. The date is June 1, 1953. The place is Westminster Abbey. What is going on here?

40. The day is July 15, 1997. The place is Miami's posh South Beach area. What's going on here?

41. The time is September 1972. The place is Munich, Germany. What is going on here?

42. The date is September 30, 1955. The place is near Salinas, California. What's going on here?

43. The date is April 19, 1995. The place is the Alfred P. Murrah Federal Building. What's going on here?

44. The year is 1903. The place is Kitty Hawk, North Carolina. What's going on here?

45. The year is 1953. The place is Dien Bien Phu. What's going on here?

46. The year is 1982. The place is the Falkland Islands. What's going on here?

47. The year is 1913. The place is Lambarene (in what was then French Equatorial Africa). What's going on here?

48. It is November 1979. The place is Tehran, Iran. What's going on here?

49. The year is 1957. The place is Little Rock, Arkansas. What's going on here?

50. The year is 1942. The place is Bataan, the Philippines. What is going on here?

51. The date is May 21, 1927. The place is Le Bourget Airport in France. What's going on here?

52. The year is 1916. The place is Verdun, France. What's going on here?

53. The date is August 1, 1966. The place is the University of Texas at Austin. What's going on here?

54. The year is 1976. The place is Soweto, South Africa. What's going on here?

55. The year is 1989. The place is Prince William Sound, Alaska. What's going on here?

56. It is April 1961. The place is known as the Bay of Pigs. What's going on here?

57. It is any year from 1942 to 1945. The place is Sobibor. What goes on there?

58. The year is 1959. The place is the Olduvai Gorge in Tanganyika (which has since become Tanzania). What's going on here?

59. The date is July 20, 1944. The place is known as Wolfschanze (Wolf's Lair). What's going on here?

60. The months are January through April 1968. The place is called Khe Sanh in South Vietnam, near the Laotian border. What's going on here?

61. The date is September 2, 1945. The place is aboard the USS *Missouri* in Tokyo Bay. What is going on here?

62. It is the early months of the year 1962. The place is the Star Club in Hamburg, Germany. What's going on here?

63. The year is 1953. The place is Sun Studios in Memphis, Tennessee. What's going on here?

64. It is April 1974. The place is Atlanta Stadium. What's going on here?

65. The time is October 1917. The place is the Winter Palace in Petrograd. What's going on here?

66. The year is 1956. The place is Budapest. What is going on?

67. The date is December 8, 1980. The place is just outside the Dakota apartment building in New York. What's happening here?

68. The dates are June 9 and 10, 1942. The place is Lidice, Czechoslovakia. What is going on here?

69. It is May 1946. The place is Cannes, France. What's going on here?

70. It is 1983. The place is just outside of the town of Antelope, Oregon. What's going on?

71. It is June 1940. The place is Paris. What's going on?

72. The year is 1946. The place is Nuremburg, Germany. What's going on?

73. The date is December 21, 1988. The place is Lockerbie, Scotland. What's going on?

74. The date is September 30, 1927. The place is Yankee Stadium in New York. What's going on here?

75. It is May 18, 1970. The place is the campus of Kent State University. What's going on here?

76. It is April 19, 1943. The place is Warsaw, Poland. What is going on here?

77. The time is August 1968. The place is Grant Park in Chicago. What's going on here?

78. The date is March 8, 1945. The place is Remagen in the Rhineland. What's going on here?

79. The year is 1992. The place is the South Central district of Los Angeles. What's going on here?

80. It is February 1972. The place is Beijing, China. What's going on here?

81. The year is 1948. The place is Roswell, New Mexico. What's going on here?

82. The year is 1993. The place is a compound outside Waco, Texas. What's going on here?

83. The date is October 1, 1975. The place is Manila. What's going on here?

84. The date is November 24, 1963. The place is the Dallas jail. What's going on here?

85. It is June 1943. The place is Detroit, Michigan. What is going on?

86. It is August 1926. The place is the English Channel. What's going on?

87. The date is August 19, 1946. The place is Hope, Arkansas. What's going on here.

88. It is May 30, 1911. The place is Indianapolis, Indiana. What's going on here?

89. The date is July 18, 1954. The place is Newport, Rhode Island. What's happening here?

90. The date is August 21, 1983. The place is the airport in Manila. What's happening here?

91. The date is January 8, 1935. The place is Tupelo, Mississippi. What's going on here?

92. The date is December 26, 1908. The place is Sidney, Australia. What's going on here?

93. The date is September 22, 1980. The place is the Lenin Shipyards in Gdansk, Poland. What's going on?

94. It is April 1975. The place is Saigon. What's going on?

95. The date is February 21, 1965. The place is the Audubon Auditorium in Harlem. What's going on?

96. It is New Year's Eve, 1959. The place is Havana, Cuba. What's going on?

97. It is Easter Sunday, 1916. The place is Dublin, Ireland. What's going on?

98. The date is February 3, 1959. The place is somewhere between Mason City, Iowa, and Ames, Iowa. What's going on here?

99. The date is May 1, 1931. The place is on Fifth Avenue in New York City. What's going on here?

100. The year is 1913. The place is the Sixty-Ninth Regiment Armory in New York City. What's going on here?

101. The date is May 9, 1994. The place is South Africa. What's going on here?

102. The date is June 28, 1914. The place is the Balkan city of Sarajevo. What's going on?

## ANSWERS

1. November 11, 1963, Dealy Plaza: President John F. Kennedy is assassinated. Texas governor Connally is wounded.

2. October 1993, the Viper Room: Twenty-three-year-old actor River Phoenix is dying of a drug overdose.

3. July 18, 1969, Chappaquiddick: Mary Jo Kopechne is drowning in Senator Ted Kennedy's car.

4. June 12, 1994, Bundy Drive: Nicole Brown Simpson and Ronald Goldman are brutally murdered.

5. June 8, 1968, the Ambassador Hotel: Robert Kennedy is assassinated by Sirhan Sirhan after winning the California presidential primary.

6. June 28, 1919, Versailles: The peace treaty that officially ends World War I is being signed.

7. July 20, 1969, the Sea of Tranquility: Men have landed on the surface of the Moon.

8. October 1935, Ethiopia: The Italian Fascist army is invading that nation in a war pitting spears against tanks. Italy wins.

9. July 1925, Dayton, Tennessee: The Scopes Trial (over the teaching of evolution in public schools) is concluding. The teacher, John Scopes, is found guilty of illegally teaching evolution.

10. April 19, 1906, San Francisco: Fires are consuming the city in the aftermath of a massive earthquake.

11. July 16, 1945, Los Alamos: The first atomic bomb is being exploded. In little

more than two weeks, it will be used against human beings.

12. December 1969, Altamont: The Rolling Stones are giving a free concert that turns deadly as Hell's Angels hired as security guards stab a man to death in front of the stage while the Stones perform "Under My Thumb." Many will see this event as the spiritual end of the '60s.

13. July 1955, Anaheim, California: Walt Disney is opening Disneyland, his first amusement park.

14. August 16, 1936, Berlin: The Berlin Olympics are ending after Hitler snubbed several victorious black athletes, including black American multimedalist Jesse Owens.

15. September 6, 1901, Pan-American Expo: President William McKinley is fatally wounded by Leon Czolgosz, an anarchist.

16. From the 1970s to the present, Silicon Valley: It is a high-tech manufacturing and development area south of San Francisco, famous for microchip design and manufacture.

17. The year 1936, Cooperstown: The Baseball Hall of Fame is established. Ruth, Cobb, Mathewson, and Wagner are the first to be recognized.

18. July, 1996, East Moriches, New York: TWA Flight 800 explodes off Long Island, killing 230.

19. April 5, 1968, Lorraine Motel: Martin Luther King, Jr., falls to a sniper's bullet fired by James Earl Ray.

20. March 5, 1982, Chateau Marmont: Comedian John Belushi is dead of a drug overdose.

21. August 8, 1974, 1600 Pennsylvania Avenue: Richard Nixon is resigning the presidency, telling staffers that his mother was a saint and advising them that "those who hate you don't win unless you hate them. And then you destroy yourself."

22. April 1, 1945, Warm Springs: FDR dies of a cerebral hemorrhage. His last words are, "I have a terrific pain in the back of my head."

23. September 8, 1935, Baton Rouge: Governor (and third-party presidential candidate) Huey Long is falling to an assassin's bullets.

24. 1964, Sproul Plaza, Berkeley: The Free Speech Movement gains national attention as America's youth proclaims itself and leaves behind the shortsighted slogan: "Don't trust anyone over thirty."

25. May 6, 1937, Lakehurst, New Jersey: The *Hindenburg* explodes in flames as it is

Ruth Shoots Gehrig, 1932

docking, ending the commercial viability of dirigible passenger flights forever.

26. January 31, 1986, Cape Canaveral: Space shuttle *Challenger* explodes killing all seven aboard, including high-school teacher Christa McAuliffe.

27. August 1969, Max Yasgur's farm: Nearly four hundred thousand people

gather for the Woodstock Music and Arts Fair.

28. The year 1964, the Gulf of Tonkin: Many now believe that nothing much was going on, but Lyndon Johnson claimed that U.S. ships had been attacked by North Vietnamese torpedo boats, and he used these supposed incidents as a means of getting Congress to give him war powers.

29. July 22, 1934, the Biograph theater, Chicago: Bank robber John Dillinger is being gunned down by FBI agents led by Melvin Purvis.

30. The year 1951, Eniwetok atoll: The first open-air tests of the hydrogen bomb are being conducted. This bomb is hundreds of times more powerful than those dropped on Nagasaki and Hiroshima.

31. November 19, 1978, Jonestown: 911 people are dying at the command of cult leader Jim Jones, head of the People's Temple.

32. July 3, 1976, Entebbe: Israeli commandoes are rescuing 106 airline passengers kidnapped by the Popular Front for the Liberation of Palestine.

33. December 3, 1984, Bhopal: A toxic chemical leak at a Union Carbide plant is killing over two thousand people and injuring fifty thousand more.

34. The years 1978–79, Love Canal: The entire town is evacuated (all 239 families) due to contamination of the land there by Hooker Chemical Company.

35. October 24, 1929, Wall Street: "WALL STREET LAYS AN EGG" is the headline in *Variety*. It is the disastrous Stock Market Crash.

36. The year 1961, the Peppermint Lounge: Joey Dee and Chubby Checker are introducing a new dance craze—the Twist.

37. May 8, 1915, the North Atlantic: The *Lusitania*, a British passenger ship, is sunk by German U-boats.

38. From 1942 to 1945, Manzanar et al.: Japanese-Americans are being confined in camps as a "security measure." Many people get rich from land confiscated from Nisei citizens. The U.S. will admit that it violated their constitutional rights a generation hence.

39. June 1, 1953, Westminster Abbey: The occasion is the coronation of Queen Elizabeth II.

40. Miami, July 15, 1997. Designer Gianni Versace is murdered.

41. September 1972, Munich: Black September terrorists are in the process of killing eleven Israeli athletes at the Olympic Games.

42. September 30, 1955, outside Salinas: James Dean is killed in an auto accident.

43. April 19, 1995, the Alfred P. Murrah Building: A bomb blast kills 169 people, apparently the work of antigovernment fanatics. In this climate of fear and antigovernment fanaticism, the National Rifle Association refers to government agents as "jack-booted thugs" in a fund-raising letter. In response, ex-president Bush resigns his longtime membership in the organization.

44. The year 1903, Kitty Hawk: The Wright brothers are making history's first flight of a heavier-than-air craft.

45. The year 1953, Dien Bien Phu: The French are losing a battle, and a colonial presence in Vietnam. This defeat will cast a long shadow into the future of the United States.

46. The year 1982, the Falklands: A brief war is raging between Great Britain and Argentina over possession of these scrubby islands. The Brits are victorious.

47. The year 1913, Lambarene: Albert Schweitzer has set up his famous hospital there.

48. November 1979, Tehran: The U.S. embassy is seized and fifty-nine Americans are taken hostage. Four women and six blacks will be released this month but the

King Shiite

The "Imam" (spiritual leader) of Iran from 1979 to 1989 humiliated the United States when he held Americans hostage for 444 days. "Death to America" was a slogan popular during his regime. Reflecting the frustration of Carter administration officials during the Hostage Crisis, press secretary Jody Powell snapped: "If I had my way, I'd ask the f—king Ayatollah to keep fifty reporters . . . then you people who have all the answers could figure how to get them out."

Ted Koppel and *Nightline* were both launched by the Ayatollah as that anchorman and that show were pressed into service to cover the Hostage Crisis.

Later, during the Iran–Contra hearings in 1987, Oliver North defended selling arms to the Ayatollah, saying it was "a neat idea."

\* \* \*

rest will be held for a total of 444 days, costing Jimmy Carter an election.

49. The year 1957, Little Rock: Governor Orval Faubus has mobilized the National Guard to prevent nine black students from integrating Little Rock's Central High School.

50. The year 1942, Bataan: Twelve thousand American and sixty-four thousand Philippine soldiers surrender to a superior Japanese force. Ten thousand of these prisoners will die on what comes to be known as the Bataan Death March.

51. May 21, 1927. Le Bourget: Lucky Lindy has landed, completing the first solo flight across the Atlantic Ocean.

52. The year 1916, Verdun: A fierce battle rages for months. The French line holds, but nearly a million French soldiers die in this long battle.

53. August 1, 1966. Austin: In the kind of event that will become all too common, Charles Whitman climbs to the top of a campus tower. From there, he methodically kills twelve people and wounds thirty-three more before he is killed by police.

54. The year 1976, Soweto: Riots in this and other black townships are violently put down by police. Over one hundred people die and Soweto is destroyed.

55. The year 1989, Prince William Sound: The oil tanker *Exxon Valdez* spills 11 million gallons of oil, making an oil slick forty-five miles long. It is the worst oil spill in U.S. history.

56. The year 1961, the Bay of Pigs: A CIA-backed anti-Castro invasion of Cuba is being repulsed in an early foreign policy disaster for the new Kennedy administration.

57. The years 1942 to 1945, Sobibor: It is a Nazi concentration camp in the Soviet Union capable of disposing of twenty thousand victims each day.

58. The year 1959, Olduvai Gorge: It is the place where the anthropologists Louis and Mary Leakey find a 1.75-million-year-old fossil skull.

59. July 20, 1944, Wolfschanze: An attempt to kill Hitler is thwarted. A heavy table shields him from the worst of a bomb blast.

60. January through April, 1968, Khe Sanh: American Marines are besieged by a numerically superior North Vietnamese army force.

61. September 2, 1945, USS *Missouri*: The Japanese are surrendering to General Douglas MacArthur.

62. The year 1962, Hamburg: The Beatles are playing here, just months before their return to Liverpool and international stardom.

63. The year 1953, Sun Studios: Elvis Presley is making a record for his mother and gaining the attention of Sam Phillips. The meeting will change the course of American music.

64. April 1974, Atlanta Stadium: Hank Aaron is breaking Babe Ruth's lifetime home-run record.

65. October 1917, the Winter Palace: The Bolsheviks are taking power in Russia. The Soviet Union is being born.

66. The year 1956, Budapest: Hungarians are staging a short-lived but heroic revolt against Soviet domination.

67. December 8, 1980, the Dakota: Mark Chapman is shooting John Lennon to death as the singer returns from his last recording date.

68. June 1942, Lidice: The SS is destroying the village and killing all its inhabitants in retaliation for the assassination of Reinhard Heydrich, the Nazi official who administer the subjugated Czechs.

69. May 1946, Cannes: It is the first Cannes Film Festival.

70. The year 1983, Antelope, Oregon: The Bhagwan Shree Rajneesh has a sizeable spiritual commune here, complete with a fleet of Rolls-Royces for his personal use. Remember him?

71. June 1940, Paris: Nazis occupy the City of Light.

72. The year 1946, Nuremburg: War crimes trials of high-ranking Nazi officials are under way.

73. December 21, 1988, Lockerbie: Pan Am Flight 103 crashes here and 259 people are dead, victims of Islamic terrorists.

74. September 30, 1927. Yankee Stadium: Babe Ruth is hitting his sixtieth home run, a record that will stand for thirty-four years.

75. May 18, 1970, Kent State: National Guardsmen are in the process of firing into a crowd of student protesters, killing four and wounding eight. Ronald Reagan, then governor of California, had called for a bloodbath to quell dissent just a week before the Kent State incident.

76. April 19, 1943, Warsaw: Jews in the Warsaw ghetto are resisting Nazi attempts to round up the last sixty thousand of them. In less than thirty days, nearly all will be dead.

77. August 1968, Chicago: A "police riot" is going on. As "the whole world is watching," Chicago police wade into antiwar protesters, injuring more than one hundred people. Answering charges of police brutality, Mayor Daley says: "The police aren't there to create disorder. The police are there to preserve disorder."

78. March 8, 1945, Remagen: Allied troops capture a vital bridge across the Rhine River, one of the final obstacles to the complete collapse of the Third Reich.

Warsaw Ghetto, 1943

79. The year 1992, South Central LA: A huge riot is going on in violent reaction to the not-guilty verdict rendered in the case against LA police officers charged with using excessive force in the arrest of Rodney King.

80. February 1972, Beijing: President Richard Nixon is visiting China, normalizing relations with that country for the first time since Mao and the communists took power in 1949.

81. The year 1948, Roswell, New Mexico: Though no definitive proof has been produced in the years since, many people believe an unidentified flying object has crashed here and that evidence of the alien visit has been covered up by the government.

82. The year 1993, Waco: Cult leader David Koresh and more than one hundred of his followers (and their children) are killed when a fire destroys the Branch Davidian compound as agents of the FBI and the ATF break the long siege of the place.

83. October 1, 1975, Manila: The "Thrilla in Manila" is being fought between Muhammad Ali and Joe Frazier. Ali will win, but it is no easy victory. Ali fights much of the fight with cracked ribs.

84. November 24, 1963, Dallas: Jack Ruby is shooting Lee Harvey Oswald.

85. June 1943, Detroit: A race riot rages. Twenty-nine people will die in the disturbance.

86. August 1926, the English Channel: Gertrude Ederle is becoming the first woman to swim the Channel. She beats the time of all the men who preceded her in the feat.

87. August 19, 1946, Hope, Arkansas: Bill Clinton is being born.

88. May 30, 1911, Indianapolis: It is the first running of the Indianapolis 500.

89. July 18, 1954, Newport: The first Newport Jazz Festival is being held. Newport is the model for hundreds of other jazz festivals to follow, large and small, throughout the world.

90. August 21, 1983, Manila: Opposition leader Benigno Aquino is assassinated as he returns to his homeland from exile in the U.S.

91. January 8, 1935, Tupelo, Mississippi: Elvis Presley is being born.

92. December 26, 1908, Sidney, Australia: Jack Johnson is becoming the first black heavyweight boxing champion, defeating Tommy Burns in a fourteenth-round TKO.

93. September 22, 1980, Gdansk: Polish labor union Solidarity is asserting its strength and signaling the final days of Poland's existence as a Soviet bloc country.

94. April 1975, Saigon: The city is falling to the Viet Cong and the North Vietnamese. The last Americans are fleeing. South Vietnam ceases to exist. Saigon is soon to become Ho Chi Minh City.

95. February 21, 1965, Harlem: Malcolm X is being gunned down by three Black Muslims.

96. New Year's Eve, 1959, Havana: The Batista regime is falling. Castro is coming to power.

97. Easter 1916, Dublin: This is the Sunday, Bloody Sunday of story and song, when Irish nationalists rose up against British rule. In the week that followed, the British army killed 450 of the rebels, and wounded more than 2,500 more. This event gave rise to the IRA and many of the troubles still present there.

98. February 3, 1959, near Ames, Iowa: This is "the day the music died," according to the Don McClean song. Buddy Holly, Richie Valens, and the Big Bopper die in a plane crash.

99. May 1, 1931, Fifth Avenue, New York: The Empire State Building is completed and opened to the public on this day.

100. The year 1913, the Sixty-ninth Regiment Armory: The International Exhibition of Modern Art, the famous "Armory show" that introduced Americans to Picasso, Braque, Duchamp, and others. The art world changes irrevocably after this.

101. May 9, 1994, South Africa: Nelson Mandela takes office as president of South Africa, a country that had held him as a political prisoner for twenty-seven years.

102. June 28, 1914, Sarajevo: Archduke Ferdinand and his wife are being assassinated, an event that will plunge the world into war.

Scoring: If you knew the answers to more than 80 of these, then you're well anchored in time and space. If you knew the answers to fewer than 40 of these, then much of what happened in this century is lost on you, and you may have been lost in much of it.

# THE MORE THINGS CHANGED . . .

## 1930s

More people can be found with a knowledge of the likes and dislikes of Mr. Gary Cooper than with the simplest idea of the main precepts of, say, Jesus Christ.

—Otis Ferguson, film critic

## 1960s

We're more popular now than Jesus Christ. I don't know which will go first. Rock and roll or Christianity.

—John Lennon, musician

# 7

# Categorically Speaking

*Trivia is a game played by those who realize that they have
misspent their youth but do not want to let go of it.*

—EDWIN GOODGOLD, 1965

Often, the events of the century seemed random. People
came and went, made themselves famous, then faded into
obscurity. Places emblazoned themselves on our attention
for a few days or weeks, then dropped off the news pages
and out of our consciousness.

But once imprinted, many of these people, places, and
things remained with us, however murkily. Sometimes all it
took to call them back was some measure of similarity to a
new person, place, or thing the media were reporting.
Though we were addicted to the new in the twentieth century, the context for new things was provided by their similarity to things we already knew. In fact, the news media
handled all stories by slipping them into the molds provided
by earlier stories of identifiable kinds. Thus it was that
though we craved novelty, mostly we got old stories re-
heated with new names.

As Shakespeare said, "There's nothing new under the
sun." Everything we know is traceable to something that
came before. The book you hold in your hand comes to you
as it does because of a hugely popular crossword puzzle fad
during the 1920s. In 1924, having noted the popularity of

crossword puzzles in the *New York World*, Richard Simon and Max Schuster decided to put out a book of crossword puzzles. Calling themselves Plaza Publishing, they did just that. Their success was mercurial, laying the foundation for the publishing empire that would, more than seventy years on, publish this book.

There are connections to be made every-where, if we follow the threads, and that is what the upcoming series of questions asks you to do. Each question is a series of nouns or proper nouns. If you know one or more of the items in the series, it's likely you'll be able to supply the category the items share.

What do the items listed below have in common? Be as specific as possible.

There are one hundred questions. A good score is anything over 80 correct. It should be easy. Degree of difficulty: 4.

## CATEGORICALLY SPEAKING

1. Cordell Hull, Warren Christopher, Henry Kissinger were all _____.

2. Gold, Omaha, Juno, Utah, Sword were all _____.

3. Lucille Bremer, Rita Hayworth, Eleanor Powell, Cyd Charise, and Ginger Rogers were all _____.

4. Brace Beamer, Clayton Moore, Klinton Spilsbury, Lee Powell, and George Seaton were all _____.

5. Stuka, Zero, Spitfire were all _____.

6. Dee Dee Meyers, Jim Brady, Pierre Salinger were all _____.

7. *Stagecoach, The Searchers, The Quiet Man, Grapes of Wrath* were all _____.

8. Tom Mix, William S. Hart, Bronco Billy Anderson were all _____.

9. Scheck, Cochran, Bailey, Shapiro were all _____.

10. Teller, Bethe, Oppenheimer, Fermi were all _____.

11. Swaggart, Bakker, Roberts, Robertson were all _____.

12. Fat Man and Little Boy were _____.

13. Eric Clapton, Ginger Baker, and Jack Bruce were collectively known as _____.

14. Lang, Van Ater, and Fuhrman were all _____.

15. Medgar Evers, Ralph Bunche, Ralph Abernathy were all _____.

16. Val Kilmer, Adam West, Michael Keaton, Robert Lowery were all _____.

17. WPA, CCC, NRA, CWA were all _____.

18. Malvina Reynolds, Buffy St. Marie, Judy Collins, Rosalie Sorrells, Tracy Chapman, and Suzanne Vega were all _____.

19. Robert Kennedy, Janet Reno, John Mitchell, Ed Meese were all _____.

20. *Rope*, *Rear Window*, and *Rebecca* were all _____.

21. Rommel, Von Stauffenberg, von Rundstedt were all _____.

22. Liona Boyd, Andrés Segovia, and Christopher Parkening were all _____.

23. Dinkins, Lindsay, Koch were all _____.

24. Heidi Fleiss, Sally Stanford, and Polly Adler were all _____.

25. Luftansa, Aerlingus, Braniff, Aeroflot were all _____.

26. Hart, Schaffner, and Marx were _____.

27. Whirlaway, Man O'War, Citation were _____.

28. Wells, Asimov, Clarke, Zelazny were all _____.

29. Brett, Roseanne, Lucy, Ellen, Candice, and Mary were all _____.

30. Sweet Caporals, Wings, Marvels, Spuds, and Murads were all _____.

31. Olivetti, Smith-Corona, and Underwood were all _____.

32. Flopsy, Mopsy, and Cottontail were all _____.

33. "Madamoiselle from Armentieres, Parlay-Voo," "Over There," and "Pack Up Your Troubles in Your Old Kit Bag and Smile, Smile, Smile" were all _____.

34. Crystal power, aromatherapy, channeling, harmonic convergence were all elements of the movement known as_____.

35. Checkers, Fala, Liberty, and Millie were all _____.

36. Clint Walker, Will Hutchins, Clu Gulager, and Robert Culp were all _____.

37. RKO, MGM, Universal, Pathe, and Fox were all _____.

38. Glaxo Wellcome, Squibb, Smith-Kline, E. J. Lilly, and Merck were all_____.

39. Wrong Way Corrigan, Howard Hughes, Wiley Post, Beryl Markham were all _____.

40. George Bush, Allen Dulles, William Casey, William Colby were all _____.

41. Mauthausen, Theresienstadt, Treblinka, Bergen-Belsen, and Dachau were all _____.

42. Tillich, Niebuhr, Teilhard de Chardin, and Cox were all _____.

43. Ben-Gurion, Meir, Begin, Peres, and Netanyahu were all _____.

44. Hart Crane, Sylvia Plath, Virginia Woolf, Ernest Hemingway were all _____.

45. Ansel Adams, Andre Kertesz, Diane Arbus, and Margaret Bourke-White were all _____.

46. Stanley Kowalski, Vito Corleone, Napoleon I, and Terry Molloy were all _____.

47. Igor Stravinsky, John Cage, Benjamin Britten, Charles Ives were all _____.

48. "Daniel," "Benny and the Jets," "Candle in the Wind," and "Goodbye Yellow Brick Road" were all _____.

49. Carroll O'Connor, Jean Stapleton, Rob Reiner, and Sally Struthers were all _____.

50. Taft-Hartley, Hawley-Smoot, Gramm-Rudman, Humphrey-Hawkins were all _____.

51. Zanuck, Thalberg, Cohn, Laemmle were all _____.

52. *The Romance of Helen Trent, Stella Dallas*, and *Girl Alone* were all _____.

53. Jeff Smith, Jacques Pepin, Graham Kerr, and Julia Child were all _____.

54. John Coltrane, Stan Getz, Dexter Gordon, Josh Redman, James Carter were all _____.

55. ENIAC and UNIVAC were _____.

56. Cubby, Annette, Jimmy, and Tommy were all _____.

57. Jobs, Wozniak, and Gates were all_____.

58. Toni Morrison, Alice Walker, Zora Neale Hurston, and Terry MacMillan were all _____.

59. "Night and Day," "Begin the Beguine," and "You're the Top" were all_____.

60. Salerno, Monte Cassino, and Anzio were all _____.

61. Russell Baker, Jimmy Breslin, Molly Ivins, and Ellen Goodman were all _____.

62. Ferlinghetti, Corso, Ginsberg, Snyder, McClure were all _____.

63. Beckett, Genet, Stoppard, Durrenmatt, and Ionesco were all _____.

64. Hootie and the Blowfish, Pearl Jam, REM, and Hole were all _____.

65. Henry K. Thaw, Evelyn Nesbit, and Stanford White were all _____.

66. Ngo Dinh Diem, Nguyen Van Thieu, Nguyen Cao Ky were all _____.

67. Marianne Moore, Louise Bogan, Elizabeth Bishop, Sylvia Plath, and Sharon Olds were _____.

68. Willie Nelson, Waylon Jennings, Kris Kristofferson, and Johnny Cash performed collectively as _____.

69. "Stopping by Woods on a Snowy Evening," "The Road Not Taken," and "The Death of the Hired Man" are all _____.

70. Carreras, Domingo, and Pavarotti were _____.

71. " 'Round Midnight," "Blue Monk," "Crepuscule With Nellie," and "Ruby My Dear" (extra point if you know what "crepuscule" means) were all _____.

72. Bobby Rydell, Fabian Forte, Tommy Sands, and Eddie Cochran were all _____.

73. Kofi Annan, Dag Hammarskjöld, and U. Thant were all _____.

74. Montel Williams, Jerry Springer, Charles Perez, Gordon Elliott were all_____.

75. Tinian, Saipan, Tarawa, Iwo Jima were all _____.

76. Arna Bontemps, Countee Cullen, Ralph Ellison, Richard Wright, and Langston Hughes were all _____.

77. Jayne Mansfield, Albert Camus, James Dean, Tom Mix, Grace Kelly, and General George Patton all _____.

78. Satchel Paige, Cool Papa Bell, and Josh Gibson were _____.

79. John Cleese, Eric Idle, and Terry Gilliam were all _____.

80. Blind Lemon Jefferson, Son House, Howlin' Wolf, and Leadbelly were all _____.

81. Jason Alexander, Julia Louis-Dreyfuss, and Michael Richards were all _____.

82. John Wayne Gacy, Ted Bundy, Jeffrey Dahmer, David Berkowitz were _____.

83. Potsdam, Yalta, Casablanca, and Tehran were all _____.

84. "The Prosperity Decade," "the Era of Excess," "the Dollar Decade," "the Jazz Age," and "the Ballyhoo Years" were all _____.

85. Darrow, Belli, Spence, and Bailey were all _____.

86. Kenesaw Mountain Landis, Peter Ueberroth, A. Bartlett Giamatti were all _____.

87. Sun, Chess, Alligator, Arhoolie, Blind Pig, Rounder, Blue Note, and Verve were all _____.

88. Corazon Aquino, Ferdinand Marcos, Emilio Aguinaldo were all _____.

89. Laika, Belka, and Strelka were _____.

90. The Hughes brothers, the Coen brothers, the Maysles brothers were all _____.

91. Uzi, Glock, Tech 9 were all _____.

92. James Joyce's *Ulysses*, D. H. Lawrence's *Lady Chatterley's Lover*, and Henry Miller's *Tropic of Cancer* were all _____.

93. Alfafa, Spanky, Buckwheat were all _____.

94. Rhubarb, Morris, Garfield, Sylvester were all _____.

95. *Sleeper, Zelig, Bullets Over Broadway, Take the Money and Run* were all _____.

96. Herbert Stempel, Charles van Doren, Joyce Brothers were all _____.

97. Ann Landers and Abigail Van Buren, Joan Fontaine and Olivia DeHavilland, Lorna Luft and Liza Minnelli were _____.

98. *Inner Sanctum, The Fat Man, The Shadow,* and *Lights Out* were all _____.

99. *Hud, Harper, Hombre, The Hustler, The Hudsucker Proxy* were all _____.

100. Srebrenica, Gorazde, Zepa, Sarajevo were all _____.

## ANSWERS

1. Hull, Christopher, and Kissinger were secretaries of state.

2. Gold, Omaha, and the rest were beaches in Normandy on D-Day.

3. Lucille Bremer and the others were Fred Astaire's dance partners.

4. Brace Beamer et al. were actors who played the Lone Ranger.

5. Stuka, Zero, Spitfire were all WW II aircraft.

6. Meyers, Salinger, and Brady were presidential press secretaries.

7. *Stagecoach* and the others were films directed by John Ford and starring John Wayne.

8. Mix, Hart, Anderson were silent movie cowboys.

9. Scheck et al. were members of the O. J. Simpson defense team.

10. Teller and the others were scientists who developed the a-bomb.

11. Swaggart, Bakker, Roberts, Robertson were televangelists.

12. Fat Man and Little Boy were the names given the bombs dropped on Hiroshima and Nagasaki.

13. Clapton, Baker, and Bruce were collectively known as Cream.

14. Lang, Van Ater, and Fuhrman were detectives who worked on the O. J. Simpson case.

15. Evers, Bunche, and Abernathy were leaders of the civil rights movement.

16. Kilmer, West, Keaton, and Lowery all played Batman. (Lowery played the Caped Crusader in a 1943 serial, worth watching on videotape for campiness and wartime attitudes.)

17. WPA, CCC, NRA, CWA were all New Deal programs.

18. Malvina Reynolds and the others were all folksingers.

19. Kennedy, Reno, and the others all headed the Justice Department.

20. *Rope, Rear Window, Rebecca* were all films directed by Alfred Hitchcock.

21. Rommel and the others were German generals in World War II.

22. Boyd, Segovia, and Parkening were classical guitarists.

23. Dinkins, Lindsay, and Koch were all New York City mayors.

24. Fleiss, Stanford, and Adler were all famous madams.

25. Luftansa, Aerlingus, Braniff, Aeroflot were airlines.

26. Hart, Schaffner, and Marx were clothiers.

27. Whirlaway, Man O'War, Citation were thoroughbred racehorses.

28. Wells, Asimov, Clarke, and Zelazny were sci-fi writers.

29. Brett, Roseanne, Lucy, et al. were sit-com stars.

30. Sweet Caporals, Wings, Marvels were brands of cigarettes.

31. Olivetti, Smith-Corona, and Underwood were typewriters.

32. Flopsy, Mopsy, and Cottontail were all characters created by Beatrix Potter in 1902.

33. "Madamoiselle from Armentieres" et al. were World War I songs.

34. Crystal power etc. were of the movement known as New Age.

35. Checkers, Fala, Liberty, and Millie were White House dogs.

36. Clint Walker and the others were 1950s Warner Bros. TV cowboys.

37. RKO, MGM, Universal, Pathe, and Fox were movie studios.

38. Glaxo Wellcome and the others were pharmaceutical companies.

39. Wrong Way Corrigan and the others were aviation pioneers.

40. George Bush and the others all headed the CIA.

41. Mauthausen and the others were Nazi concentration camps.

42. Tillich, Niebuhr, and the rest were theologians.

43. Ben-Gurion and the others were Israeli prime ministers.

44. Hart Crane, Sylvia Plath, and the others were literary suicides.

45. Ansel Adams, Andre Kertesz, and the others were photographers.

46. Stanley Kowalski et al. were roles played by Marlon Brando.

47. Stravinsky, Cage, Britten, and Ives were twentieth-century composers.

48. "Daniel" and the others were Elton John/Bernie Taupin songs.

49. O'Connor and the others were the cast of *All in the Family*.

50. Taft-Hartley and the others were acts of Congress.

51. Zanuck, Thalberg, Cohn, Laemmle were movie studio moguls.

52. *Helen Trent* and the others were radio soap operas.

53. Jeff Smith and the others were television chefs.

54. Coltrane, Getz, Gordon, Redman, and Carter were jazz sax players.

55. ENIAC and UNIVAC were computers of the 1950s.

56. Cubby, Annette, Jimmy, and Tommy were all Mouseketeers.

57. Jobs, Wozniak, and Gates were all computer pioneers.

58. Morrison, Walker, and the others were black women writers.

59. "Night and Day" and the others were all Cole Porter songs.

60. Salerno et al. were battles fought in Italy during WWII.

61. Russell Baker and the rest were syndicated newspaper columnists.

62. Ferlinghetti and the others were Beat Generation poets.

63. Beckett and colleagues were playwrights.

64. Hootie et al. were popular rock bands of the '90s.

65. Thaw, Nesbit, and White were principals in the Stanford White murder of 1906, as notorious for its time as the Simpson case.

66. Diem, Thieu, and Ky were South Vietnamese leaders during U.S. military involvement there.

67. Moore, Bogan, Bishop, Plath, and Olds were poets.

68. Nelson, Jennings, Kristofferson, and Johnny Cash performed collectively as the Highwaymen.

69. "Stopping by Woods on a Snowy Evening," "The Road Not Taken," and "The Death of the Hired Man" are poems by Robert Frost.

70. Carreras, Domingo, and Pavarotti were operatic tenors.

71. " 'Round Midnight" et al. were Thelonious Monk compositions (Crepuscule means "twilight"; Nellie was Monk's wife).

72. Rydell, Forte, Sands, and Cochran were '50s rock sensations.

73. U. Thant and the others were secretaries general of the United Nations.

74. Williams and the others were daytime TV talk show hosts.

75. Tinian and the others were WW II island battles in the Pacific.

76. Bontemps, Cullen, and the others were black American writers.

77. Jayne Mansfield and the others all died in automobile accidents.

78. Paige, Bell, and Gibson were stars of the Negro Baseball Leagues when the game was still segregated.

79. Cleese, Idle, and Gilliam were members of Monty Python's Flying Circus, the British comedy group that began in the '60s.

80. Blind Lemon Jefferson and the others were bluesmen.

81. Alexander, Louis-Dreyfuss, and Richards were George Costanza, Elaine Benis, and Kozmo Kramer on TV's *Seinfeld*.

82. Gacy, Bundy, Dahmer, and Berkowitz were serial killers.

83. Potsdam and the others were sites of Allied summit conferences during World War II.

84. "The Prosperity Decade" et al. were names applied to the 1920s.

85. Darrow, Belli, Spence, and Bailey were famous lawyers.

86. Landis and the others were major league baseball commissioners.

87. Sun, Chess, Alligator, et al. were record/CD labels.

88. Aquino, Marcos, Aguinaldo were Philippine leaders.

89. Laika, Belka, and Strelka were dogs, the first animals in space.

90. The Hughes, Coen, and Maysles brothers were filmmaking teams.

91. Uzi, Glock, Tech 9 were all guns popular with gangs in the '90s.

92. *Ulysses*, *Lady Chatterly's Lover*, and *Tropic of Cancer* were all books once banned in the U.S.

Reefer Madness, 1936

93. Alfafa, Spanky, Buckwheat were characters in *Little Rascals/Our Gang* comedies of the '30s and '40s.

94. Rhubarb, Morris, and the others were famous cat characters.

95. *Sleeper, Zelig,* and the others were Woody Allen films.

96. Stempel and the others were all contestants on *Twenty-One,* the rigged '50s quiz show.

97. Landers and Van Buren, Fontaine and DeHavilland, Luft and Minnelli were sisters.

98. *Inner Sanctum* and the others were radio shows.

99. *Hud* and the others were all movies starring Paul Newman.

100. Srebrenica and the others were cities in the former Yugoslavia.

Scoring: If you insist on categorizing yourself based on how many of these categories you knew, then the categories are as follows: 81–100 correct, categorically splendid; 61–80 correct; categorically above average; 41–60 correct; a middling category; 0–40 correct, there weren't many questions in your categories here.

# 8

# Sex, Drugs, and Rock 'n' Roll

*The majority of pop stars are just idiots in every respect.*

—SADE, 1985

If you had tried to tell people at midcentury that in forty years it would be possible to buy color tapes that played on their television sets, they probably wouldn't have believed you. Few people had even seen television then, and virtually no one had seen color television. If you had added to your prediction that it would be possible, quite legally and without raising fuss or comment, to buy a tape to play on your television set that featured the daughter of a living president cavorting in the nude, people would have thought you mad. After all, at midcentury, people couldn't even buy books with the F-word printed in them. Nudity was confined to the raunchiest of underground venues, to stag films usually made overseas and smuggled into the country. At midcentury, even the sanitized girl-next-door sexuality of *Playboy* was three years away from making its first appearance.

It is difficult, in fact, to quite recall just how sexually repressive the country was at midcentury. Since then, the change in mores and attitudes has been seismic. Others can decide if all that change has been socially liberating or culturally calamitous, but none can deny that in terms of graphic language and images, the atmosphere of the 1990s would be truly shocking to a drop-in time traveler from the 1950s. A casual glance at current afternoon TV fare or a peek inside a video store would surprise even the most forward-looking sophisticate of the Eisenhower era.

So this chapter isn't just about sex, drugs, and rock 'n' roll. It's about change. We've all learned to adapt to change during this century. As change accelerated, so did our adaptations to it. What tends to get lost in all this is how things were. The danger in forgetting how things once were is that we become inclined to the idea that the way things are now is the way things have to be. Remembering the past reminds us that the status quo is not fixed. Perhaps the questions to come will help you to remember the way we were, or failing that, introduce you to the way things used to be.

## SEX, DRUGS, AND ROCK 'N' ROLL

*Sequence 1*

The first fifty questions offer you a choice of answers, but they're still a stiff challenge to memory. The degree of difficulty here is: 8.

1. The president whose daughter appeared nude in *Playboy* magazine and video was:

a. Richard Nixon

b. Jimmy Carter

c. Gerald Ford

d. Ronald Reagan

e. Lyndon Johnson

2. The cartoon character banned by the Hays Office in 1935 because of "immortality" was:

a. Sadie the Vamp

b. Betty Boop

c. Mata Hari

d. the Flora Dora girl

e. Olive Oyl

f. Theda Bara

3. The name of Frank Zappa's '60s band was:

a. Dweezil

b. Mother of God

c. The Mothers of Invention

d. Moon Unit

e. the Warlocks

4. "I did drugs to keep going. But performing in itself is a drug. And taking cocaine is like being a hemophiliac in a razor factory." The guy who said that (in 1988) also said "nanu, nanu" and "Shazbat." He was:

a. Jonathan Winters

b. Eddie Murphy

c. Robin Williams

d. Martin Lawrence

e. Richard Pryor

**5.** Her plays *Sex* and *Drag* added spice to the 1920s. Earlier, she'd been known as "the Baby Vamp," appearing in burlesque at age fourteen. She was:

a. Vilma Banky

b. Joan Crawford

c. Mae West

d. Clara Bow

e. Mary Pickford

f. Isadora Duncan

**6.** In the 1970s, *Deep Throat* became the first "porn" film to make going to a porn film socially acceptable. The title of the film also became a part of our political history as the name for the mystery informant in the Watergate case. The star of *Deep Throat* was:

a. Linda Lovelace

b. Blaze Starr

c. Georgina Spelvin

d. Marilyn Chambers

**7.** Speaking of pornography, Erica Jong said: "After the first ten minutes, I want to go home and screw. After the first twenty minutes, I never want to screw again as long as I live." Erica Jong is remembered as:

a. a failed Supreme Court nominee

b. the first president of the National Organization for Women

c. a best-selling novelist

d. a famous Hollywood casting director

e. one of John Kennedy's mistresses

**8.** Of the following, which was never a member of the Grateful Dead?

a. "Pigpen" McKernan

b. Sonny Boy Williamson

c. Phil Lesh

d. Bob Weir

e. Jerry Garcia

f. Bill Kreutzmann

**9.** In 1957, the song "Party Doll" was just too racy for many radio stations, though it would be difficult for anyone in the 1990s to understand why. The man who had a hit with "Party Doll" was:

a. Frankie Avalon

b. Buddy Knox

c. Ronnie Hawkins

d. Fabian

e. Elvis Presley

f. Bobby Sherman

**10.** "Free as a Bird" and "Real Love" are distinctive songs in rock history because:

a. their melodies were taken from works of Beethoven

b. one of the singers was long dead when the songs were completed

c. '60s icon Neil Young performed the songs with '90s band Pearl Jam

d. they were hits for Pat Boone, Little Richard, and, years later, Liz Phair

**11.** "One of Us" was praised by Rush Limbaugh as a sign that '90s youth were making a return to fundamentalist Christianity, but the singer of the song refused Limbaugh permission to play it on his TV show. The singer was:

a. Melissa Etheridge

b. Alanis Morrisette

c. Bjork

d. Joan Osborne

e. Tracy Chapman

f. Madonna

**12.** Of the following, which was never associated with the musical trend known as bossa nova?

a. Stan Getz

b. Antonio Carlos Jobim

c. Astrid Gilberto

d. Charlie Byrd

e. Charlie Parker

f. Laurindo Almeida

**13.** "Girl You Know It's True" made pop music history in 1990 when:

a. it both won and lost a Grammy

b. it was the first hit record made entirely by computer

c. it was the first record released by Virgin Records

d. it was the first record marketed as "gangsta" rap

**14.** Snooky Lanson was a household name in the 1950s because:

a. he was the disk jockey who gave the world the phrase "rock 'n' roll"

b. he was the first American drug dealer to be arrested with more than a million dollars worth of drugs in his possession

c. he was a singer on *Your Hit Parade,* an early music show on radio and television

d. his song "Snooky's Boogie" was the first record to "cross over," selling equally well in black and white markets

**15.** Of the following, which one was never romantically linked with Madonna?

a. Warren Beatty

b. Charlie Sheen

c. Dennis Rodman

d. Carlos Leon

e. Sean Penn

**16.** "If you want anything, all you have to do is whistle. You know how to whistle, don't you? Just put your lips together and blow." It's a famous line from a 1940s film classic. The actress who infused the line with sex appeal was:

a. Rita Hayworth

b. Ingrid Bergman

c. Lauren Bacall

d. Betty Grable

e. Mae West

f. Shelley Winters

**17.** A controversial 1996 advertisement for an Amsterdam liquor store chain employed a picture of a noted world leader and a caption that read: "11 special vodkas for the real connoisseur." That world leader was:

a. Vaclav Havel

b. Bill Clinton

c. John Major

d. Boris Yeltsin

e. Nelson Mandela

f. Lech Walesa

**18.** *And God Created Woman* was a film that created an international sex symbol in the 1950s. That sex symbol was:

a. Sophia Loren

b. Mamie Van Doren

c. Brigitte Bardot

d. Diana Dors

e. Claudia Cardinale

f. Jeanne Moreau

**19. Bartles and Jaymes were:**

a. two make-believe enologists created by Ernest and Julio Gallo

b. a 1960s folk-rock duo, part of the "British invasion"

c. ragtime piano team

d. 1980s country music duo

**20. The Diggers were**

a. a funk group of the 1980s

b. a group that provided free food in the Haight-Ashbury during the 1960s

c. a trendy London-based clothing shop that marketed fashions to the drug culture of the 1970s

d. Merle Haggard's first backup band

**21. A '90s phrase, "roofie rape," described:**

a. a rape performed as part of a fraternity initiation

b. an outbreak of big-city rapes committed on roofs of apartment buildings

c. rapes committed by Rufus "Roofie" Arnold, a New Jersey serial rapist who gained media attention by sending flowers to his victims after the crime

d. rape committed when the victim was under the influence of Rohypnol, a drug ten times more powerful than Valium.

22. *Superfly* was more popular than it should have been in the 1970s. It was a film that seemed to glorify people who made money selling:

a. cocaine

b. marijuana

c. LSD

e. aphrodisiacs

f. crack

23. In the 1920s, Virginia Dare was the name of:

a. a tonic for anemia that became popular because it was 22 percent alcohol

b. the most famous speakeasy proprietress in New York

c. Al Capone's mistress

d. a child who was trapped in a well for three weeks

24. In the 1940s, the Production Code Administration (for which read "censors") decreed that an on-screen kiss could last no longer than:

a. one second

b. three seconds

c. ten seconds

d. thirty seconds

25. If you were a kid in the 1970s (and maybe even if you weren't) then you will probably know that Gene Simmons and Ace Frehley were:

a. the guys who started MTV

b. members of a band known as Kiss

c. members of a band known as Yes

d. members of a band known as Genesis

e. the guys who produced TV's *Soul Train*

26. In the 1950s, Hugh Hefner defined playboys as guys who "enjoy mixing up cocktails and an hors d'oeuvre or two . . . and inviting in a female for a quiet discussion of Picasso, Nietzsche, jazz, sex." One such Nietzsche aficionado was his heavily publicized girlfriend of the late '60s. She attempted a career as a country western singer, and was often seen on *Hee Haw*. Her name was:

a. Shannon Tweed

b. Barbi Benton

c. Vanessa Williams

d. Jessica Hahn

e. Donna Rice

f. Minnie Pearl

27. He was the photographer whose homoerotic images got Jesse Helms so riled up in the late 1980s. In the process, Helms nearly killed government funding for the arts. He was:

a. Ansel Adams

b. Robert Mapplethorpe

c. Richard Avedon

d. Weegee

e. Andy Warhol

f. Harvey Milk

28. Howard Hughes designed a pushup brassiere for her 1940s screen debut. "This is really just a very simple engineering problem," he said at the time. The woman whose endowments created the problem was:

a. Marilyn Monroe

b. Lana Turner

c. Jane Russell

d. Jayne Mansfield

e. Terry Moore

f. Kim Novak

29. Of the following musicians, which four did not die in a plane or helicopter crash?

a. Jim Croce

b. Sam Cooke

c. Buddy Holly

d. Otis Redding

e. Robert Johnson

f. Stevie Ray Vaughn

g. Jim Morrison

h. Richie Havens

30. It was said of her that "she did everything he did, except she did it backwards and in high heels." The two of them were:

a. George Burns and Gracie Allen

b. Nureyev and Fonteyn

c. Marge and Gower Champion

d. Irene and Vernon Castle

e. Fred Astaire and Ginger Rogers

f. Gene Kelly and Debbie Reynolds

31. The Stone Poneys was an LA rock group that served to launch the career of singer:

a. Natalie Merchant

b. Bjork

c. Cyndi Lauper

d. Linda Ronstadt

f. Emmy Lou Harris

32. Songs like "You've Got a Friend," "It's Too Late," and "I Feel the Earth Move" combined to make this album a virtual soundtrack for the early 1970s. The album was called:

a. *Teaser and the Firecat*

b. *Every Picture Tells a Story*

c. *Tapestry*

d. *Heart Like a Wheel*

e. *American Beauty*

f. *Nashville Skyline*

33. One of the following was noted for some '90s appearances with the grunge rockers known as Pearl Jam. Which one?

a. Neil Diamond

b. Neil Young

c. Sam Neill

d. Neal Cassady

e. Neil Sedaka

f. Neil Armstrong

**34.** Sharon Stone became the sex symbol of the 1990s, and all she had to do was cross her legs. The movie in which she did that so notoriously was:

a. *Fatal Attraction*

b. *Basic Instinct*

c. *Primal Fear*

d. *Primal Attraction*

e. *Fatal Instinct*

f. *Basic Fear*

g. *Primal Instinct*

**35.** *Gish* was the first album; Billy Corgan was the songwriter/guitarist/vocalist. The '90s band was known as:

a. Blind Melon

b. Soundgarden

c. Sonic Youth

d. Smashing Pumpkins

e. Oasis

**36.** Of the following, which one was not a drummer?

a. Mickey Hart

b. Gene Krupa

c. Ringo Starr

d. Anton Figg

e. Art Blakey

f. Cannonball Adderley

g. Charlie Watts

**37.** He was the pathfinder of the genre known as "Free Jazz." Reviewers didn't quite know what to make of him and his white plastic saxophone when he first appeared in the late 1950s. He was:

a. Pharoah Sanders

b. Coleman Hawkins

c. John Coltrane

d. Richie Cole

e. Ornette Coleman

f. Dexter Gordon

**38.** This legendary singer, whose hits included "Into Each Life Some Rain Must Fall," said: "I thought my singing was pretty much hollering." That singer was:

a. Glenn Yarbrough

b. Janis Joplin

c. Huddie Ledbetter

d. Ella Fitzgerald

e. Joe Cocker

f. Patti Labelle

**39.** Sex researchers Masters and Johnson wrote a book that challenged the way we looked at sexuality. The book was:

a. *The Hite Report*

b. *Everything You Wanted to Know About Sex But Were Afraid to Ask*

c. *Sex*

d. *The Female Eunuch*

e. *Sexual Behavior in the Human Male*

f. *Human Sexual Response*

40. The album: *Jagged Little Pill*. The decade: 1990s. The award: Grammy. The artist: Alanis Morrisette. Her country of origin:

a. U.S.

b. Canada

c. England

d. Australia

e. Ireland

f. South Africa

41. The song "I Put a Spell on You" is a minor but enduring classic of the 1950s. The song was performed by:

a. Eddie "Clean Head" Vinson

b. Johnny Otis

c. Screamin' Jay Hawkins

d. Ronnie Hawkins and the Hawks

e. The Big Bopper

42. That wasn't Audrey Hepburn's voice we heard in the film *My Fair Lady*. The singer who sang those songs was:

a. Julie Andrews

b. Marni Nixon

c. Patti Page

d. Ethel Merman

43. "Hi de hi de hi de ho" became a national catchphrase in 1930. It's from Cab Calloway's signature tune, entitled:

a. "Big Noise from Winnetka"

b. "Happy Feet"

c. "Minnie the Moocher"

d. "Boney Moroney"

e. "Hi-de-ho"

44. "[They] puke on stage? That's not showmanship. They gotta get themselves an act." That's rock pioneer Bo Diddley talking in 1978, and he was talking about the British band whose album *Never Mind the Bollocks* launched the punk trend. That band was:

a. The Clash

b. The Police

c. The Sex Pistols

d. The Dead Kennedys

e. The Ramones

45. "Sometimes when I look at my children, I say to myself, Lillian, you should have stayed a virgin." Which presidential mother said that?

a. Richard Nixon's mom

b. Bill Clinton's mom

c. Calvin Coolidge's mom

d. Jimmy Carter's mom

46. "You can't trust politicians. It's all lies . . . and it applies to any rock star who wants to make a political speech as well." This was the opinion of British rocker and Live-Aid organizer Bob Geldof in 1978. When he made the comment, Geldof's band was called:

a. Oingo Boingo

b. Tears for Fears

c. Boomtown Rats

d. The Pogues

e. The Smiths

47. "High Hopes" was a theme song for the 1960 Kennedy campaign. "Don't Stop Thinkin' About Tomorrow" was a song used in Bill Clinton's 1992 campaign. From the following list, pick the people who performed those respective campaign songs.

a. Tony Bennett

b. Frank Sinatra

c. Vic Damone

d. Jack Jones

e. Robert Goulet

f. Grand Funk Railroad

g. The Mamas & the Papas

h. Melanie

i. Fleetwood Mac

j. Carly Simon

48. "I'm Henery the Eighth, I am, I am. I got married to the widow next door. She's been married seven times before.

Every one was a Henery, She wouldn't have a Willy or a Sam." The song was first performed in 1911, but it was a hit again in the 1960s during the period the press dubbed "the British Invasion." The group that made it a '60s novelty hit was:

a. Chad and Jeremy

b. Eric Burdon and the Animals

c. Them

d. Herman's Hermits

e. Danny and the Juniors

49. You had your coke spoon on a chain around your neck, you had your platform shoes and an eight-track player blaring "That's the Way I Like It" in your 280-Z. Advertisers in the '90s thought you might want to live all that again. According to one marketer: "Despite all the craziness—all the drug use, all the casual sex—people find it a more innocent time." He meant the '70s, by the way, and the trendiest New York club of that decade was:

a. The Peppermint Lounge

b. Whiskey A Go Go

c. Studio 54

d. The Viper Lounge

e. The Hard Rock Café

50. A '90s mail-order music company advertised "44 Wacky Hits from the Fun '40s." Of the following, which is not a "wacky hit from the Fun '40s"?

a. "Aba Daba Honeymoon," Debbie Reynolds & Carleton Carpenter

b. "I'm Looking Over a Four Leaf Clover," Art Mooney

c. "Rag Mop," the Ames Brothers

d. "Transfusion," Nervous Norvis

e. "Mairzy Doats," The Merry Macs

## SEX, DRUGS, AND ROCK 'N' ROLL

*Sequence 2: Wasted*

Get drunk and be somebody.
—Street corner philosophy, 1950s

I bought into the whole romantic myth of Fitzgerald's crackup. The truth is there ain't a great deal of romance in blood, vomit, and inarticulate ramblings.
—Jay McInerney, 1996

We spent a great deal of time and money taking leave of our senses over the last hundred years. Marijuana is thought to be among the top three cash crops in the country. Alcohol sales are staggering, pun intended. That reliance on mind-altering substances came with an ever-increasing social price tag as the century wore on. From the '60s on, "wasted" was a popular slang expression for someone who was drunk or stoned. But the waste was literal, too, in lives shortened, talents dimmed, pain increased.

Should you think I exaggerate, check your knowledge of the waste represented in the following questions. What is sad is how readily this stuff comes to mind. Level of difficulty: 6 (if you're sober), 9 (if you're not).

51. Malcolm Lowry died of alcoholism,

and he wrote a classic novel about a man

Pearl
Called "the first major girl sex symbol of rock," she was dead at age twenty-seven. Also dead at twenty-seven: Jim Morrison, Jimi Hendrix, Kurt Cobain.

dying of alcoholism. That novel was titled _____.

52. He once dated Janis Joplin, later served as George Bush's drug czar, and still later compiled *The Book of Virtues*. His name? _____

53. He played lead guitar in one of the world's greatest rock and roll bands. Legend has it that he went to Switzerland on occasion for complete transfusions of blood to cure him of his heroin addiction. He is _____.

54. This novelist was an early experimenter with LSD. It is said that those experiments helped him to create Randle Patrick McMurphy, Chief Bromden, and the other memorable characters in his first novel. Name the novel or the novelist. _____

55. Keyboardist Jonathan Melvoin overdosed on heroin, and in doing so, he inspired others to use. His band? _____

56. When it came to drugs, the slogan associated with her name was "Just say no." It didn't prove very effective. Who was she? _____

57. "Tune in, turn on, drop out." He gave us these immortal words, and he often practiced what he preached. This former Harvard professor was _____.

58. This one-time Panamanian strongman was the only foreign head of state deposed by a foreign power for suspicion of international drug dealing. He was _____.

59. This Canadian runner forfeited an Olympic gold medal because he used steroids. He was _____.

60. Al Pacino played a real-life narcotics agent in this eponymous 1973 movie. The narc and the movie were both named _____.

61. Out in Palm Springs, there's a rehab facility named after this former first lady, herself a victim of addiction. The name of the clinic is _____.

62. This big-city mayor was caught smoking crack on videotape. He was later reelected. Name him. _____

63. This grim depiction of a man's descent into the last stages of alcoholism won three Academy Awards in 1945. The name of the film was _____.

64. The father of "Gonzo Journalism," his drug and alcohol use is legendary. He is _____.

65. "One pill makes you larger, and one pill makes you small," she sang. And she, too, had her share of problems with drugs and alcohol. She is _____.

66. This Mets pitcher, star of the 1986 Worlds Series, went through a drug rehabilitation program in 1987. He is _____.

67. In her book, *Story of a Life Interrupted*, she told of her recreational drug use with Nicole Simpson. Her name was _____.

68. He led a force called "The Untouchables," and he was the most famous Prohibition-era illegal substance fighter. His name was _____.

69. "You can get anything you want at Alice's restaurant." The singer and the song were part of the '60s drug culture. Who was that singer? _____

70. John Travolta pierced through to this actress's heart with an adrenaline injection in *Pulp Fiction*. Name the actress. _____

71. He played Popeye Doyle, fighting drug smuggling in *The French Connection*. Name the actor. _____

72. This presidential candidate's wife disclosed her serious alcohol problem in her book *So Now You Know*. Her name was _____.

73. He wrote a book called *The Man With the Golden Arm*. It was about a drummer/heroin addict. The novelist's name was _____.

74. This novelist, creator of *The Call of the Wild*, wrote about his own battles with alcohol in a book called *John Barleycorn*. Name the writer. _____

75. *Junkie* was his first book, *Naked Lunch* his second. His name was _____.

76. He played Count Dracula in the 1930s. He was a heroin addict. Martin Landau won an Oscar for playing him in a 1994 film. Name this Hungarian-born actor. _____

77. He and his wife, Zelda, both had mental problems exacerbated by alcohol abuse. *The Crack-up* was his

book about those problems. Name

him. _____

78. He virtually reinvented jazz. He was known as "Bird." He was dead of a drug overdose at age thirty-five. His name was _____.

79. Her real name was Eleanora Fagan. "Lover Man" was a signature tune. Heroin killed her at the age of forty-four. She was _____.

80. Sherlock Holmes was a drug user. He used a 7 percent solution. The writer/physician who created Holmes was _____.

81. This Welsh poet's last words were "eighteen straight whiskeys, that must be a record." An American singer/ songwriter later took the poet's first

name and made it his last name. The dead poet is _____.

82. Actress Susan Hayward played a famous '30s alcoholic singer in the movie *I'll Cry Tomorrow*. The singer she played? _____

83. His real name was Leonard Alfred Schneider. His autobiography was called *How to Talk Dirty and Influence People*. He overdosed in 1966. His stage name was _____.

84. He tried marijuana once, but he didn't inhale. He was _____.

85. *Long Day's Journey Into Night* was this dramatist's treatment of his own family's problems with drug and alcohol addictions. Name the playwright. _____

86. He was known as Dr. Nick, the doctor who supplied Elvis Presley with prescription drugs. He, and all such doctors, also carry the nickname taken from the title of an Aretha Franklin hit. That nickname is _____.

87. *Midnight Express*, a 1978 movie about drug smuggling and Turkish prisons, was written in bombastic fashion by a man who would become one of the most controversial directors of the 1990s. That man was _____.

88. *On the Road* romanticized drug and alcohol use in the 1950s. Its author died of alcoholism in the 1960s. He was _____.

89. *When a Man Loves a Woman* was a 1994 movie about a woman alcoholic played by _____.

90. Best known by his first name and last initial, the founder of Alcoholics Anonymous was _____.

91. She was an additional embarrassment to the Nixon administration. She was the often-drunk wife of the attorney general. Her name was _____.

92. In his autobiography, this Welsh-born actor claims to have performed *Hamlet* after consuming a quart of vodka. Name him. _____

93. "The Lizard King." He died in Paris under mysterious circumstances thought to be related to alcohol. Name him. _____

94. His song with the line "Let's get to the point/Let's smoke another joint" was

controversial in 1995. Name the singer. _____

95. He was a Sex Pistol, but he misfired. Name him. _____

96. Asked how he got his inspiration, this Mississippi novelist replied: "If I have to choose between nothing and alcohol, I'll take alcohol." _____.

97. His "grunge" band had a major hit with the song "Smells Like Teen Spirit." He committed suicide after a long history of heroin addiction. Name him. _____

98. Probably the most famous drummer in jazz history, he fought a battle with drug addiction in the '30s and '40s. He was _____.

99. In *Easy Rider*, the '60s cult classic, Peter Fonda and Dennis Hopper play a couple of drug dealers named _____ and _____.

100. This novelist, failed filmmaker, and would-be mayor of New York stabbed his wife during a drinking bout in the early 1960s. His name was _____.

101. He was the flamboyant auto executive who marketed a car that carried his last name. He was charged with and then acquitted of drug trafficking in the 1980s. His name was _____.

## SEX, DRUGS, AND, ROCK 'N' ROLL

*Sequence 3: Groupies*

If we date the birth of rock 'n' roll to the release of Bill Haley's "Rock Around the Clock" in 1954, then rock music is closing in on the half-century mark. Haley died in 1981, Chuck Berry turned seventy in 1996, and had he lived, Elvis would have been sixty-five in the year 2000. Surviving second-generation rockers like Keith Richards were grandparents. Though he wasn't retired, Bob Dylan was a member of AARP, or eligible for membership. Even the third-generation rockers were beginning to show their ages. In the last few years of the century, Madonna barely beat the alarm on her biological clock, '70s teenybopper fantasy Peter Frampton was pushing fifty, as was '80s rock diva Cyndi Lauper. Twenty-something fourth-generation bands were scrambling to leave their mark before they, too, were displaced by whatever would next pass for novelty. Time laid down a steady beat, and everybody had to dance to it.

Like it or hate it, rock music provided the sound track for half the century. And if your personal movie was augmented with a rock sound-track, chances are you'll be able to move smoothly through the sequence below.

Complete the names of the bands below. If you were any kind of devotee of rock 'n' roll, you'll whip right through these. Level of difficulty: 6.

102. Danny and the _____

103. _____ and the Destroyers

104. Stevie Ray Vaughn and

_____

105. _____ and the Belmonts

106. Billy J. Kramer and the

_____

107. _____ and the Animals

108. Emerson, Lake, & _____

109. _____ and the

Heartbreakers

110. Bill Haley and the _____

111. _____ and the Teenagers

112. ? and the _____

113. _____ and the Vandellas

114. Bruce Hornsby and the

_____

115. _____ and the Pacemakers

116. Gloria Estefan and _____

117. Booker T. and the _____

118. _____ and the Pips

119. Big Head Todd and the

_____

120. _____ and the Imperials

121. Sly and the _____

122. _____ and the All-Stars

123. Frankie Valli and the _____

124. _____ and the E. Street

Band

125. Southside Johnny and the

_____

126. _____ and the Banshees

127. Buddy Holly and the _____

128. _____ and the Blue Notes

129. Iggy and the _____

130. _____ and the Playboys

131. Big Brother and _____

132. _____ and the Attractions

133. Commander Cody and

the _____

134. _____ , Stills,

_____ , & Young

135. Joey Dee & the _____

136. _____ and the Dominos

137. Echo & the _____

138. _____ , Wind & Fire

139. Ronnie Hawkins and the

_____

140. _____ and the Shondells

141. KC & the _____

142. _____ and the News

143. Sam the Sham and the

_____

144. _____ and the Blowfish

145. Gene Vincent and the _____

146. _____ and Dean

147. Mickey and _____

148. _____ and the Maytals

149. Bob Marley and the _____

150. _____ and the Gang

151. Smokey Robinson and the

_____

152. _____ and the Union Gap

153. Tony Orlando and _____

154. _____ and the Detroit Wheels

155. Jonathan Richman and the _____

156. _____ and the Texas Jewboys

157. Joan Jett and the _____

158. _____ and Oates

159. Ashford and _____

160. _____ and the Raiders

## SEX, DRUGS, AND ROCK 'N' ROLL

*Sequence 4: Jazz and Blues*

Jazz is the distinctly American art form of the twentieth century. In its different voices, it lends definition to each decade. Innovations and changes in styles march down the century, with each generation of players reinventing the music for a new generation of listeners. Ragtime, Dixieland, le jazz hot, swing, bebop, big bands, the birth of the cool, Third Stream, progressive, West Coast, free jazz, fusion, acid jazz. Along the way, distinctive players and composers left indelible signposts on the musical landscape, songs that will forever be associated with their names. In the sequence below, your task is to match that player or composer with the song he or she "owns."

If you're a jazz and blues fan, this has a degree of difficulty of 2. If you're someone who likes music, but is not an avid jazz and blues fan, this has a difficulty level of 6. If, like many, you don't listen to music, then this whole chapter has been pretty much of a bust.

161. "Mojo Workin' " _____     a. Django Reinhardt

162. "Take the A Train" _____     b. B. B. King

163. "Take 5" _____     c. Charles Mingus

164. "A Love Supreme" _____     d. Dinah Washington

165. "Everyday I Have the Blues" _____     e. Muddy Waters

166. "One O'Clock Jump" _____     f. Dizzy Gillespie

167. "Desafinado" _____     g. Billie Holiday

168. " 'Round Midnight"

h. Woody Herman

169. "Hound Dog" ____

i. Benny Goodman

170. "A Tisket a Tasket"

j. Horace Silver

171. "Bright Lights, Big City" ____

k. Thelonious Monk

172. "Good Night Irene" ____

l. Modern Jazz Quartet

173. "Crossroads Blues" ____

m. Duke Ellington

174. "Better Git It in Your Soul" ____

n. Ella Fitzgerald

175. "What a Difference a Day Makes" ____

o. Charlie Parker

176. "Salt Peanuts" ____

p. Lester Young

177. "Song For My Father" ____

q. Fats Waller

178. "Misty" ____

r. Stan Getz

179. "Stompin' at the Savoy" ____

s. Leadbelly

180. "Nuages" ____

t. Big Mama Willie Mae Thornton

181. "Woodchopper's Ball"

u. John Coltrane

182. "Lover Man" ____

v. Robert Johnson

183. "Django" ____

w. Erroll Garner

184. "Ornithology" ____

x. Jimmy Reed

185. "Ain't Misbehavin' " ____

y. Dave Brubeck

186. "Jumpin' With Symphony Sid" ____

z. Count Basie

## ANSWERS

### SEX, DRUGS, AND ROCK 'N' ROLL

*Sequence 1*

1. President whose daughter appeared nude was: d. Ronald Reagan.

2. The banned cartoon character was: b. Betty Boop.

3. Frank Zappa's band was: The Mothers of Invention.

4. He said "performing is a drug": c. Robin Williams.

5. "The Baby Vamp" was: c. Mae West.

6. The star of *Deep Throat* was: a. Linda Lovelace.

7. Erica Jong is remembered as: c. a best-selling novelist.

8. b. Sonny Boy Williamson was a blues pioneer who died in 1948, when most of the Dead were still in diapers.

9. The "Party Doll" singer was: b. Buddy Knox.

10. "Free as a Bird" and "Real Love" are distinctive songs in rock history because: b. one of the singers (John Lennon) was long dead when the songs were completed.

11. "One of Us" was a song by: d. Joan Osborne.

12. The one not associated with bossa nova was: e. Charlie Parker.

13. "Girl You Know It's True" is notable because: a. it both won and lost a Grammy (for Milli Vanilli, who had their Grammy taken away when it was revealed that they didn't actually sing on the record that bore their name).

14. Snooky Lanson was: c. a singer on *Your Hit Parade*.

15. Not romantically linked with Madonna was: b. Charlie Sheen.

16. "Just put your lips together and blow" was a line delivered by: c. Lauren Bacall.

17. The world leader used to pitch vodka was: d. Boris Yeltsin.

18. *And God Created Woman* gave the world: c. Brigitte Bardot.

19. Bartles and Jaymes were: a. two make-believe enologists created by Ernest and Julio Gallo.

20. The Diggers were: b. a group that provided free food in the Haight-Ashbury during the 1960s.

21. "Roofie rape" was: d. rape committed when the victim was under the influence of Rohypnol.

22. *Superfly* glorified people who sold: a. cocaine.

23. Virginia Dare was: a. a tonic with 22 percent alcohol content.

24. In the 1940s, an on-screen kiss could last: b. three seconds.

25. Gene Simmons and Ace Frehley were: b. members of Kiss.

26. Hefner's '60s "main squeeze" was: b. Barbi Benton.

27. The controversial photographer was: b. Robert Mapplethorpe.

**Metal Head**

Nearly 80 million albums sold worldwide.

You're now the idol of millions. The American Dream really does exist, it really paid off. You can call Uncle Sam bullshit, call the president a moron, and they still give you money and women still want to have your babies.

—Gene Simmons, Kiss bassist, discussing the perks of rock stardom while promoting a world tour, 1996

\* \* \*

28. Actress for whom Hughes designed a pushup bra was: c. Jane Russell.

29. The musicians who did not die in a plane or helicopter crash were: b. Sam Cooke, e. Robert Johnson, g. Jim Morrison, and h. Richie Havens.

30. "She did everything he did, except she did it backwards and in high heels." Together they were: e. Fred Astaire and Ginger Rogers.

31. The Stone Poneys featured: d. Linda Ronstadt.

32. "You've Got a Friend" was from the album: c. *Tapestry.*

33. Crossing generations, the one who appeared with Pearl Jam was: b. Neil Young.

34. Sharon Stone's breakthrough movie was: b. *Basic Instinct.*

35. *Gish* was the first album for: d. Smashing Pumpkins.

36. The nondrummer was: f. Cannonball Adderley.

37. The player with the white sax was: e. Ornette Coleman.

38. She wasn't "hollering." She was: d. Ella Fitzgerald.

39. The Masters and Johnson book was: f. *Human Sexual Response.*

40. Alanis Morrisette comes from: b. Canada.

41. "I Put a Spell on You" was performed by: c. Screamin' Jay Hawkins.

42. The singer who dubbed *My Fair Lady* was: b. Marni Nixon.

43. "Hi de hi de hi de ho" is from: c. "Minnie the Moocher."

44. Bo Diddley was talking about: c. the Sex Pistols.

45. The presidential mother who had occasional second thoughts was: d. Jimmy Carter's mom.

46. Geldof's band was called: c. Boomtown Rats.

47. "High Hopes" was by b. Frank Sinatra, and "Don't Stop Thinkin' About Tomorrow" was by i. Fleetwood Mac.

48. "I'm Henry the Eighth, I am" was a hit for: d. Herman's Hermits.

49. The trendiest New York club of the '70s was: c. Studio 54.

50. The song that was not of the 1940s was: d. "Transfusion," Nervous Norvis.

**SEX, DRUGS, AND ROCK 'N' ROLL**

*Sequence 2: Wasted*

51. Lowry's classic of terminal alcoholism was: *Under the Volcano.*

52. Bush's drug czar was: William Bennett.

53. The blood changer was: Keith Richards.

54. The novelist who created Randle Patrick McMurphy was: Ken Kesey. The novel was *One Flew Over the Cuckoo's Nest.*

55. Jonathan Melvoin played with: Smashing Pumpkins.

56. "Just say no" is associated with: Nancy Reagan.

57. "Tune in, turn on, drop out" are the words of: Timothy Leary.

58. The former Panamanian strongman was: Manuel Noriega.

59. The runner who forfeited the gold: Ben Johnson.

60. Al Pacino battled drugs as: Serpico.

61. The Palm Springs facility is called: The Betty Ford Clinic.

62. The crack-smoking mayor was: Washington, D.C.'s Marion Barry.

63. The Academy Award–winning film was: *The Lost Weekend.*

64. The father of "Gonzo Journalism" was: Hunter S. Thompson.

65. The woman who sang "One pill . . ." was: Grace Slick.

66. The Mets star of the 1986 World Series was: Dwight Gooden.

67. *Story of a Life Interrupted* was by: Faye Resnik.

68. Leader of "The Untouchables" was: Elliott Ness.

69. "Alice's Restaurant" was a song by: Arlo Guthrie.

70. *Pulp Fiction* actress who got a shot to the heart: Uma Thurman.

71. Popeye Doyle was played by: Gene Hackman.

72. *So Now You Know* was written by: Kitty Dukakis.

73. *The Man With the Golden Arm* was written by: Nelson Algren.

74. *John Barleycorn*, another name for whiskey, was written by: Jack London.

75. *Junkie* and *Naked Lunch* were written by: William Burroughs.

76. The junkie-actor who played Count Dracula was: Bela Lugosi.

77. *The Crack-up* was written by: F. Scott Fitzgerald.

Lady Day
 You can be up to your boobies in white satin, with gardenias in your hair and no sugar cane for miles, but you can still be workin' on a plantation.

—BILLIE HOLIDAY, 1915–59

\* \* \*

78. "Bird" was: Charlie Parker.

79. At forty-four, heroin killed: Billie Holiday.

80. Holmes was created by: Arthur Conan Doyle.

81. "Eighteen straight whiskeys . . ." were the last words of: Dylan Thomas.

82. Actress Susan Hayward played: Lillian Roth.

83. Leonard Alfred Schneider's stage name was: Lenny Bruce.

84. The man who didn't inhale was: William Jefferson Clinton.

85. *Long Day's Journey Into Night* was by: Eugene O'Neill.

86. Dr. Nick was one of many doctors known as: Dr. Feelgood.

87. *Midnight Express* was written by: Oliver Stone.

88. The dipsomaniac author of *On the Road* was: Jack Kerouac.

89. *When a Man Loves a Woman* starred: Meg Ryan.

90. The founder of Alcoholics Anonymous: Bill W.

91. The Nixon-era attorney general's wife was: Martha Mitchell.

92. The vodka-powered *Hamlet* was: Richard Burton.

93. "The Lizard King" was dead at twenty-seven, and he was: Jim Morrison.

94. "Let's smoke another joint" was sung by: Tom Petty.

95. The Sex Pistol was: Sid Vicious.

96. Novelist who found inspiration in bourbon was: William Faulkner.

97. "Smells Like Teen Spirit" was sung by: Kurt Cobain.

98. Jazz drummer who fought drug addiction: Gene Krupa.

99. Fonda and Hopper played: Wyatt and Billy.

100. The wife-stabbing novelist was: Norman Mailer.

101. The auto executive charged with and acquitted of drug trafficking was: John DeLorean.

## SEX, DRUGS, AND ROCK 'N' ROLL

### Sequence 3: Groupies

102. Danny and the Juniors

103. George Thorogood and the Destroyers

104. Stevie Ray Vaughn and Double Trouble

105. Dion and the Belmonts

106. Billy J. Kramer and the Dakotas

107. Eric Burdon and the Animals

108. Emerson, Lake, & Palmer

109. Tom Petty and the Heartbreakers

110. Bill Haley and the Comets

111. Frankie Lymon and the Teenagers

112. ? and the Mysterians

113. Martha (Reeves) and the Vandellas

114. Bruce Hornsby and the Range

115. Gerry and the Pacemakers

116. Gloria Estefan and Miami Sound Machine

117. Booker T. and the MGs

118. Gladys Knight and the Pips

119. Big Head Todd and the Monsters

120. Little Anthony and the Imperials

121. Sly and the Family Stone

122. Jr. Walker and the All-Stars

123. Frankie Valli and the Four Seasons

124. Bruce Springsteen and the E. Street Band

125. Southside Johnny and the Asbury Jukes

126. Siouxsie and the Banshees

127. Buddy Holly and the Crickets

128. Harold Melvin and the Blue Notes

129. Iggy and the Stooges

130. Gary Lewis (one of Jerry's real kids) and the Playboys

131. Big Brother and the Holding Company

132. Elvis Costello and the Attractions

133. Commander Cody and the Lost Planet Airmen

134. Crosby, Stills, Nash, & Young

135. Joey Dee & the Starliters

136. Derek and the Dominos (an Eric Clapton manifestation)

137. Echo & the Bunnymen

138. Earth, Wind & Fire

139. Ronnie Hawkins and the Hawks (the band that became The Band)

140. Tommy James and the Shondells

141. KC & the Sunshine Band

142. Huey Lewis and the News

143. Sam the Sham and the Pharaohs

144. Hootie and the Blowfish

145. Gene Vincent and the Blue Caps

146. Jan and Dean

147. Mickey and Sylvia

148. Toots and the Maytals

149. Bob Marley and the Wailers

150. Kool and the Gang

151. Smokey Robinson and the Miracles

152. Gary Puckett and the Union Gap

153. Tony Orlando and Dawn

154. Mitch Ryder and the Detroit Wheels

155. Jonathan Richman and the Modern Lovers

156. Kinky Friedman and the Texas Jewboys

157. Joan Jett and the Blackhearts

158. Hall and Oates

159. Ashford and Simpson

160. Paul Revere and the Raiders

**SEX, DRUGS, AND ROCK 'N' ROLL**

*Sequence 4: Jazz and Blues*

161. "Mojo Workin' ": e. Muddy Waters

162. "Take the A Train": m. Duke Ellington

163. "Take 5": y. Dave Brubeck

164. "A Love Supreme": u. John Coltrane

165. "Everyday I Have the Blues": b. B. B. King

166. "One O'Clock Jump": z. Count Basie

167. "Desafinado": r. Stan Getz

168. " 'Round Midnight": k. Thelonious Monk

169. "Hound Dog": t. Big Mama Willie Mae Thornton

170. "A Tisket a Tasket": n. Ella Fitzgerald

171. "Bright Lights, Big City": x. Jimmy Reed

172. "Good Night Irene": s. Leadbelly

173. "Crossroads Blues": v. Robert Johnson

174. "Better Git It in Your Soul":
c. Charles Mingus

175. "What a Difference a Day Makes":
d. Dinah Washington

176. "Salt Peanuts": f. Dizzy Gillespie

177. "Song For My Father": j. Horace
Silver

178. "Misty": w. Erroll Garner

179. "Stompin' at the Savoy": i. Benny
Goodman

180. "Nuages": a. Django Reinhardt

181. "Woodchopper's Ball": h. Woody
Herman

182. "Lover Man": g. Billie Holiday

183. "Django": l. Modern Jazz
Quartet (they also did some definitive
interpretations of "Nuages")

184. "Ornithology": o. Charlie Parker

185. "Ain't Misbehavin' ": q. Fats Waller

186. "Jumpin' With Symphony Sid":
p. Lester Young

Scoring: A clear head and a good memory should ensure a score above 90. Alas, for many of us who spent too much time preoccupied with the things in this chapter, a clear head and a good memory are no sure thing. Still, if the chapter provided even a few flashbacks, you could have answered 90 of these. If you knew little of this stuff, you've missed out on a significant chunk of the twentieth-century experience, the good of it and the ill of it.

# THE MORE THINGS CHANGED
# . . . GREAT IDEAS OF ROCK 'N' ROLL

## 1967

C'mon people now, smile on your brother./Everybody get together and love one another right now.

>—Lyrics from a song by the Youngbloods, 1967,
> sung at innumerable protests and be-ins

## 1996

It's about time/We got to get together now./It's about time/People stick together now.

>—Lyrics from a song by the Beastie Boys,
> sung at Tibetan Freedom Day, 1996

# 9

# Rhymes of Our Times

*Work and pray,/Live on hay,/You'll eat pie/In the sky,/ When you die.*

—*JOE HILL, IWW ORGANIZER, EXECUTED IN 1915*

Rhyme is a mnemonic device; it prods the memory. Poetry is characteristically rhymed not only for esthetic reasons, but because, in the days before print, it helped early bards remember their own words during recitations. Before printing, such memory stimulants were a practical necessity.

In the sequences that follow, rhyme is meant to help you retrieve some of what you know about the twentieth century. In each set of four questions, the answers rhyme. The rhyming answers are intended to jog your memory, under the theory that we all know more than we think we know, that more lingers in our memories than we credit.

Despite that, this series may prove to be a bit difficult. It contains some obscure material. Even questions with answers that seem more widely known or obvious have been constructed in ways to make them more challenging, but the echo of rhymed answers should help you overcome those challenges and help you retrieve more than you thought you knew about the times of your life.

Still, few people will be able to get them all. I attempted to answer the questions myself, less than six months after

I'd written them, and I had to recheck several answers. Memory is like a cat; it comes and goes as it pleases.

So, try your memory on the following. This 220-question series has a degree of difficulty of 8.

## RHYMES OF OUR TIMES

1. Rudolph Hess's prison was

_____.

2. Half of the original Odd Couple was

_____.

3. In 1952, the rebels in the Kenyan uprising were called _____.

4. The leader of China's "Long March" would come to be popularly known as

_____.

\* \* \*

5. He wrote the lyrics and the music for "A Little Night Music." _____

6. He was secretary-general to the UN, but he also was a Nazi officer during World War II. _____

7. The national greeting in Israel, which means "to life," is _____.

8. The Royals often vacation at the palace at _____.

\* \* \*

9. Racist America sought a "Great White Hope" to defeat heavyweight champion _____.

10. One of baseball's first Hall of Famers, this New York Giant's pitching career was ended after he was gassed in World War I. He was _____.

11. He was twice an unsuccessful presidential candidate, and once U.S. ambassador to the United Nations.

_____.

12. She was a top fashion model of the 1990s. _____.

* * *

13. If you were a member of the Queens-based rock group that virtually invented "punk" in the late '70s, you were a _____.

14. A World War II action film that starred David Niven, Gregory Peck, and Anthony Quinn. It was a top box office hit of 1961. Its title was _____.

15. Prohibition made him rich; a razor slash to his face gave him his nickname. He died of syphilis. His name was _____.

16. The famous Canadian quintuplets of the 1930s were born to the family known as _____.

* * *

17. The baseball stadium that opened in New York in 1964 was named _____.

18. He was an Air Force general in World War II who later advocated using nuclear weapons in Vietnam. "Let's bomb them back to the stone age" was his motto. He was George Wallace's running mate in the presidential election of 1968. _____

19. This swing-era band leader was introduced with the signature line "Swing and sway with _____."

20. She was the star of *Pillow Talk* and other squeaky-clean sex comedies of the 1950s and early '60s. _____

* * *

21. Among other things, she's famous for having written, "A rose is a rose is a rose." _____

22. It was a critical moment in the war. At Remagen, American forces crossed the river _____.

23. This fashion designer, big in the 1970s and after, marketed a perfume called Obsession. _____

24. Baseball Hall of Famer, this sixteen-time All-Star was known as "Mr. Tiger" after playing right field for twenty years with the Detroit team. He led the American League in batting for 1955 with an average of .340. His name was _____.

\* \* \*

25. In abbreviated form, John Lewis, Milt Jackson, Connie Kay, and Milt Hinton are collectively better known as _____.

26. He starred as Cyrano de Bergerac in the French film of that name. He also seemed to appear in nearly all French films of the 1980s. His name is _____.

27. In the '60s, she was the Dragon Lady of South Vietnamese politics. Do you remember _____?

28. The '80s rappers who hit their peak (such as it was) with the album *As Nasty As They Wanna Be.* _____

\* \* \*

29. He was Mary Tyler Moore's boss. _____

30. Brit actor who paid a prostitute for services and was publicly sorry for it through an entire movie promotion tour was _____.

31. This notorious actor/pianist/wit of the '40s and '50s wrote a memoir called

*A Smattering of Ignorance,* and he once said of Doris Day, "I knew her before she was a virgin." He was _____.

32. He was lead vocalist with Led Zeppelin. _____

\* \* \*

33. This French director's classic films include *The 400 Blows* and *Jules and Jim.* _____

34. French premier when World War I ended, he was a strong nationalist nicknamed "The Tiger." _____

35. Married to Jane Pauley, he was the cartoonist who created *Doonesbury.* _____

36. The bumbling police detective played by Peter Sellers was _____.

\* \* \*

37. He was the commander of the good ship *Calypso.* _____

38. He was prime minister of Canada, and his wife ran a bit wild in the 1970s. _____

39. A grande dame of French cinema, she was the star of *Jules and Jim.* _____

40. Poet/filmmaker/artist, his best known work is *The Blood of a Poet,* a pioneering film of 1930. _____

\* \* \*

41. Jazz royalty, he was the pianist/band leader who wrote "One O'clock Jump." _____

42. This serial killer was a part-time clown. _____

43. Chester Gould created this square-jawed comic strip hero in 1931. _____

44. This Reagan administration CIA director died during the Iran-Contra investigations. _____

* * *

45. The nationalists/communists who drove the French out of Vietnam were known as the _____.

46. His autobiography was called *My Wicked, Wicked Ways*, and his sexual escapades created a national catchphrase. _____

47. This was the most popular inexpensive perfume of the 1950s.

_____

48. Another name for a dirigible, these were used to bomb London during World War I. _____

* * *

49. His theories drove much scientific and popular thought throughout the century. In 1930, he published *Civilization and Its Discontents*. A cigar smoker, he died after a long battle with cancer of the jaw in 1939. _____

50. He was the embodiment of Hopalong Cassidy. _____

51. In the 1930s, he was an Oklahoma bank robber killed in an Ohio cornfield by FBI agents led by Melvin Purvis.

_____

52. He was the actor who played Jim Ignatowski on *Taxi*. _____

* * *

53. He was the iron-fisted leader who held Yugoslavia together for nearly half a century. _____

54. Mussolini's first name was

_____.

55. The O. J. Simpson case judge was

_____.

56. The last "divine" ruler of Japan was

_____.

* * *

57. The lead singer of the Police was

_____.

58. The victim of the videotaped LA

police beating was _____.

59. James Arness played the title role

in the 1952 sci-fi classic known as

_____.

60. Flash Gordon's nemesis was the

Merciless one known as _____.

* * *

61. This animal trainer/adventurer was

famous for the motto "Bring 'em Back

Alive." _____

62. An animated character, Daisy was

his girlfriend's name. _____

63. American poet, in 1986 she won the

National Book Critics Circle Award for

her book *The Triumph of Achilles.*

_____

64. Trendy restaurateur/chef of the

1980s and '90s. _____

* * *

65. He created *Candid Microphone* and

*Candid Camera.* _____

66. Fontaine was the other half of this

theatrical team. _____

67. This word is Vietnam-era Marine

slang for a foot soldier. _____

68. Erich Maria Remarque's novel of

World War I was _____.

* * *

69. They first gained broad recognition

backing up Bob Dylan at Big Pink.

_____

70. A 1978 Steven King best seller was

_____.

71. The region in Europe wrested from Czechoslovakia and given to Germany by the Munich Pact of 1938 was

_____.

72. *The Whole Earth Catalogue* was a countercultural phenomenon of the early 1970s. Its creator/editor was

_____.

\* \* \*

73. This anthropologist became famous after publishing *Coming of Age in Samoa.* _____

74. This disk jockey's career was destroyed in the Payola scandal of the 1950s. _____

75. The late-'60s Rolling Stones album that featured "You Can't Always Get What You Want" and "Midnight Rambler." _____

76. This golfer won the Masters in 1949, 1952, and 1954. _____

\* \* \*

77. This vice-president spelled potato with an "e" on the end. _____.

78. President Clinton tried marijuana once, but said he "_____."

79. Traceable to the first decade of the twentieth century, this word was slang for a woman. _____

80. A computer innovation of the 1990s, this was an electronic means of correspondence. _____

\* \* \*

81. A 1950s dance fad popularized on *American Bandstand.* _____

82. A 1990s German chancellor.

_____

83. The college football extravaganza in Pasadena. _____

84. He took power in Cambodia (Khmer Republic) after Prince Sihanouk was deposed in 1970. _____

\* \* \*

85. This 1970s television character's leather jacket is on display in the Smithsonian. _____

86. Renowned Metropolitan opera star for twenty-five seasons, she had a range of two and a half octaves. _____

87. Women's stockings, introduced in 1939 to replace stockings made of silk.

_____

88. American artist, his work ushered in the pop art school of the 1960s.

_____

\* \* \*

89. What the O in O. J. Simpson stands for. _____

90. Oliver North's loyal secretary.

_____

91. Popular line from the song for the movie *Ghostbusters*, used to promote that '80s film, repeated ad nauseum.

_____

92. Desi Arnaz's wife, until 1960.

_____

\* \* \*

93. This African-American singer/dancer was the toast of Paris in the 1920s, but she suffered discrimination when she returned home in the '30s and again in the '50s. _____

94. Richard Nixon's religious affiliation was _____.

95. Scandalous Erskine Caldwell novel of the 1930s. _____

96. If you played NBA basketball for the team in Los Angeles, you were a _____.

* * *

97. The name of the woman who ended Gary Hart's presidential aspirations was _____.

98. This entertainer's story is told in *Funny Girl.* _____

99. This black American soprano's roles included Aida, Cleopatra, and Bess (in *Porgy and Bess*). _____

100. The Hollywood madame who provided sexual companionship to the stars was _____.

* * *

101. Hot '90s director whose first film was *Reservoir Dogs.* _____

102. Hot '70s director who turned very cold after directing *Heaven's Gate,* Hollywood's most costly flop.

_____

103. The most popular of many nicknames for Babe Ruth. _____

104. The part played by John Travolta in *Welcome Back Kotter.* _____

* * *

105. Single-named pop singer of the 1990s whose hits include "Human Behavior" and "Violently Happy."

_____

106. It was a slang word for penis before it entered popular usage as an all-purpose word for anyone rather out of it. _____

107. This conservative was probably the most famous rejected nominee to the

The Jazz Singer

Supreme Court. His nomination was turned down in 1987. _____

108. The kind of makeup worn by Al Jolson in *The Jazz Singer*, the first talking picture, was _____.

\* \* \*

109. "Miracle" antidepressant drug of the 1990s. _____

110. "Who loves ya, baby?" was this TV detective's signature line. He was known as _____.

111. Highly addictive cocaine-derived street scourage of the '80s and '90s. It's called _____.

112. This former child star of the '30s became America's ambassador to the UN. _____

\* \* \*

113. This controversial architect was responsible for the modernist pyramid now outside the Louvre. _____

114. This observance was initiated in 1972 as part of the growing awareness of ecological concerns. _____

115. This Swiss-born master of modern painting was noted for the humor and whimsy of his abstract compositions,

which included *The Revolution of the Viaducts*. _____

116. This entertainer was known as "the big mouth." By the end of her career, she was reduced to doing denture cleanser commercials. Her name was

_____.

\* \* \*

117. Male/female comedy team of the late 1950s/early 1960s _____

118. Jackie O's maiden name.

_____

119. When this flash-in-the-pan singing sensation of the early 1950s sang "Cry," he really did. _____

120. French entertainer who sang "Thank Heaven for Little Girls," among others. _____

\* \* \*

121. It was once the Belgian Congo, but in 1971 it became _____.

122. She was born in Russia. She was a teacher in Milwaukee. She was one of the few female heads of state during the century. _____

123. A popular line of skateboard sportswear in the 1990s. _____

124. Australian feminist who became famous (and notorious) when she published *The Female Eunuch* in 1971.

_____

\* \* \*

125. California Congressman Bono's former wife. _____

126. Coach Paul Bryant's nickname.

_____

127. George Orwell's real name.

_____

128. The reactionary political hysteria in the U.S. in the years following the Russian Revolution came to be known as the _____.

\* \* \*

129. Norman Mailer's 1979 book about murderer Gary Gilmore _____

130. It originated in the 1960s, and it's head-shop slang for a kind of marijuana or hashish pipe. _____

131. Fay Wray starred in this 1933 movie classic. _____

132. Tribal people of the Vietnamese highlands who fought beside American troops in that country. Thousands of them fled to the U.S. after the war was lost. _____

\* \* \*

133. Kurt Cobain's widow's band. _____

134. World War II hero, Kansas Senator, and GOP leader. _____

135. In espionage jargon, it's a person who infiltrates another agency to gather information. _____

136. Elvis Presley's fourth movie, set in Louisiana. _____

\* \* \*

137. Classic Jack Schaeffer western, written when the author had never been west of the Ohio River. The novel was later made into a movie starring Alan Ladd. _____

138. One of America's greatest writers died in 1910. His real name was Samuel Clemens, but his better known nom de plume was _____.

139. Judy Garland's husband's name in *A Star Is Born.* _____

140. Jazz saxophone giant whose improvisations were described as "sheets of sound." _____

\* \* \*

141. Kentucky Fried Chicken's founder was _____.

142. The fields in France that became a bloody battleground in both world wars were known as _____.

143. She wrote an advice column for over forty years. _____

144. Schwarzkopf, Westmoreland, and Pershing were all _____.

\* \* \*

145. Comic strip character Blondie's married name. _____

146. Jerry Garcia's group. _____

147. British philosopher who collaborated with Bertrand Russell to write *Principia Mathematica*.
_____

148. Hollywood's most famous costume designer. _____

\* \* \*

149. This 1970s country singer was known as "the Silver Fox." "Behind Closed Doors" was his biggest hit.

_____

150. House Speaker Newt Gingrich's mother said her son called the first lady a _____.

151. Nickname for the director of *Rear Window.* _____

152. What Whitaker Chambers was to Alger Hiss. _____

\* \* \*

153. Haitian leader returned to power by U.S. forces in the 1990s. _____

154. This American revolutionary wrote *Ten Days That Shook The World*. He's buried in the Kremlin. _____

155. The name of the character played by Patrick McNee on *The Avengers*. _____

156. In broadcasting jargon, when a television network delivers pictures to its affiliates, that's called a _____.

\* \* \*

157. He's the most famous oil rig firefighter, a job classification not much needed in the nineteenth century. _____

158. In 1966, this national health insurance program for the elderly was implemented. _____

159. Michael Jordan's nickname is _____.

160. This 1990s rocker's critically acclaimed first album was called *Exile in Guyville*. _____

\* \* \*

161. The road machine also known as a "hog." _____

162. The legendary reggae superstar. _____

163. In Vietnam, it was a slang term for the Viet Cong. _____

164. With the precision slang is known for, this '70s "Valley" slang word can mean "excellent" or "awful." _____

\* \* \*

165. Though surely not new to the twentieth century, we often heard the Arabic word for a religious war against heretics. That word? _____

166. Neo-Edwardian '60s British fashion trend, opposites of "rockers," whose adherents affected a "look" known as _____.

167. Elizabeth Taylor's third husband was _____.

168. Father and son senators from Connecticut: the father was formally censured for misuse of campaign funds in 1967, his son was later elected to his father's former seat. _____

\* \* \*

169. Campaign song and slogan for the 1952 Republican presidential candidate. _____

170. It was supposed to last for a thousand years, but it ended in a Berlin bunker in 1945. _____

171. He played MTM's husband, Rob Petrie. _____

172. Heavyweight Tyson's nickname. _____

\* \* \*

173. Where movie stars go when they die. _____

174. Tony Orlando's backup singers. _____

175. Hitler's girlfriend. _____

176. Jewish-American social realist artist _____

\* \* \*

177. According to her diary, she resolutely believed that people were good. _____

178. Slang term for methamphetamine, or speed. _____

179. Psychoanalyst and protégé of Freud, he wrote *The Trauma of Birth*.

_____

180. What weighed thirty tons and was called a "Sherman"? _____

\* \* \*

181. Martial-arts cinema pioneer who died mysteriously at thirty-two.

_____

182. This magazine, started in the 1970s by the same man who'd had a success with *Penthouse*, was fixed on the future.

_____

183. Woody's Allen's stepdaughter/girlfriend/wife. _____

184. The member of the A-Team who wore a Mohawk. _____

\* \* \*

185. In the Disney version of Peter Pan, he was Captain Hook's righthand man.

_____

186. President of South Korea during the Korean War. _____

187. Cree Indian folksinger who appeared on *Sesame Street* and *The Electric Company*. Her songs included "Now That the Buffalo's Gone."

_____

188. Janis Joplin hit penned by Kris Kristofferson. _____

\* \* \*

189. Alan Greenspan virtually was the Federal Reserve for years. That agency was commonly referred to as

_____.

190. "An antidote to civilization," these vacation villages first appeared in the '50s, but gained popularity throughout

the second half of the century.

_____

191. Television show about a talking

horse. _____

192. The U.S. Navy gave us this word

for toilet in the 1930s, and we've kept it

ever since. _____

* * *

193. The CBS sports guy whose

signature phrase was "tell it like it is."

_____

194. What campaign supporters urged

Harry Truman to do. _____

195. Actor who costarred in *The Piano*

and *Taxi Driver.* _____

196. The '50s commercial for this

popular brand of shampoo featured a

pearl dropped into it to demonstrate the

product's density. _____

* * *

197. Group organized in 1935 to help

people stay sober. _____

198. Expression associated with Willie

Mays. _____

199. Popular young bluesman of the

1980s and '90s: "Strong Persuader" was a

hit album for _____.

200. June 6, 1945, was _____.

* * *

201. '60s term for wealthy world

travelers. _____

202. The place for opera in New York:

_____

203. In *Playboy*, she's known as a

"playmate," but in *Penthouse* she's

known as a _____.

204. The computer equivalent of a

national party line. _____

205. The White House counsel who told Richard Nixon there was a cancer on his presidency. _____

206. Rock group whose leader, Freddy Mercury, died of AIDS. _____

207. The Catholic bishop who had a popular television show in the 1950s.

_____

208. *Captain Midnight*'s sponsor.

_____

* * *

209. She died tragically young, but she wrote *Raisin in the Sun* before she passed. She was _____.

210. In the '68 Olympics, he did a seven-foot, four-inch backward high jump. Think "flop," and you'll think of his name. _____

211. "Bloody Sunday" was a day in 1973 when British troops shot thirteen unarmed demonstrators. The Irish city where it happened was _____.

212. The protopunk lead singer of Blondie was _____.

* * *

213. We used to call it Peking, but now we call it _____.

214. It seems really stupid now, but members of Sinatra's Rat Pack were once thought to be cool when they said, "_____."

215. Chuck Berry's last top-forty hit was a salacious little ditty about his penis entitled _____.

216. The phrase "sent up the river" referred to a place in upstate New York we came to know better from movies

about "the big house." That place was

_____.

\* \* \*

217. This musician's nickname was short for "satchel mouth." _____

218. The artificial sweetener introduced in 1958. _____

219. On an episode of *Seinfeld*, Kramer and George's father come up with an idea for a bra for men. They call it

_____.

220. The famous World War II flag-raising took place on a Pacific atoll the Marines called _____.

## ANSWERS

1. Rudolph Hess's prison was Spandau.

2. Half of the original Odd Couple was Mathau.

3. The rebels in Kenya were called Mau Mau.

4. The leader of China's "Long March" was Chairman Mao.

\* \* \*

5. The composer of "A Little Night Music" was Sondheim.

6. The former Nazi secretary-general to the UN was Waldheim.

7. In Israel, "to life" is L'chaim.

8. The Royals often vacation at Blenheim.

\* \* \*

9. A "Great White Hope" was sought to defeat Jack Johnson.

10. The Giants's pitcher gassed in WW I was Christy Mathewson.

11. The unsuccessful candidate was Adlai Stevenson.

12. The '90s model whose name rhymes here was Christy Turlington.

\* \* \*

13. If you were in that group, you were a Ramone.

14. The WW II action film in question was *The Guns of Navarone*.

15. The mobster known as "scarface" was Alphonse Capone.

16. The famous 1930 quintuplets were named Dionne.

* * *

17. The ballpark that opened in New York in 1964 was Shea.

18. George Wallace's running mate was Curtis LeMay.

19. "Swing and sway with Sammy Kaye."

20. The star of *Pillow Talk* was Doris Day.

* * *

21. "A rose is a rose" was the work of Gertrude Stein.

22. The bridge at Remagen crosses the Rhine.

23. The fashion designer and marketeer was Calvin Klein.

24. Baseball Hall of Famer "Mr. Tiger" was Al Kaline.

* * *

25. John Lewis and company were known as the MJQ.

26. That top French film star was Gerard Depardieu.

27. The Dragon Lady of South Vietnam was Madame Nhu.

28. The '80s rap bad boys were 2 Live Crew.

* * *

29. Mary Tyler Moore's boss was Lou Grant.

30. The Brit actor who paid a prostitute was Hugh Grant.

31. The actor/pianist/wit was Oscar Levant.

32. The lead vocalist for Led Zeppelin was Robert Plant.

* * *

33. The French director of *The 400 Blows* was François Truffaut

34. The French premier nicknamed "The Tiger" was Clemenceau.

35. The cartoonist who created *Doonesbury* was Garry Trudeau.

36. The Peter Sellers detective was Inspector Clouseau.

* * *

37. The commander of the *Calypso* was Jacques Cousteau.

38. The '70s Canadian prime minister was Pierre Trudeau.

39. The female star of *Jules and Jim* was Jeanne Moreau.

40. The poet/filmmaker/artist in question was Jean Cocteau.

\* \* \*

41. The band leader who wrote "One O'clock Jump" was Count Basie.

42. The clown/killer was John Wayne Gacy.

43. Chester Gould was the creator of Dick Tracy.

44. The Reagan administration CIA director was William Casey.

\* \* \*

45. The French were driven out of Vietnam by the Viet Minh.

46. *My Wicked, Wicked Ways* was the autobiography of Errol Flynn.

47. The most popular inexpensive perfume of the '50s was My Sin.

48. Dirigibles used to bomb London during WWI were Zeppelins.

\* \* \*

49. The "Father of Psychoanalysis" was Sigmund Freud.

50. The actor who embodied Hopalong Cassidy was William Boyd.

51. The '30s thief killed by Melvin Purvis was Pretty Boy Floyd.

52. On *Taxi*, Jim Ignatowski was played by Christopher Lloyd.

\* \* \*

53. Yugoslavia's leader for nearly half a century was Tito.

54. Mussolini's first name was Benito.

55. Simpson case judge was Ito.

56. The last "divine" ruler of Japan was Hirohito.

\* \* \*

57. The lead singer of the Police was Sting.

58. The victim of the LA police beating Rodney King.

59. James Arness played the title role in *The Thing*.

60. Flash Gordon's nemesis was Ming.

\* \* \*

61. This animal trainer/adventurer was Frank Buck.

62. Daisy's boyfriend was Donald Duck.

63. The poet who won the National Book Critics Circle Award for *The Triumph of Achilles* was Louise Gluck.

64. The trendy chef of the 1980s and '90s was Wolfgang Puck.

\* \* \*

65. The creator of *Candid Camera* was Allen Funt.

66. Fontaine's partner was Alfred Lunt.

67. In Vietnam, a foot soldier was a grunt.

68. Erich Maria Remarque's novel was *All Quiet on the Western Front*.

\* \* \*

69. Bob Dylan's backup at Big Pink was The Band.

70. The 1978 Steven King best seller was *The Stand*.

71. The region wrested from Czechoslovakia was The Sudetenland.

72. The creator of *The Whole Earth Catalogue* was Stewart Brand.

\* \* \*

73. *Coming Of Age in Samoa* was the work of Margaret Mead.

74. The Payola disk jockey was Alan Freed.

75. The late-'60s Rolling Stones album was *Let It Bleed*.

76. The Masters winner in 1949, 1952, and 1954 was Sammy Snead.

\* \* \*

77. The VP who spelled potato with an "e" was Dan Quayle.

78. Clinton tried marijuana once, but he "didn't inhale."

79. When the century was new, a woman was a frail.

80. Computer correspondence is e-mail.

\* \* \*

81. The 1950s dance fad was the Stroll.

82. The 1990s German chancellor was Helmut Kohl.

83. The college football extravaganza in Pasadena is the Rose Bowl.

84. The man who took power in Cambodia after Sihanouk was Lon Nol.

\* \* \*

85. That leather jacket in the Smithsonian belonged to the Fonz.

86. The Metropolitan opera star was Lily Pons.

87. Women's stockings that replaced silk were nylons.

88. The artist who paved the way for pop art was Jasper Johns.

* * *

89. The O in O. J. stands for Orenthal.

90. Oliver North's loyal secretary was Fawn Hall.

91. The popular line from *Ghostbusters* was "Who ya gonna call?"

92. Desi's wife was Lucille Ball.

* * *

93. The toast of Paris in the 1920s was Josephine Baker.

94. Richard Nixon was a Quaker.

95. The Erskine Caldwell novel was *God's Little Acre*.

96. If you played for LA, you were a Laker.

* * *

97. Gary Hart's career-ending playmate was Donna Rice.

98. *Funny Girl* is about Fanny Brice.

99. The soprano whose name rhymes with Brice is Leontyne Price.

100. The Hollywood madame was Heidi Fleiss.

* * *

101. *Reservoir Dogs* was directed by Quentin Tarantino.

102. The director of *Heaven's Gate* was Michael Cimino.

103. Babe Ruth's most popular nickname was the Bambino.

104. In *Welcome Back Kotter*, Travolta played Vinnie Barbarino.

* * *

105. The singer who had a hit with "Human Behavior" was Bjork.

106. The slang word for penis is dork.

107. The rejected nominee to the Supreme Court was Judge Bork.

108. Al Jolson wore burnt cork.

* * *

109. The antidepressant drug of choice in the '90s was Prozac.

110. "Who loves ya, baby?" were the words of Kojak.

111. The drug that changed the nation was called crack.

112. Ambassador to the UN under Nixon was Shirley Temple Black.

*   *   *

113. That controversial architect was I. M. Pei.

114. The envirobservance initiated in 1972 was Earth Day.

115. The Swiss painter was Paul Klee.

116. "The big mouth" was also known as Martha Raye.

*   *   *

117. The comedy team was Nichols and May.

118. Jackie O's maiden name was Bouvier.

119. The guy who sang "Cry" was Johnny Ray.

120. The singer who sang "Thank Heaven for Little Girls" was Maurice Chevalier.

*   *   *

121. In 1971, the Belgian Congo became Zaire.

122. One of the few female heads of state was Golda Meir.

123. Popular skateboard sportswear of the 1990s was No Fear.

124. The feminist who wrote *The Female Eunuch* was Germaine Greer.

*   *   *

125. Bono's former wife was Cher.

126. Coach Paul Bryant's nickname was Bear.

127. George Orwell's real name was Eric Blair.

128. The reactionary political hysteria was known as the Red Scare.

*   *   *

129. Norman Mailer's book about Gary Gilmore was *Executioner's Song*.

130. A kind of marijuana or hashish pipe is a bong.

131. Fay Wray starred in *King Kong*.

132. The tribal people of the Vietnamese highlands were the Hmong.

*   *   *

133. Kurt Cobain's widow's band was called Hole.

134. World War II hero, etc. was Bob Dole.

135. A person who infiltrates another agency is a mole.

136. Elvis Presley's fourth movie was *King Creole*.

\* \* \*

137. The Jack Schaeffer western was *Shane*.

138. One of America's greatest writers was Mark Twain.

139. Judy Garland's husband's name in *A Star Is Born* was Norman Maine.

140. The jazz saxophone giant was John Coltrane.

\* \* \*

141. Kentucky Fried Chicken's founder was Harland Sanders.

142. Those bloody French fields were known as Flanders.

143. The advice columnist is, of course, Ann Landers.

144. Schwarzkopf, Westmoreland, and Pershing were all commanders.

\* \* \*

145. Blondie's married name was Bumstead. (Her maiden name was Boopadoop.)

146. Jerry Garcia's group was the Grateful Dead.

147. Bertrand Russell's collaborator was Alfred North Whitehead.

148. Hollywood's most famous costume designer was Edith Head.

\* \* \*

149. "The Silver Fox" was Charlie Rich.

150. Gingrich's mother said the Speaker called Ms. Clinton a bitch.

151. *Rear Window* director's nickname was Hitch.

152. Whittaker Chambers was a snitch.

\* \* \*

153. The Haitian leader returned to power was Aristide.

154. American radical buried in the Kremlin: John Reed.

155. The character played by Patrick McNee: Steed.

156. When a network delivers pictures to its affiliates, that's called a feed.

* * *

157. The most famous oil rig firefighter was Red Adair.

158. The health insurance program begun in 1966 was Medicare.

159. Michael Jordan's nickname is Air.

160. *Exile in Guyville* was the work of Liz Phair.

* * *

161. A "hog" was a Harley (as in Davidson).

162. The legendary reggae superstar was Bob Marley.

163. Slang for Viet Cong was Charlie.

164. The '70s "Valley" slang for great or lousy was gnarly.

* * *

165. The Arabic word for a religious war was jihad.

166. The neo-Edwardian '60s British fashion trend was mod.

167. Elizabeth Taylor's third husband was Mike Todd.

168. The father and son senators from Connecticut were Dodd.

* * *

169. The 1952 Republican presidential slogan was "I Like Ike."

170. In a Berlin bunker in 1945: The Third Reich.

171. Rob Petrie was played by Dick Van Dyke.

172. Heavyweight Tyson's nickname was Iron Mike.

* * *

173. When they die, movie stars go to: Forest Lawn.

174. Tony Orlando's backup singers were Dawn.

175. Hitler's girlfriend was Eva Braun.

176. The Jewish-American social realist artist was Ben Shahn.

* * *

177. The girl who believed that people were good was Anne Frank.

178. Slang term for meth is crank.

179. The protégé of Freud was Otto Rank.

180. A thirty-ton Sherman was a tank.

\* \* \*

181. The martial arts cinema pioneer was Bruce Lee.

182. This magazine that was fixed on the future was *Omni*.

183. Woody's Allen's stepdaughter/girlfriend/wife was Soon-Yi.

184. The member of the A-Team who wore a Mohawk was Mr. T.

\* \* \*

185. Captain Hook's righthand man was Mr. Smee.

186. The president of South Korea was Syngman Rhee.

187. The Cree Indian folksinger was Buffy Sainte-Marie.

188. The Janis Joplin hit was "Me and Bobby McGee."

\* \* \*

189. Alan Greenspan led the Fed.

190. Those vacation villages are called Club Med.

191. The show about a talking horse was called *Mr. Ed*.

192. The U.S. Navy word for toilet is the head (near the bulkhead, see?).

\* \* \*

193. "Tell it like it is," said Howard Cosell.

194. Harry Truman was supposed to give 'em hell.

195. *The Piano* and *Taxi Driver* costar was Harvey Keitel.

196. The popular brand of shampoo was Prell.

\* \* \*

197. The group organized in 1935 was AA.

198. The expression associated with Willie Mays was, "Say hey."

199. The popular young bluesman of the 1980s and '90s was Robert Cray.

200. June 6, 1945 was D-Day.

\* \* \*

201. The '60s term for wealthy world travelers was jet set.

202. The place for opera in New York was the Met.

203. In *Penthouse* she's a pet.

204. The computer party line is the Net.

\* \* \*

205. The Nixon White House counsel was John Dean.

206. The rock group led by Freddy Mercury was Queen.

207. The '50s Catholic TV bishop was Sheen.

208. *Captain Midnight*'s sponsor was Ovaltine.

\* \* \*

209. The playwright who wrote *Raisin in the Sun* was Lorraine Hansberry.

210. The "Fosbury Flop" was done by Dick Fosbury.

211. "Bloody Sunday" happened in Londonderry.

212. The protopunk lead singer of Blondie was Debbie Harry.

\* \* \*

213. It was once Peking, but we now call it Beijing.

214. Sinatra's Rat Pack used to say, "Ring a ding ding."

215. Chuck Berry's last top-forty hit was titled "My Ding a Ling."

216. Up the river referred to Sing Sing.

\* \* \*

217. Satchel mouth was shortened to Satchmo.

218. The artificial sweetener introduced in 1958 was Sweet 'n Low.

219. The name of the bra for men on *Seinfeld* was the bro.

220. The Marines called the atoll Iwo.

Scoring:

If you knew
most all of these,
tell your ma,
and she'll be pleased.
If you could not
rhyme a bunch,
then you're probably
out to lunch.

# 10

# By Any Other Name

*I confused things with their names.*

—*JEAN-PAUL SARTRE*

As Sartre did, many of us confused things with their names. Politicians, propagandists, publicists, and promoters counted on us doing that. To be well informed in the twentieth century, we often needed to know more than one word for a thing, or know the meanings that sometimes lurked beneath the surface of words.

Gobbledygook is a twentieth-century word, coined by an American politician after World War II, about the same time George Orwell was introducing us to the concept of "doublespeak." Perhaps it wasn't coincidental that both words came into being at about the same time, contemporaneous with the beginning of the Cold War, when governments on both sides of the Iron Curtain were busy hiding their activities behind a smokescreen of words.

For various reasons, we were seldom satisfied to call a thing by a single name. We needed alternative words for purposes of politeness, euphemism, exaggeration, hype, obfuscation, and aggrandizement. So, for people and for things, we often had alternative names, acronyms, sobriquets, appellations, and evasions.

And that's what the next hundred questions are about.

Do you know the other names the following people and things have been known by?

This series is not easy. It has a degree of difficulty of 8.

## BY ANY OTHER NAME

1. "The supermarket to the world" was also known as _____.

2. He was rock 'n' roll's "Lizard King." _____

3. In World War I it was known as "shell shock." In World War II it was "combat fatigue." After Vietnam, it was known as PTSD, which stands for

P _____ T _____

S _____ D _____.

4. "The Sunshine Act" of 1976 was more officially known as _____.

5. MOSSAD is another name for _____.

6. The "It" Girl of the 1920s was _____.

7. "The Comeback Kid" of twentieth-century American politics was _____.

8. The general known as "Old Blood and Guts" was _____.

9. He was dubbed "the Darth Vader of American Politics." _____

10. The comedian known as the "Great Stone Face" was _____.

11. *ID4* was the trendy '90s abbreviation for the blockbuster movie known as _____.

12. Before the press dubbed him "the Boston Strangler," he was known to his neighbors as _____.

13. The president known as the "trustbuster" was _____.

14. It was once called Ceylon, but when the century ended it was known as _____.

15. "The house that Ruth built" was also known as _____.

16. In the world of 1990s home entertainment, DTVs were _____.

17. An "Atari star" was '80s showbiz jargon for _____.

18. The musician known as "Killer" was _____.

19. WYSIWYG was '80s hacker jargon for _____.

20. In the '90s, the press dubbed him "Dr. Death." _____

21. "The Vagabond Lover" of '20s music was _____.

22. "Snail Mail" was '90s slang for _____.

23. In the '90s it became 3-Com Park, but before that it was known as _____.

24. "The King of Swing" during the '30s was _____.

25. "The King of Jazz" of the '20s was _____.

26. The actor known as "the Duke" was, of course, _____.

27. The "artist formerly known as Prince" was known to his mother as _____.

28. During World War II, the Axis Powers were _____ , _____ , and _____.

29. On Wall Street, an IPO is _____.

30. "The Juice" was another name for

_____.

31. It began the century as Burma, and

it ended the century as _____.

32. In the '20s and '30s, Scarface was a

nickname for _____.

33. "Sidewalk Surfin' " was a 1965 hit

record for Jan and Dean. "Sidewalk

surfin' " came to be known as

_____.

34. A. A. Milne's "Bear of Little Brain"

was better known as _____.

35. "The Man of Steel" was, of course,

_____.

36. "The Queen of Mean" was what the

media dubbed _____.

37. Closed in 1963, "the Rock" was

another name for _____.

38. The rock in "a piece of the rock" is

_____.

39. In modern military nomenclature,

ANZAC was an acronym for

A _____ N _____

Z _____ A _____

C _____.

40. The "Girl in the Red Velvet Swing"

was _____.

41. He billed himself as "the hardest-

working man in show business" and "the

Godfather of Soul." His name was

_____.

42. After weeks of captivity with the

Symbionese Liberation Front, Patty

Hearst took the revolutionary name of

_____.

43. Founded in 1964, the PLO was the

P _____ L _____

O _____.

44. In the last two decades in corporate America, the "glass ceiling" was a phrase that glossed the reality of _____.

45. In the world of mortgage and real estate, "redlining" was another word for _____.

46. "Corporate downsizing" was a phrase commonly heard in the last decade of the century. It was a euphemism for _____.

47. "Terminate with extreme prejudice" was a CIA euphemism for _____.

48. A "grief counselor" was euphemistic jargon developed in what industry to describe what occupation? _____

49. "Workforce Imbalance Correction" was a euphemism for _____.

50. "Preventive detention" was a concept promoted by Attorney General John Mitchell during the Nixon administration. What it was, was

_____.

51. He was known as "the man in black." _____

52. Campaign rhetoric dubbed him "the man from Hope." _____

53. He was known as "the man of a thousand faces." _____

54. What '70s athlete was known as "Smokin' Joe"? _____

55. "A blind pig" was '20s slang for

_____.

56. We began to hear about PAC money in the 1970s. PAC was an abbreviation for _____.

57. An early rap group of the '80s called themselves NWA. The initials hid the words _____.

58. This Irish playwright was also known as "the Borstal Boy" after an autobiographical work with the same name. He was _____.

59. "Lion of Judah" was another name for Ethiopian emperor _____.

60. Red Grange, football immortal of the 1920s, was popularly known as _____.

61. This Yankee first baseman and Hall of Famer was also known as "the Iron Horse." He was _____.

62. The 1940s Hollywood star known as "the sweater girl" was _____.

63. Senator Pothole was a name of derision applied to _____.

64. Tom Wolfe dubbed it "the Me decade." He was referring to _____.

65. *Anna and the King of Siam* later became the musical *The King and I.* What was once Siam is now _____.

66. In the 1980s, just before the Soviet Union dissolved, Mikhail Gorbachev initiated a policy called Glasnost. That meant _____.

67. In 1980, Ronald Reagan proclaimed "the Eleventh Commandment." What was that? _____

68. The 1990s saw the opening of "the Chunnel," which was _____.

69. He died in 1931, but he shaped the century. He was known as "the wizard of Menlo Park." Who was that?

_____

70. GATT was much debated in the 1990s. What did the initials stand for?

_____

71. Since the 1930s, entertainers have worked "the Borscht Belt," which remains a name for _____.

72. The Great White Way is another name for _____.

73. The Mann Act was enacted into law in 1910. It was a law meant to combat "white slavery." What was that?

_____

74. In Vietnam, an "FNG" was a _____.

75. In the 1950s, he was dubbed the comedian with "the button-down mind." Who was that? _____

76. You couldn't pick up a paper in the 1970s without reading about OPEC. The initials stood for _____.

77. PATCO. President Reagan destroyed it in the early 1980s. What was it? _____

78. In Vietnam, American soldiers shared combat with ARVN troops. What did ARVN stand for? _____

79. Smog. It's a portmanteau word that entered the language after World War II. The two words it's composed of are _____ and _____.

80. In the 1950s, this senator from Illinois was known as "Mr. Conservative." He was _____.

81. The word is fading from our vocabulary, but in the 1920s everyone knew what a flivver was. Do you? _____

82. Neal Cassady was Jack Kerouac's friend. Kerouac immortalized him in the influential '50s novel *On the Road.* Cassady is known in that novel as _____.

83. The phrase "inside the Beltway" became a cliché in the 1990s. What did it delineate? _____

84. In World War II, a BAR man operated a B _____ A _____ R _____.

85. In the mid-1920s, H. L. Mencken coined the phrase "Bible Belt" to describe what region? _____

86. In the lexicon of the Cold War, a "Pinko" was _____.

87. "The track of the American chicken" was a derisive 1960s phrase (and bumper sticker) used to describe _____.

88. Jim Crow schools were _____.

89. If you were attending the "submarine races" during the '50s and '60s, what you were really doing was _____.

90. In the world of cloaks and daggers, what was a mole? _____

91. For nearly half the century we heard about the KGB. What was that? _____

92. In the '90s, we often heard about "Indies." What were they? _____

93. TCBY was an '80s franchise that sold frozen yogurt. What did the initials stand for? _____

94. FCC Chairman Newton Minow called it "a vast wasteland," and the phrase stuck. What was he talking about? _____

95. If you owned stock, you probably checked the NASDAQ daily, so surely you knew that the initials stood for

N _____ A _____

S _____ D _____

A _____ Q _____.

96. The Lend-Lease Program—when and what was that? _____

97. Freedom Riders—who were they, and when were they in the news? _____

98. They were known as V-girls during the World War II years. What did that mean? _____.

99. The Six-Day War. When was that (the decade) and who were the combatants? _____

100. On *Saturday Night Live*, they were the actor/comedians who played the two wild and crazy guys. They were _____ and _____.

## ANSWERS

1. Archer-Daniel-Midlands called itself "supermarket to the world."

2. Jim Morrison was the self-proclaimed "Lizard King."

3. P.T.S.D. was Post Traumatic Stess Disorder.

4. "The Sunshine Act" is officially known as The Freedom of Information Act, which grants Americans access to places (and documents) relating to the people's business.

5. The Israeli Secret Service is known as MOSSAD.

6. Clara Bow was the "It" Girl.

7. William Jefferson Clinton was known as "The Comeback Kid."

8. General George Patton was also known as "Old Blood and Guts."

9. Bob Dole was dubbed "the Darth Vader of American Politics."

10. Buster Keaton was known as the "Great Stone Face."

11. *Independence Day* was promoted as *ID4* because it was slated to open on the July 4, 1996. It actually opened on the third.

12. Albert deSalvo was the man who came to be known as "the Boston Strangler" after confessing to killing thirteen women in the mid-'60s.

13. Theodore Roosevelt was known as the "trustbuster."

14. Sri Lanka (which means "resplendent land" in Sinhalese) was known as Ceylon until 1972.

15. Yankee Stadium was also known as "the house that Ruth built."

16. DTVs (or Direct to Video) were movies never released to theaters.

17. If, after a bright debut, you did a fast fade to obscurity, you were known as an "Atari star."

18. Jerry Lee Lewis called himself "Killer."

19. WYSIWYG stood for "What you see is what you get."

20. Assisted-suicide crusader Dr. Kevorkian was dubbed "Dr. Death."

21. Rudy Vallee was also known as "the Vagabond Lover."

22. Mail delivered by the U.S. Postal Service was "Snail Mail."

23. The San Francisco Giants used to play ball at Candlestick Park.

24. Benny Goodman was "the King of Swing."

25. "The King of Jazz" was Paul Whiteman. Though the jazz he played was much diluted, he had a role to play in

making jazz popular with a mainstream audience.

26. John Wayne was known as "the Duke."

27. Prince Rogers Nelson was the "artist formerly known as Prince."

28. Germany, Japan, and Italy were the Axis Powers.

29. An IPO is an Initial Public Offering.

30. O. J. Simpson was "The Juice."

31. Myanmar is the place once known as Burma.

32. Al Capone was known as "Scarface." (He was also known as "Snorky," a nickname he much preferred.)

33. "Sidewalk surfin' " was skateboarding.

34. Pooh was Milne's "Bear of Little Brain." (Incidentally, befitting the century's drift, Milne's son, the model for Christopher Robin, grew up to become a soldier in WWII.)

35. Superman was "the Man of Steel."

36. Hotel owner Leona Helmsley was "the Queen of Mean."

37. Alcatraz was "the Rock."

"The Girl in the Red Velvet Swing"
Evelyn Nesbit: Her husband's trial for the murder of architect Standford White was as big in the first decade of the century as the O. J. Simpson trial was in the last decade.

The murder took place in front of a large gathering at Madison Square Garden in 1906. After shooting White in the head three times, Henry Thaw, a wealthy lunatic, told the arresting officer: "He ruined my wife."

Like Simpson, Thaw was an abusive husband. He spent nine years in an insane asylum and divorced his wife after his release in 1915. Evelyn Nesbit died in 1967.

In the 1970s, novelist E. L. Doctorow used the real-life characters in his novel *Ragtime*. Novelist Norman Mailer played the architect in the movie made from the novel.

38. Prudential Insurance features Gibraltar in its corporate logo, so the rock could be said to be either the Prudential (the company) or Gibraltar.

39. ANZAC equals Australian New Zealand Army Corps.

40. Evelyn Nesbit was known as the "Girl in the Red Velvet Swing."

41. James Brown was "the hardest-working man in show business."

42. Tania was the name Patty Hearst adopted.

43. The PLO was the Palestine Liberation Organization.

44. "Glass ceiling" was a phrase denoting systemic discrimination that blocked the advancement of women and minorities in businesses and organizations.

45. "Redlining" was (and is) the practice of discrimination in denying mortgage loans based on the race of the loan applicant.

46. "Corporate downsizing" was a euphemism for firing people.

47. To "terminate with extreme prejudice" was a CIA euphemism for killing someone, as used in the world of Cold War spies.

48. In the jargon of the funeral industry, "grief counselor" was a euphemism for the undertaker or mortician.

49. A "Workforce Imbalance Correction" was another euphemism for firing people. (We needed many such euphemisms in the '90s as corporate services shrank and executive salaries soared.)

50. "Preventive detention" was a plan to lock people up to prevent them from doing what law enforcement suspected they might be planning to do, a clear violation of First Amendment guarantees. We should remember this assault on freedom, and others like it. As Jefferson said a couple of centuries ago, "The price of freedom is eternal vigilance." It was this kind of thing he had in mind.

51. Country singer Johnny Cash was known as "the man in black."

52. Bill Clinton was "the man from Hope."

53. Silent movie star Lon Chaney was "the man of a thousand faces."

54. "Smokin' Joe" was the moniker of boxer Joe Frazier.

55. "A blind pig" was a speakeasy, or illegal drinking establishment.

56. PAC stood (and stands) for Political Action Committee, a way of raising funds

to buy clout with a candidate or for a cause.

57. NWA was an abbreviation for Niggers With Attitudes. Their first hit album was *Straight Outta Compton*, which included the controversial song "F—K the Police."

58. "The Borstal Boy" was Dublin playwright and legendary tippler Brendan Behan, 1923–64.

59. The "Lion of Judah" was Ethiopian emperor Haile Selassie, who ruled that country for half a century.

60. Red Grange was known as "the Galloping Ghost."

61. Lou Gehrig was "the Iron Horse."

62. Lana Turner was known as "the sweater girl."

63. New York's Alphonse D'Amato was dubbed Senator Pothole.

64. The 1980s were known as "the Me decade."

65. What was once Siam is now Thailand.

66. Glasnost was Gorbachev's policy of a new openness in Soviet politics, an easing of restrictions on speech and advocacy.

67. Reagan's "Eleventh Commandment" decreed that no Republican would speak ill of another Republican.

68. "The Chunnel" was the tunnel under the Channel, the English Channel between France and England.

69. "The wizard of Menlo Park" was Thomas Alva Edison.

70. GATT was the General Agreement on Tariff and Trade.

71. "The Borscht Belt" is a chain of resorts in the Catskill Mountains that cater to a predominantly Jewish clientele.

72. Broadway is also known as the Great White Way.

73. "White slavery" was a polite way to say prostitution. The phrase dates back to a nineteenth-century play that bore that title.

74. An "FNG" was a "F—kin' New Guy."

75. Bob Newhart was the comedian with "the button-down mind."

76. OPEC was (and remains) the Organization of Petroleum Exporting Countries.

77. PATCO was the Professional Air Traffic Controllers Organization.

78. ARVN was the Army of Vietnam.

79. Smog is a word built from smoke and fog.

80. "Mr. Conservative" was Illinois senator Everett Dirksen.

81. A flivver was another word for an automobile—more specifically, not a very good automobile.

82. Neal Cassady is called Dean Moriarty in *On the Road*.

83. The Beltway is the highway that virtually encircles Washington, D.C., therefore the phrase "inside the Beltway" denotes the nation's capital. Connotations of the phrase suggest that people (politicians) inside the beltway are insular and out of touch with the realities known to the rest of us.

84. A BAR man operated a Browning Automatic Rifle.

85. Mencken coined the phrase "Bible Belt" to describe the South.

86. A "Pinko" was one who wasn't quite a Red, but was sympathetic to many of the ideas of communists.

87. The peace symbol was called "the track of the American chicken."

88. Jim Crow schools were segregated schools. (The phrase "Jim Crow" dates back to the eighteenth century, when blacks were referred to as "crows," and to the nineteenth century, when Jim Crow was a dance done by slaves and later by minstrels.)

89. "Submarine races" described the act of parking for the purpose of "making out."

90. In the language of espionage, a "mole" was a spy working inside the agency or organization he or she was spying upon.

91. Literally, the KGB was the Komitet Gosudartstvennoi Bezopasnosti, or Committee of State Security, the Soviet secret police.

92. "Indies" were independently made films. Such films were made outside the studios, and were independently financed. Many of the biggest film directors of the century's last decade got started as independents.

93. TCBY stood for The Country's Best Yogurt.

94. "A vast wasteland" was Minow's characterization of television programming.

95. The NASDAQ was the National Association of Securities Dealers Automated Quotations system.

96. Under FDR, the Lend-Lease Act (of 1941) allowed a still-neutral U.S. to furnish war materials to Great Britain, China, and the Soviet Union.

97. In 1961, Freedom Riders were students (and others) who left northern cities and colleges to protest segregation in the South by integrating interstate buses. Many were beaten for their efforts.

98. V-girls (or Victory girls) were young women said to be rather free with sexual favors for servicemen.

99. The Six-Day War took place in 1967 when Israeli forces were victorious over Egypt and its Arab allies.

100. Steve Martin and Dan Ackroyd played the "two wild and crazy guys."

Scoring: If you had the right answers for 80 or more of these, then you have a way with words, and with other words.

If you scored somewhere near the middle (say, 40–60 correct), then you had a middling score. Since this series, like most, defies categories, what such a score suggests is that you know some things, and don't know others.

If you knew fewer than 30 of these, you may be a bit word deficient, or inattentive to what some people called some other people and things. In other words, you didn't do well here.

# 11

## Words, Perfect and Otherwise

We were word driven, our dreams and desires bullied by the words of poets, politicians, and publicists, our passions, enthusiasms, hopes, and fears crafted into catchphrases. Our hunger for novelty found expression in the way we spoke. The turnover in new expressions was one of the hallmarks of a century characterized by rapid change; the time it took for a phrase to move from new to ubiquitous to cliché became increasingly brief as the century wore on.

Remember those little candy hearts we gave each other on Valentine's Day when we were kids? The ones with words or phrases like "Be Mine," "Kiss Me," and "I'm Yours" printed on them? You should remember. Those candies have been a tradition since 1902, the year the Necco Candy Company started making them.

But it turns out that the sayings change on those itty-bitty candies and, in their small way, the changes reflect the ebb and flow of fashions in language. So it is, then, that in the 1990s, the company dumped such words and phrases as "Dig Me," "Cha Cha," "Far Out," "Why Not," and "Crazy." Though some of those slogans had been offered on the candies for forty years, they had to go. No '90s kid would readily know them, the company reasoned. Also gone were "Solid" and "Hang Ten." The replacement slogans? "Fax Me" and "E Mail Me" hit the stores as the century drew to a close. Fourth-graders with fax machines? Oh, the times, oh, the mores.

Those times and mores can be recaptured in the memorable words and phrases of the past.

## WORDS, PERFECT AND OTHERWISE

### Sequence 1

Popular culture echoes through the following phrases. Do you still hear the echoes? Level of difficulty: 4.

1. "Return with us now to those thrilling days of yesteryear." The phrase will forever be associated with _____.

2. "M'm M'm Good" was the core of a very successful advertising campaign for _____.

3. "Not a cough in a carload." This one goes back more than fifty years. If you heard or read it once, you heard or read it a thousand times. The brand name it advertised was _____.

4. Ella Fitzgerald (and others) made TV commercials for this product in which glass broke when she hit a high note. The question we were asked was: "Is it live, or is it _____?"

5. This one is too easy. If you were alive in this century, then you surely know that "two all-beef patties, special sauce, lettuce, cheese" were words used to sell _____.

6. "Head for the border." These are words from another saturation advertising blitz. We remember the words not because they're clever or meaningful, but because we heard them

so often advertising the franchise known as _____.

7. "I made him an offer he couldn't refuse." These words have entered the culture, perhaps indelibly. Since you surely know they're from *The Godfather*, I'll ask if you remember the name of the writer. Well, do you? _____

8. "I don't belong to any organized political party. I'm a Democrat." The time was the 1930s, the speaker one of the country's most beloved humorists. His name was Will Rogers. Do you remember where he was from?

_____

9. "Read my lips! No new taxes." The phrase probably won him one election and cost him another. The presidential candidate he beat was _____ ,

and the candidate who beat him was

_____.

10. For about twenty years it was customary for stadium-level musicians to give names to their tours. One of the top-grossing tours of the century was the "Steel Wheels Tour," a tour made by

_____.

11. "You are a lost generation." It was a label applied by Gertrude Stein, and it stuck. That generation was

_____.

12. "Hog Butcher for the World. Tool Maker, Stacker of Wheat . . . City of the Big Shoulders." The words were Carl Sandburg's. The city they describe is

_____.

13. The popular press labeled them "the fab four" and the "mop tops." You know

they were the Beatles, but do you remember the name of their Liverpool-based manager? _____

14. In the 1960s, a book became popular pushing the idea that, in organizations, employees tended to rise to their level of incompetence, then lock in at that level. The idea, and the book that embodied it, were both known as _____.

15. According to T. S. Eliot's seminal 1922 poem "The Wasteland," it is "the cruellest month." Which month? _____

16. Congresswoman Pat Schroeder called his "the Teflon-coated presidency," because she said nothing stuck to him. The name did, however. The president she was talking about? _____

17. Newspapers dubbed this racketeer as "the Teflon Don," but that bit of description proved premature in the case of _____.

18. "If it doesn't fit, you must acquit." The year these words were uttered was _____ and the person who uttered them was _____.

19. "We're number two. We try harder." That was a famous 1960s advertising slogan for _____.

20. "I think it pisses God off if you walk by the color purple in a field somewhere and don't notice it." Who wrote that line? _____

# WORDS, PERFECT AND OTHERWISE

## Sequence 2

This sequence gives you a bit of help. It's a multiple-choice sequence, but like the one before, it's fairly eclectic. It's also a bit more difficult. Level of difficulty: 6.

21. "The best lack all conviction, while the worst/Are full of passionate intensity." For many, these lines evoked a powerful truth about our times. The line is from a poem called "The Second Coming." The poet was:

a. Dylan Thomas

b. W. B. Yeats

c. Robert Frost

d. T. S. Eliot

22. A popular phrase had it that they were "overpaid, overfed, oversexed, and over here." They were:

a. oil field workers in 1970s Kuwait

b. U.S. servicemen in France during World War I

c. U.S. servicemen in England during World War II

d. Japanese businessmen on "sex junkets" to Thailand in the 1980s

23. Gore Vidal called him "a triumph of the embalmer's art," and Gerald Ford said, "No, I don't think he dyes his hair.

He's just prematurely orange." They were dissing:

a. Strom Thurmond

b. Bob Dole

c. Robert Redford

d. Ronald Reagan

24. "I tawt I taw a puddy tat." That's Tweety, and he's usually talking about Sylvester. The studio they both worked for was:

a. Warner Brothers

b. Miramax

c. Disney

d. United Artists

25. "The words of the prophet are written/on the subway walls and tenement halls." The lines are by:

a. Bob Dylan

b. Bruce Springsteen

c. Paul Simon

d. Paul McCartney

e. Tracy Chapman

26. This product was touted as having a "micronite filter," which proved to be a popular innovation in the 1950s. The product with the micronite filter was:

a. the Culligan water purifier

b. the Chevrolet auto air-conditioning system

c. Kent cigarettes

d. the Acme humidifier

27. "Goodbye Norma Jean,/Though I never knew you at all./You had the grace to hold yourself/While those around you crawled." The song was about pop icon Marilyn Monroe. The title of the song was:

a. "Candle in the Wind"

b. "Goodbye Norma Jean"

c. "A Song for You"

d. "The Rose"

e. "Goodbye Yellow Brick Road"

28. A mugger barks the ultimatum, "Your money or your life." Long pause. The mugger repeats: "C'mon, I said your money or your life." The reply: "I'm thinking, I'm thinking." The bit was a comedy classic from the radio days of:

a. Fred Allen

b. George Burns

c. Jack Benny

d. Groucho Marx

e. Abbott and Costello

American Dreamers

Screen icon marries baseball icon, January 14, 1954: Marilyn Monroe and Joe DiMaggio are wed. DiMaggio is inducted into the Baseball Hall of Fame a year later, in 1955. Of the marriage, Norman Mailer, himself a literary icon, said: "The highest prize in the world of men is a woman on your arm and living there in your heart loyal to you."

In 1956, the by-then-divorced Monroe will marry Arthur Miller. Of Marilyn, one-time costar Tony Curtis said: "Kissing [her] was like kissing Hitler."

Monroe was a "star" for less than ten years. DiMaggio played pro ball for fifteen years. The marriage lasted less than two years.

29. "Float like a butterfly, sting like a bee." The words belong to:

a. Mao Zedong

b. Sugar Ray Leonard

c. Rudolph Nureyev

d. Howard Cosell

e. Muhammad Ali

f. Joe Louis

30. "Okie used to mean you was from Oklahoma. Now it means you're scum." The writer of that line was:

a. William Faulkner

b. John Steinbeck

c. William Styron

d. John Ford

e. Tennessee Williams

31. "Whether you like it or not, history is on our side. We will bury you." The speaker of these famous, tension-enhancing words was:

a. Josef Stalin

b. Adolf Hitler

c. Benito Mussolini

d. Idi Amin

e. Nikita Khrushchev

f. Newt Gingrich

32. "My brain? That's my second favorite organ." Many people, including his fans, questioned Woody Allen's sense of priority some twenty years after he first uttered this line in the movie:

a. *Sleeper*

b. *Crimes and Misdemeanors*

c. *Manhattan Murder Mystery*

d. *Hannah and her Sisters*

e. *Annie Hall*

f. *The Purple Rose of Cairo*

33. Complete this famous 1973 line from feminist Florynce Kennedy: "If men could get pregnant, abortion would be:

a. legal

b. required

c. a sacrament

d. no problem

e. a joke

f. free

34. At a dinner for Nobel Prize winners, President John Kennedy said: "I think it's the most extraordinary collection of talent, of human knowledge, that has ever been gathered at the White House—with the possible exception of when:

a. Franklin and Eleanor lived here"

b. Thomas Jefferson dined alone"

c. George Washington was president"

d. Abraham Lincoln inhabited these rooms"

e. the Democrats last held the White House"

35. He drank his martinis "shaken, and not stirred." He was:

a. Ian Fleming

b. Dean Martin

c. Foster Brooks

d. The Thin Man

e. James Bond

36. "I used to be Snow White . . . but I drifted" were words attributed to:

a. Bette Davis

b. Mae West

c. Bette Midler

d. Marlene Dietrich

e. Madonna

f. Demi Moore

37. Ars gratia artis. It means "art for art's sake," but that meaning notwithstanding, the words were on the logo of:

a. Chrysler Corporation

b. Trump Towers

c. MGM Studios

d. Sotheby's

e. the L.L. Bean catalogue

f. Budweiser beer

38. "Supercallifragilisticexpialidocious" was the word. The movie that gave it currency was:

a. *Mary Poppins*

b. *The Love Bug*

c. *The Sound of Music*

d. *Peter Pan*

e. *101 Dalmations*

f. *The Lion King*

39. Complete this famous line by Harry S. Truman. "I don't give 'em hell. I just tell the truth and:

a. there's hell to pay"

b. watch 'em cry"

c. they think it's hell"

d. that's the hell of it"

40. "War is Peace. Freedom is Slavery. Ignorance is Strength." In George Orwell's book *1984*, phrases like this are known as:

a. self-canceling

b. The Big Lie

c. newspeak

d. agit-prop

e. double talk

f. contradictions in terms

## WORDS, PERFECT AND OTHERWISE

*Sequence 3*

Fill in the blanks. Level of difficulty: 6.

41. A lamentation by humorist Alexander Woollcott, which we still are repeating more than sixty years after he wrote it: "All the things I really like to do are either illegal, _____ , or _____ ."

42. Mae West said it in the movie *Diamond Lil*: "Is that a gun in your pocket, or are you just _____ ."

43. Dean Rusk said it to John Kennedy during the Cuban Missile Crisis in 1962. His words? "We're eyeball to eyeball, and I think the other fellow just _____."

44. It's a song from *Evita*, the musical by Tim Rice and Andrew Lloyd Webber. "Don't Cry for Me, _____"

45. The line is from the movie *Field of Dreams*. Fill in the blank. "If you build it, _____."

46. Way back when, the ads for *Easy Rider* proclaimed: "He went looking for America, but _____."

47. Mao Zedong's line was expropriated self-defeatingly by a number of American radicals in the 1960s. What Mao said was: "Political power grows out of the _____."

48. Hillary Clinton took the title of her 1996 book from an African proverb that goes: "It takes _____."

49. Texas Guinan is remembered as the most colorful speakeasy proprietress of the prohibition era. She is also remembered for the way she greeted her patrons, saying: "Hello _____."

50. It was lapel-button wisdom during the Flower Power days of the '60s. If you were there, you'll remember that it went, "Today is the first day of _____."

51. It was also in those days that Eldridge Cleaver said; "If you're not part of the solution, you're _____."

52. The Clinton administration's way of dealing with the question of gays in the

military was: "Don't _____.

Don't _____."

53. During World War II, we were exhorted to be careful about what we said. As the slogan had it: "Loose lips _____."

54. Cold War sloganeering insisted that, all things considered, we were "Better dead _____."

55. The most famous slogan to come out of President Clinton's first national campaign, a reminder from James Carville to stay focused. That slogan insisted: "It's the _____, stupid."

56. It was written for a British musical called *The Beauty Shop*, which appeared in 1908. You're certain to suppose that "She sells _____ down by the sea

shore./The _____ she _____ are _____ , I'm sure."

57. Among the century's best-remembered lines of poetry, known even to people who never read the stuff. Dylan Thomas defied death when he raged: "Do not go gentle into that _____."

58. In 1958, Harry Truman made the following distinction about how we perceive economic downturns: "It's a _____ when your neighbor loses his job; it's a _____ when you lose your own."

59. You may be surprised to learn that the song dates back to 1902, but surely you know the name that goes in the blank spaces: "Won't you come home

_____? Won't you come home? I cried the whole night long."

60. From *Casablanca*, the classic 1942 film, Bogart's last words to Bergman: "It doesn't take much to see that the problems of three little people don't amount _____ in this crazy world. Someday you'll understand that. Now, now. Here's _____ , kid."

## WORDS, PERFECT AND OTHERWISE

*Sequence 4*

Another multiple-choice sequence. Level of difficulty: 4.

61. Take a guess. In 1906, president-to-be Woodrow Wilson said: "Nothing has spread socialistic feeling in this country more than the use of:

a. marijuana."

b. alcohol."

c. the automobile."

d. Christian teachings."

e. scare tactics."

62. In 1992, beating victim Rodney King made a fervent appeal to an incendiary Los Angeles—and the world. He said: "People:

a. let's knock this off."

b. can't we just get it together."

c. can't we all get along."

d. we gotta chill."

63. The words "subway vigilante" Bernard Goetz said to the last of the men he shot in 1984: "You don't look so bad:

a. Take that."

b. Want more?"

c. Here's another."

d. Now maybe you'll leave me alone."

64. "Hi ho, hi ho, it's off to work we go," was sung by:

a. the seven dwarfs

b. the three little pigs

c. the magnificent seven

d. the Chicago 7

e. the coal miner's daughter

65. The year: 1963. The place: the Lincoln Memorial. The speaker: Martin Luther King. The words: "When we let freedom ring, when we let it ring from every village and hamlet, from every

state and every city, we will be able to speed up that day when all of God's children, black men and white men, Jews and Gentiles, Protestants and Catholics will be able to join hands and sing in the words of the old Negro spiritual:

a. I have a dream today."

b. Free at last! Free at last! Thank God almighty, we are free at last!"

c. we shall overcome someday."

d. Go tell it on the mountain."

e. Amazing grace, how sweet the sound/that saved a wretch like me."

66. According to the Geneva Conventions governing the conduct of war, a captured enemy soldier could be asked to divulge no more than:

a. his superior officer's name and his unit assignment.

b. his address, his social security number, and his mother's maiden name.

c. the troop strength of his unit.

d. his name, rank, and serial number.

67. In 1971, when he was Nixon's national security advisor, Henry Kissinger said, "Power is the ultimate:

a. high."

b. turn on."

c. aphrodisiac."

d. satisfaction."

e. orgasm."

68. The Weathermen, a '60s radical underground organization, took its name from a Bob Dylan song that went, "You don't need a weatherman:

a. to know a hard rain's gonna fall."

b. out on Highway 61."

c. to know that the times they are a'changin'."

d. to know which way the wind blows."

e. when you're knock, knock, knockin' on Heaven's door."

69. Franz Kafka's most famous short story begins with the line, "As Gregor Samsa awoke one morning from uneasy dreams he found himself transformed in his bed into a gigantic:

a. ego."

b. insect."

c. buffoon."

d. breast."

e. worm."

70. In January of 1991, Saddam Hussein welcomed the start of the Gulf War, saying:

a. "The mother of battles has begun."

b. "Let the games begin."

c. "Take no prisoners."

d. "Praise Allah."

71. Published in 1902, Owen Wister's novel *The Virginian* gave us a movie, a television series, and the immortal line:

a. "Stick 'em up."

b. "When you call me that, smile."

c. "Get up, you stinkin' tub of guts."

d. "Get along, little doggies."

e. "Goodbye, Old Paint, I'm leavin' Cheyenne."

72. In Vietnam-era parlance, a Huey was:

a. a raw recruit

b. a helicopter

c. a brief but intense exchange of small-arms fire

d. a male prostitute

e. a USO show with Playboy bunnies, named after Hugh Hefner

73. It was first heard in the first decade of the century, but this cliché come-on has remained with us. It goes: "I love my wife, but:

a. oh you kid."

b. take my wife, please."

c. she's got nothing on you."

d. there's a limit to love."

74. A song that spoke to American polarization in 1969 included these lines: "I'm proud to be an Okie from Muskogee, a place where even squares can have a ball." The singer/songwriter was:

a. Waylon Jennings

b. Johnny Cash

c. David Allan Coe

d. Merle Haggard

e. Porter Wagoner

75. Dorothy Parker asked Ernest Hemingway, "Exactly what do you mean by 'guts'?" In words that seemed to define his ethos, Hemingway replied:

a. "To bend, but not break."

b. "To stand tall."

c. "Grace under pressure."

d. "To take crap from no man."

e. "Indifference to pain."

76. Complete this phrase that epitomizes the McCarthy era: "Are you now, or have you ever been:

a. a threat to the security of the United States?"

b. a member of the Communist party?"

c. disloyal to your country?"

d. guilty of giving information to the Soviet Union?"

77. They both saw the same movie, or did they? President Woodrow Wilson praised it as "like writing history with lightning," while W. E. B. Du Bois called it "a cruel slander of a defenseless race." They were both commenting on a film based on a novel called *The Klansman.* That film was:

a. *Way Down East*

b. *Birth of a Nation*

c. *Greed*

d. *Uncle Tom's Cabin*

e. *Gone With the Wind*

78. J. Robert Oppenheimer quoted words from the Bhagavad Gita when he said: "I am become Death, the shatterer of worlds." The occasion that prompted him was:

a. The dropping of the atom bomb on Hiroshima

b. The bombing of Pearl Harbor

c. The discovery of the AIDS virus

d. The first thermonuclear test explosion in New Mexico

e. The liberation of Auschwitz by U.S. troops

79. But was it worth it? Do you remember, or can you guess, which political wife said, "I have sacrificed everything in my life that I consider precious in order to advance the political career of my husband."

a. Hillary Clinton

b. Rosalyn Carter

c. Barbara Bush

d. Betty Ford

e. Patricia Nixon

First Ladies, 1991

80. "Woodstock" was the title of the song, and the lyrics said, "We are stardust, we are golden." Actually, they were muddy. The song's composer was:

a. David Crosby

b. Joni Mitchell

c. Joan Baez

d. John Sebastian

e. Judy Collins

f. Grace Slick

81. If you're a historian, you'll have heard of political boss Mark Hanna. If you're not, you'll have to guess which president he was talking about when he said, "And now look. That damn cowboy is President of the United States." Which one was it?

a. Theodore Roosevelt

b. Lyndon Johnson

c. Ronald Reagan

d. William Taft

82. A major American play of the twentieth century contains these words: "I can't stand a naked light bulb any more than I can a rude remark or a vulgar action." The words are so distinctively his you're sure to know that the playwright was:

a. Edward Albee

b. Arthur Miller

c. Sam Shepherd

d. Tennesse Williams

e. Eugene O'Neill

83. In his farewell address, he did us a favor when he warned of the dangers of "the military-industrial complex." He was:

a. Dwight Eisenhower

b. Jimmy Carter

c. Harry Truman

d. Winston Churchill

e. Herbert Hoover

f. Charles DeGaulle

84. "You talkin' to me?" If you're a film buff, you know these words were spoken by Robert DeNiro talking to his own mirror image while playing a character named:

a. Vinnie Barbarino

b. Merle Travis

c. Travis Bickle

d. Dwight Yoakam

e. Jake LaMotta

f. Rupert Pupkin

85. "Men seldom make passes/At girls who wear glasses." The poet was:

a. Phyllis Diller

b. Dorothy Parker

c. Bonnie Parker

d. Harper Lee

e. I. W. Harper

f. Ogden Nash

86. His image is now considered a racist stereotype, but the phrase "feet don't fail me now" lingers in the culture. The character (or characters) who spoke those words?

a. Satchel Page

b. Stepin Fetchit

c. Al Jolson

d. Amos 'n' Andy

e. Mantan Moreland

f. Eddie "Rochester" Anderson

87. "You've come a long way, baby," was a successful advertising campaign exploiting the women's movement. The product the phrase was used to sell was:

a. L'Eggs pantyhose

b. Charlie perfume

c. Kentucky Fried Chicken

d. Virginia Slims cigarettes

e. Tampax

f. Maidenform bras

88. "Ethnic cleansing." As phrases go, this one was particularly obscene even in a century in which there was much competition in the verbal obscenity category. The phrase arose out of:

a. Bosnia-Herzegovina

b. Lebanon

c. El Salvador

d. Nazi Germany

e. South Africa

f. Cambodia

89. "Long live Death. Down with intelligence." This was a rallying cry used by the eventual victors of the Spanish Civil War. Their victory brought what leader to power?

a. Tito

b. Aguinaldo

c. Aquino

d. Franco

e. Castro

90. "I can't deny the fact that you like me! You really like me!" It seems that what made this little speech memorable was its naked hunger for approval. The occasion was the 1984 Academy Awards. The speaker was:

a. Meryl Streep

b. Jane Fonda

c. Sally Field

d. Bette Davis

e. Meg Ryan

f. Tom Hanks

91. "ET, phone home." The kids in the movie *E.T.* coaxed the extraterrestial out of the shed in the backyard using:

a. M&Ms

b. Cheerios

c. carrots

d. Jujubees

e. Milk Duds

f. Reese's Pieces

92. His Nobel Prize acceptance speech in 1950 was among the more eloquent of that genre. In it, he said, "I believe that man will not merely endure; he will prevail." That speaker was:

a. William Faulkner

b. Bertrand Russell

c. Ernest Hemingway

d. Jean-Paul Sartre

e. Sinclair Lewis

f. Dylan Thomas

93. "You have a right to remain silent." That's just one of the rights of a person being arrested, and in 1966 the Supreme Court ruled that anyone being taken into police custody must be informed of those rights. The decision came out of the case known as:

a. *Rowe* v. *Wade*

b. *Miranda* v. *the State of Arizona*

c. *Brown* v. *Board of Education*

d. *Bakke* v. *U.C. Davis*

e. The Sherman Anti-Trust Act

94. He was the Hollywood mogul who became famous for saying things like "a verbal contract isn't worth the paper it's printed on" and "Anybody who goes to a psychiatrist ought to have his head examined." That mogul was:

a. Samuel Goldwyn

b. Michael Eisner

c. Michael Ovitz

d. Daryl Zanuck

e. Jay Gatsby

f. Irving Thalberg

95. "Oh no, it wasn't the airplane. It was beauty killed the beast." That's the last line of:

a. *Beauty and the Beast*

b. *Godzilla*

c. *King Kong*

d. *The Creature From the Black Lagoon*

96. "If black people kill black people every day, why not have a week and kill white people." These words sparked political controversy in 1992. The speaker of those words was:

a. Louis Farrakhan

b. Sister Souljah

c. Ice-T

d. Dennis Rodman

e. Clarence Thomas

97. "Every Man a King." It's a famous slogan associated with:

a. Benito Mussolini

b. Imperial Margarine

c. Huey P. Long

d. Franklin Roosevelt

e. Father Divine

f. Reverend Jim Jones

98. Of the Russian Revolution of 1917, Emma Goldman said, "If there's no dancing, count me out." Fifty years later, a popular song said, "But if you're talkin' 'bout destruction/Don't you know that you can count me out." That song was by:

a. Led Zeppelin

b. the Rolling Stones

c. the Jefferson Airplane

d. the Beatles

e. the Doors

99. Hannah Arendt coined the phrase in 1961. Of Adolf Eichmann and the death camps, she wrote: "The fearsome word-and-thought defying banality of:

a. oppression."

b. totalitarianism."

c. hate."

d. murderers."

e. evil."

100. "That's All Folks," were the words of Porky Pig. Porky Pig was produced by:

a. Warner Brothers

b. Disney

c. RKO

d. Universal Studios

## ANSWERS

### WORDS, PERFECT AND OTHERWISE

*Sequence 1*

1. "Return with us now" is associated with the Lone Ranger.

2. "M'm M'm Good" advertised Campbell's Soup.

3. "Not a cough in a carload" advertised Old Gold cigarettes.

4. "Is it live, or is it Memorex?"

5. "Two all-beef patties, etc." were words used to sell Big Macs.

6. "Head for the border" sold us Taco Bell.

7. "I made him an offer" were words written by Mario Puzo.

8. Will Rogers was born in Colagah, Indian Territory, which would later become Oklahoma.

9. George Bush beat Mike Dukakis, and was, in turn, beaten by Bill Clinton.

10. The 1989 "Steel Wheels Tour" was made by the Rolling Stones.

11. "You are a lost generation" was the generation of young men in the 1920s disillusioned by the senseless carnage of World War I.

12. The "City of the Big Shoulders" was Chicago.

13. The manager of "the fab four" was Brian Epstein.

14. The '60s book on incompetence was *The Peter Principle*.

15. In "The Wasteland," "the cruellest month" is April.

16. "Teflon-coated presidency" was the one served by Ronald Reagan.

17. "The Teflon Don" was John Gotti.

18. "If it doesn't fit" was uttered in 1995 by Johnny Cochran.

19. "We're number two" was the slogan for Avis Car Rental.

20. "The color purple" were words by Alice Walker.

## WORDS, PERFECT AND OTHERWISE

*Sequence 2*

21. "The best lack all conviction, while the worst/Are full of passionate intensity." The poet was b. W. B. Yeats.

22. Those said to be "overpaid, oversexed, and over here" were c. U.S. servicemen in England during World War II.

23. Gore Vidal and Gerald Ford were dissing d. Ronald Reagan.

24. Tweety and Sylvester worked for a. Warner Brothers.

25. "The words of the prophet are written/On the subway walls and tenement halls" are lines by c. Paul Simon.

26. The product with the micronite filter was c. Kent cigarettes.

27. The title of the song was a. "Candle in the Wind."

28. The comedy classic was from the radio days of c. Jack Benny.

29. "Float like a butterfly, etc." The words belong to e. Muhammad Ali.

30. "Okie used to mean you was from Oklahoma" was written by b. John Steinbeck.

31. "Whether you like it or not, history is on our side. We will bury you." That was e. Nikita Khrushchev.

32. Woody Allen put his brain in second place in the movie a. *Sleeper.*

33. "If men could get pregnant, abortion would be c. a sacrament."

34. Kennedy said: "I think it's the most extraordinary collection of talent . . . at the White House—with the possible exception of when b. Thomas Jefferson dined alone."

35. The man who drank his martinis "shaken, and not stirred" was e. James Bond.

36. "I used to be Snow White . . . but I drifted" were words attributed to b. Mae West.

37. "Ars gratia artis" is on the logo of c. MGM Studios.

38. "Supercallifragilisticexpialidocious" is from a. *Mary Poppins.*

39. "I don't give 'em hell. I just tell the truth and c. they think it's hell."

40. "War is Peace. Freedom is Slavery. Ignorance is Strength." These are examples of c. newspeak.

## WORDS, PERFECT AND OTHERWISE

### Sequence 3

41. "All the things I really like to do are either illegal, immoral, or fattening."

42. "Is that a gun in your pocket or are you just glad to see me."

43. "We're eyeball to eyeball, and I think the other fellow just blinked."

44. Don't Cry for Me, Argentina.

45. "If you build it, they will come."

46. "He went looking for America, but couldn't find it anywhere."

47. "Political power grows out of the barrel of a gun."

48. The First Lady's title: *It Takes a Village.*

49. Texas Guinan's greeting: "Hello suckers."

50. "Today is the first day of the rest of your life."

51. Eldridge Cleaver said: "If you're not part of the solution, you're part of the problem."

52. "Don't ask. Don't tell."

53. "Loose lips sink ships."

54. "Better dead than red."

55. "It's the economy, stupid."

56. "She sells sea shells down by the sea shore./The sea shells she sells are sea shells, I'm sure."

57. "Do not go gentle into that good night."

58. "It's a recession when your neighbor loses his job; it's a depression when you lose your own."

59. "Won't you come home Bill Bailey? Won't you come home?"

60. "It doesn't take much to see that the problems of three little people don't amount to a hill of beans in this crazy world. Someday you'll understand that. Now, now. Here's lookin' at you, kid."

## WORDS, PERFECT AND OTHERWISE

*Sequence 4*

61. "Nothing has spread socialistic feeling in this country more than the use of c. the automobile."

62. Rodney King said: "People, c. can't we all get along?"

63. Bernard Goetz said: "You don't look so bad, c. here's another."

64. "Hi ho, hi ho, it's off to work we go," was sung by: a. the seven dwarfs.

65. "... black men and white men, Jews and Gentiles, Protestants and Catholics will be able to join hands and sing in the words of the old Negro spiritual, b. Free at last! Free at last! Thank God almighty, we are free at last!"

66. A captured enemy soldier could be asked no more than d. his name, rank, and serial number.

67. Henry Kissinger said: "Power is the ultimate c. aphrodisiac."

68. The Dylan song went: "You don't need a weatherman d. to know which way the wind blows."

69. "As Gregor Samsa awoke one morning from uneasy dreams he found himself transformed in his bed into a gigantic b. insect."

70. Saddam Hussein welcomed the start of the Gulf War, saying, a. "The mother of battles has begun."

71. *The Virginian* gave us the immortal line, b. "When you call me that, smile."

72. In Vietnam-era parlance, a Huey was: b. a helicopter.

73. "I love my wife, but" a. "oh you kid."

74. "Okie from Muskogee" was a song by d. Merle Haggard.

75. Hemingway defined "guts" as c. "grace under pressure."

76. "Are you now, or have you ever been b. a member of the Communist party?"

77. Wilson and Du Bois were both commenting on b. *Birth of a Nation.*

78. When Oppenheimer said: "I am become Death, the shatterer of worlds" the occasion was d. the first thermonuclear test explosion in New Mexico.

79. The political wife who said "I have sacrificed everything" was e. Patricia Nixon (in 1975).

80. "Woodstock" was written by b. Joni Mitchell.

81. Mark Hanna called a. Theodore Roosevelt a "damn cowboy."

82. "I can't stand a naked light bulb" are words by d. Tennesse Williams.

83. The president who warned us of "the military-industrial complex" was a. Dwight Eisenhower.

84. "You talkin' to me?" were the words of a character named c. Travis Bickle (in *Taxi Driver,* 1976).

85. The poet who wrote "Men seldom make passes/At girls who wear glasses" was b. Dorothy Parker.

86. "Feet don't fail me now," is a phrase associated with b. Stepin Fetchit.

87. "You've come a long way, baby," was used to sell d. Virginia Slims cigarettes.

88. "Ethnic cleansing" arose out of a. Bosnia-Herzegovina.

89. "Long live Death. Down with intelligence" was a rallying cry that helped bring to power d. Franco.

90. "You like me. You really like me." The speaker was c. Sally Field.

91. The kids coaxed the extraterrestial out using f. Reese's Pieces.

92. "I believe that man will not merely endure; he will prevail." That speaker was a. William Faulkner.

93. "You have a right to remain silent." The words are traceable to the case known as b. *Miranda* v. *the State of Arizona.*

94. "A verbal contract isn't worth the paper it's printed on," and other similar malaprops are associated with a. Samuel Goldwyn.

95. "Oh no, it wasn't the airplane. It was beauty killed the beast" is the last line of c. *King Kong*.

96. "Why not have a week and kill white people" were the words of b. Sister Souljah.

97. "Every Man a King" is associated with c. Huey P. Long.

98. The popular song that said "you can count me out" was by d. the Beatles.

99. "The fearsome word-and-thought defying banality of e. evil."

100. Porky Pig was produced by a. Warner Brothers.

Scoring: At mid-century, a comedian asked, "How do I know what I think until I see what I say?" In this test, you didn't know the famous words you knew until you found out the ones you didn't know. If you knew 80 or more of these bon mots, exclamations, jingles, and japes, then you can congratulate yourself on knowing and remembering. If, however, you knew fewer than 30 of these, then much of the wit, wisdom, and detritus of the century has simply passed you by, unheard or unrecorded.

# THE MORE THINGS CHANGED . . . FINANCIAL SECRETS OF THE SON OF GOD

## 1924

*The Man Nobody Knows* was a best-selling book of the 1920s. The book saw Jesus Christ as the most effective salesman who ever lived, and plundered the Christ story for business tips. Of Christ, the author wrote: "He would be a national advertiser today, I am sure, as he was a great advertiser in His own day. He thought of His life as a business."

## 1996

In 1996, a best-selling book entitled *Jesus: CEO* was messianic with son-of-God models for managers, and a similar tome called *The Management Methods of Jesus* found biblical precedent for corporate downsizing. Other spiritual guides to riches included such gems as: "Timing was key in the success of Jesus. Make it work for you too."

# 12

# A Brief History of Fear

*History . . . is a nightmare from which I am trying to awake.*

—JAMES JOYCE, ULYSSES, *1922*

In 1962, the year of the Cuban Missile Crisis, I was nineteen years old, working in a defense plant. The phrase "defense plant" seems dated now, needing a clarifying sentence. Defense plants made weaponry. Defense plants usually had but a single client: the Pentagon.

In any case, those of us working at "defense plants" were routinely told that, in the event of a nuclear exchange, we were certainly a priority target. That, in itself, was redundant since this particular defense plant was in Los Angeles, and the accepted wisdom of the time was that, come Armageddon, Los Angeles would surely be among the first places hit. LA, then and now, had a certain apocalyptic feel; there was so much in all directions, so many lights, so much disconnection. It felt like the end of everything: the continent, the future, history itself.

Still, we all worked in routine calm, exchanging jokes and pleasantries, passing compliments about new shirts or skirts, talking about sports and smog. Meanwhile, *The Los Angeles Times* was running a series of feature stories about a guy who was building a fallout shelter in his backyard up in the canyons north of Hollywood. The articles were replete with diagrams about how *Times* readers could build one just like it. With such a shelter, with its air filtration system and its supply of canned food and bottled water, there was a chance for postapocalyptic survival, if you could fend off the desperate neighbors.

That fall, the shelter was destroyed when a wildfire roared up the canyon. The *Times* gave its destruction very little space. At the office, we all laughed about it. Weeks later, when the Cuban Missile Crisis heated up and we were all pretty sure that the game was up, that the world was coming to an end, I was amazed at how calm we all were.

Until, that is, one of the plant's air-raid sirens went off accidentally on the third day of the crisis, with Soviet ships steaming toward Cuba and a U.S. blockade bringing Armageddon within too easy reach of the imagination. When that siren went off, the place became bedlam. People were running toward exits in every direction. Some were praying.

It was all over in a minute or so, a disembodied voice over the PA system telling us to be calm, that it was a matter of faulty wiring or a prankster, I forget which. But the fear we had hidden beneath the jokes and attention to our work, under pleasantries and talk of television, that fear had been unleashed. Now we knew the fear dwelt in all our separate hearts, and somehow that made it even scarier.

We were profoundly embarrassed, of course, ashamed to have let the fear show.

The Cuban Missile Crisis passed.

Kennedy passed, and later Khrushchev. Throughout all that time, we lived in what the media rather casually referred to as a "balance of terror." In the '80s, when President Ronald Reagan, warming up for one of his weekly radio broadcasts, joked before a live microphone that missiles had been launched against the Soviet Union, many people my age didn't find it very funny.

And eventually, the Cold War passed, too. Surprisingly, new fears arose to replace those Cold War fears.

Though we didn't invent fear in the twentieth century, we surely refined it, massaged it, nuanced it. We created new venues for fear through new media. New fears were promulgated and traditional fears were exacerbated. Old fears bred of ignorance and superstition survived despite gains in education and advances in science. Though Franklin Roosevelt told us that "the only thing we have to fear is fear itself," we managed to create, manipulate, and exploit fears of nearly everything else, while still managing to remain afraid of fear itself.

The history of the twentieth century is surely a history of fear and anxiety. If you doubt this, follow me through the following little prose poem composed of adjectives and nouns the media concocted to define our fears. By force of will or fortunate circumstances you may have evaded these fears and anxieties, but it's unlikely you avoided hearing about them.

## TWO-WORD TERRORS

Hair loss, liver disease, high cholesterol, fatty deposits, economic downturn, radioactive waste, Lyme disease, oil dependency, alien abduction, nuclear winter, global warming, greenhouse effect, ozone depletion, generation gap, red menace, white flight, black power, yellow peril, gray sickness, domino theory, drug addiction, culture shock, budget deficit, mental illness, shell shock, battle fatigue, falling arches, tooth decay, gang bangers, storm troopers, computer virus, moral decline, urban blight, gum disease, creeping socialism, toxic chemicals, ethnic cleansing, Final Solution, air pollution, smog alert, child abuse, illegal immigration, tax increase, job displacement, women's lib, population explosion, product tampering, consumer fraud, senile dementia, Alzheimer's disease, kidney stones, industrial waste, selective service, draft board, missile gap, trade deficit, national debt, unsightly blemishes, skin rash, bad breath, body odor, athlete's foot, bank foreclosure, heart attack, nervous breakdown, crime wave, bank failure, arterial sclerosis, big business, corporate greed, big government, Big Brother, market correction.

Fear was a reasonable emotion in a century that saw so much aggression, so much threatening change, and so much destructive force. We feared each other—socially, ethnically, biologically, culturally. We sometimes feared our own government, and we often feared the governments of other countries. We feared things visible and things invisible. To watch the news each night was to call up the menu of fear. A vast worry machine fed us worries each day.

But, as Mark Twain once said, "Worry is interest paid on a debt we may never owe." The questions that follow tap that balance sheet of worry, not so as to frighten ourselves all over again, but to remind us of the interest we paid, and of the debts that were real and the debts we never contracted. Though we worried plenty about these things, some of what follows is about interest we paid on debts we didn't come to owe. Owed or not, we paid these dues.

This series has a difficulty level of 4. You are expected to do well because the questions are relatively easy, and in the twentieth century, we were all experts on fears.

## A BRIEF HISTORY OF FEAR

1. Restrictive covenants were:

a. exclusive 1960s witchcraft circles in Manhattan

b. agreements between property owners not to sell to minorities

c. restrictions used by Protestants against Catholics in Northern Ireland

d. a '70s heavy metal band popular with Satan worshipers

2. "Duck and cover" was a jingle known to most schoolchildren in the 1950s. It was meant to teach them:

a. what to do when attacked by bullies

b. what to do when frightened in the dark

c. what to do in case of a nuclear attack

d. what to do when taking a fall

3. The word "banzai" was dreaded by American forces in the Pacific during World War II. It was a Japanese battlecry. It means:

a. death to the round eye

b. the Emperor forever

c. rising sun

d. ten thousand years

4. In the lexicon of American race relations, the word "ofay" meant:

a. oaf

b. foe

c. welfare

d. police officer

e. landlord

5. Rodan, Mothra, and Godzilla were all:

a. makes of Asian automobiles

b. companies that expired in the stock market crash of 1929

c. Japanese movie monsters

d. specially bred hibiscus

6. During the sit-in period of the 1960s, this Georgia restaurant owner kept axe handles in a barrel by the door. They were meant for customers to use in the event any "Negroes" attempted to enter the premises. The resulting publicity launched him into the governor's mansion. The axe-iomatic governor was:

a. George Wallace

b. Strom Thurmond

c. Lester Maddox

d. Ford Maddox Ford

e. Lester Scruggs

f. Jesse Helms

7. During the "mad cow disease" scare of 1996, a rumor spread that England's 11 million cow herd would be used to:

a. find the 11 million unexploded land mines left in Cambodia

b. feed the hungry in sub-Saharan Africa

c. make frozen gravy to be sent as relief to Bosnia

d. make a hundred-acre landfill park in Liverpool

8. In 1918–19, in the aftermath of World War I, the world suffered a global scourge that killed 20 million people, four times the number that had died in the war. (It's statistically probable that you lost a relative in this calamity.) That scourge was:

a. a worldwide crop failure

b. an influenza epidemic

c. a global tuberculosis outbreak

d. a monetary collapse

## 9. "Overkill" was an expression:

a. used in the Cold War to describe how many more people would die in a nuclear exchange than were necessary to immobilize an enemy state

b. used in World War II, translated from the German word "blitzkrieg"

c. used on Madison Avenue to describe a saturation advertising campaign

d. used by fundamentalists to decry the violence in American films

## 10. "Everybody should rise up and say, 'Thank you, Mr. President, for bombing Haiphong.'" The woman's name was Martha Mitchell. Her husband:

a. was a POW in North Korea

b. was attorney general of the United States

c. was the Speaker of the House

d. was a noted antiwar activist

## 11. Fluoridation was controversial in the 1950s. Many feared it because:

a. it was a blanket nerve gas attack used in the Korean War

b. it was the process of putting an additive in municipal water supplies

c. it was a toxic paint finish used on GM automobiles

d. it was the process of taking X-rays of the feet in shoe stores

## 12. "The right of an honest American to own a firearm . . . is more important than the life of any leader who ever lived." Or so said a letter writer to *Time* magazine in the aftermath of Robert Kennedy's assassination. The handgun that killed Robert Kennedy was:

a. a nine-millimeter

b. a .357 magnum

c. a .22-caliber revolver

d. a .38 Special

e. a .25-caliber automatic

f. an Army .45

## 13. Enola Gay was:

a. the real name of WWII Japanese propagandist better known as Tokyo Rose

b. John Reed's lover and fellow American communist, played by Diane Keaton in the movie *Reds*

c. the name of the plane that carried the first nuclear weapon to be used against human beings

d. the name of the woman who "outed" k. d. lang

## 14. It's a famous line from the movie *Apocalypse Now*, so famous that you can probably complete it. Robert Duvall said it, and it goes: "I love the smell of napalm in the morning. It smells like . . .

a. America."

b. manhood."

c. victory."

d. my dad's gas station back in Skokie."

e. barbeque."

(Note for readers born after 1960: Napalm was a jellied petroleum product packed in bombs. When napalm hit the skin, it was virtually inextinguishable as it burned through flesh. It was manufactured by Dow Chemical, a target of many antiwar protests. Once, in the '60s, a peace group announced it would napalm a dog on the steps of San Francisco City Hall. The group had no intention of doing that, but the resulting public outrage and horror made the point that we shouldn't do to people in Vietnam what we wouldn't do to a dog. The point may also have been made that a dog at home was more real to us than a war ten thousand miles away.)

15. "Ring around the collar" was a commercial pushing the idea that a husband's dirty neck was his wife's responsibility. The commercial also pushed:

a. the "New" Wisk

b. the "New" Tide

c. the "New" Dreft

d. the "New" Oxydol

16. "Often a bridesmaid, never a bride," was an enormously successful advertising campaign of the 1920s. The phrase remains with us, though you may not recall that the product it was intended to sell was:

a. Clairol

b. Listerine

c. Chanel No. 5

d. Odor Eaters

e. Kotex

f. Max Factor lipstick

17. For a time, in the early days of the AIDS epidemic, it was erroneously feared by some scientists that AIDS could be transmitted by:

a. birds

b. mosquitoes

c. ants

d. houseflies

e. spider webs

18. In the 1950s and '60s, there were groups that sought to have *Robin Hood* removed from school libraries. Some of those groups even succeeded. They sought to have the story kept from children because they feared it could be seen as a story about:

a. English homosexuals living in the woods

b. communistic values

c. disrespect for constituted authority

d. tax revolt

19. The song "Gloomy Sunday" was banned from airplay in the 1930s because it was feared that:

a. the song encouraged extramarital sex

b. the song encouraged suicide

c. the song encouraged people to quit their jobs

d. the song discouraged church attendance

(The song was recorded decades later by Irish singer Sinéad O'Connor in the 1990s.)

20. The Turner Movie Channel planned to show *Birth of a Nation* on a Sunday in October 1995, but postponed the cable presentation after:

a. Jesse Jackson requested it

b. commercial sponsorship dried up

c. a dispute with the film company

d. the O. J. Simpson verdict

21. In the mid-1980s, Ronald Reagan called it the "Evil Empire." He was talking about:

a. the Democratic party

b. the liberal media

c. the Soviet Union

d. defense industry profiteers

e. the American Civil Liberties Union

22. Feared by scads of children, Cruella de Ville was a villain in the Disney feature:

a. *Beauty and the Beast*

b. *Aladdin*

c. *Lady and the Tramp*

d. *One Hundred and One Dalmatians*

23. When Franklin Roosevelt made that speech in which he said "the only thing we have to fear is fear itself," the occasion was:

a. the declaration of war against Japan in 1941

b. the declaration of victory over Japan in 1945

c. the enactment of the first New Deal programs in 1933

d. his first inaugural address in 1933

24. "I saw the best minds of my generation destroyed by madness" are the first words of one of the century's most notorious poems. It became a cultural landmark when it prompted obscenity charges in the 1950s. The poem was written by:

a. e. e. cummings

b. Allen Ginsberg

c. Lawrence Ferlinghetti

d. T. S. Eliot

e. Langston Hughes

f. William Burroughs

25. If you were afraid of the Mau Mau, it was the 1950s, and you were a white person living in:

a. Kenya

b. Haiti

c. Madagascar

d. South Africa

e. Vietnam

f. Japan

26. "Arbeit Macht Frei" were words found over the entrance to this infamous place. The place was:

a. Slaughterhouse 5 in Dresden

b. the Reichstag in Berlin

c. Auschwitz

d. Checkpoint Charlie

e. the bunker where Hitler died

27. "Lions, and tigers, and bears. Oh my" were frightened words chanted by characters in:

a. *The Lion King*

b. *Winnie the Pooh*

c. *The Wizard of Oz*

d. *Charlie and the Chocolate Factory*

e. *James and the Giant Peach*

28. A popular novel and film of the 1970s exploited fears of demonic possession. The title of both film and book was:

a. *The Omen*

b. *The Uninvited*

c. *The Exorcist*

d. *The Witches of Eastwick*

e. *Rosemary's Baby*

29. He worked for J. Edgar Hoover, one of the century's most successful fearmongers, and was the man who led the team that killed John Dillinger. He was FBI Agent:

a. Elliot Ness

b. Clyde Tolson

c. Clyde Barrow

d. Melvin Purvis

e. Robert Stack

30. In the last half-century, scientists have warned that cancer could be contracted by:

a. eating fried hamburgers

b. drinking coffee

c. sitting in the sun

d. worry and stress

e. drinking alcohol

f. eating fatty foods

g. smoking

h. asbestos

i. air pollution

j. sitting on a contaminated toilet seat

k. all of the above

l. all of the above, except j (and k)

31. The only thing Superman feared was:

a. rejection by Lois Lane

b. discovery of his true identity

c. Kryptonite

d. phone booths

e. Lex Luthor

32. *Scream* was a hugely popular horror film of the 1990s. Its best-known actress was killed off in the first fifteen minutes of the movie. Her name?

a. Parker Posey

b. Jennifer Jason Leigh

c. Drew Barrymore

d. Winona Ryder

33. The name Alan Greenspan generated a good deal of fear because:

a. he was the SS overlord who conceived of the "Final Solution," and devised the concentration camp idea

b. he was an early AIDS victim who spread the virus throughout San Francisco

c. he alerted the world to the dangers of global warming

d. he held the power to raise interest rates.

34. *Unsafe At Any Speed* was a book that heightened our fears about auto safety. Its author was:

a. Lee Iacocca

b. Ralph Nader

c. John DeLorean

d. Edsel Ford

e. Senator Al Gore

f. Preston Tucker

35. An easy one, even if you weren't born yet. In the 1950s, people took to digging holes in their backyards. The holes were meant for living in in the aftermath of a nuclear war. The holes were popularly known as:

a. postapocalypse dwelling units

b. doomsday digs

c. fallout shelters

d. atom anthills

e. Red fear follies

f. ground zero

36. In films, the first time this ghoul frightened us was in 1921 in the German film *Nosferatu,* and he would frighten us many more times in the century. Nosferatu is better known as:

a. Frankenstein

b. the Wolf Man

c. Dracula

d. Satan

e. the Mummy

37. Few words were more feared than "cancer." In keeping with his tough-guy image, this screen star had a lung removed in 1963, emerging from the operation with the defiant words, "I licked the Big C." But cancer returned, joining other ailments to take him in 1979. That defiant star was:

a. Burt Lancaster

b. Edward G. Robinson

c. John Wayne

d. Yul Brynner

e. Steve McQueen

f. Jack Palance

## 38. Fear of taking a shower swept the country in the early 1960s after:

a. news of water pollution first made the news

b. the movie *Psycho* gained popularity

c. a report on waterborne microorganisms was made public

d. the AMA issued health warnings against showering because it was thought to create drying of the skin

e. the John Birch Society alleged that fluoride in the water supply would cause people to turn to communism

## 39. "Let us never negotiate out of fear. But let us never fear to negotiate." These famous words were uttered by:

a. John Kennedy in 1961 during the Cold War

b. Lyndon Johnson in 1968 during the Vietnam War

c. Neville Chamberlain in 1939 on the eve of World War II

d. Saddam Hussein in 1991 on the eve of the Gulf War

## 40. Writer Ayn Rand's biggest fear:

a. that governments would fail to look after the unfortunate

b. the erosion of individuality

c. that women would marry for purely economic reasons

d. that the oceans were being polluted

## 41. Paranoia ruled the final days of Jim Jones, who engineered the deaths of some nine hundred of his followers in Guyana in 1978. He was the leader of:

a. the Symbionese Liberation Army

b. the Children of God

c. the Children of the Corn

d. the People's Temple

e. the People's Church

f. the People's Mission

## 42. Lewis Hershey. His very name sent a shiver up the spines of many young people in the 1960s. They feared him because he was:

a. Lyndon Johnson's drug enforcement czar

b. the head of the Selective Service system

c. the man who designed the Scholastic Aptitude Test

d. the director of the National Guard

## 43. Fellow travelers. Some Americans feared them in the 1940s, '50s, and '60s. They were:

a. thieves who preyed on tourists

b. Soviet spies who infiltrated the U.S. government

c. people who sympathized with many of the ideals and goals held by communists

d. the silent community support in the South for the work of the Ku Klux Klan

**44.** He frightened people as the original Phantom of the Opera in 1925, and he became known as "the man of a thousand faces." He was:

a. Lionel Barrymore

b. Boris Karloff

c. Bela Lugosi

d. Lon Chaney

e. Ramon Navarro

f. Christopher Lee

**45.** During the years 1914–17, "three on a match" was considered bad luck because:

a. tuberculosis could be contracted in sharing close proximity while lighting cigarettes

b. the number "three" was considered unlucky during that decade

c. to match three cards in the Tarot deck was a sign of impending death

d. to light three cigarettes with one match gave WWI snipers time to draw a bead on trenchbound soldiers

**46.** Though it was a mark of honor, no one wanted to be a "Gold Star Mother." A "Gold Star Mother" was:

a. a Vietnam-era mother who turned in her draft-dodger son

b. an American mother who had lost a son in World War II

c. a WWII-era German woman who had produced more than three children for the Fatherland

d. an American mother whose son had confirmed enemy kills in air battles over Europe during World War I

**47.** Hannibal Lecter was a name to conjure fear with. He was:

a. a midwestern serial killer of the 1950s

b. a man who murdered five wives in Paris in the 1920s

c. a character in *Silence of the Lambs*

d. a character in *The Shining*

e. Jeffrey Dahmer's ill-fated roommate

**48.** The Maginot Line was:

a. a fashion line that failed so badly in 1930 that it nearly brought down the Paris haute couture empire

b. the cocaine traced to the notorious French Connection drug dealers in Marseilles

c. the fortified French line of defense against Germany in the days before World War II

d. the string of Paris taxis that took troops to the front lines in World War I

**49.** Of the following words or phrases, which were not around for us to worry about in 1970? (The conditions may have existed, but the question is about whether the phrase had made its appearance.)

a. bad hair day

b. HIV positive

c. downsizing

d. Lyme disease

e. computer viruses

f. global warming

g. the yuppie flu

h. toxic shock syndrome

i. Legionnaire's disease

j. secondhand smoke

## 50. For the last thirty years of the century, the word "geek" was a feared insult. If someone called you that, it meant that you were socially unacceptable, weird, dweeby. Earlier in the century, the word had been narrower in its meaning. In those days, a geek was:

a. an inept office boy

b. one who bit the heads off chickens and snakes in carnival sideshows

c. an artificial inseminator of thoroughbred horses

d. a general assistant on silent film crews

## 51. In the 1960s and '70s, the word Oreo was an insult in some slang usages. It was used metaphorically to describe:

a. someone sweet, but without substance

b. someone who was black on the outside, but white on the inside

c. a conformist, like every other one of his or her kind

d. a bad relationship partner, especially one that was hard to give up

## 52. Paraquat was:

a. a virulent avian disease that nearly wiped out the Australian parakeet population in the 1950s

b. a defective brand of sealing wax used in home canning that led to a botulism outbreak in 1915

c. an herbicide used to spray South American marijuana fields in the 1970s

d. the alien's name in the movie *Alien*

## 53. According to Freudian theory, the part of our personalities we need to worry most about is:

a. the ego

b. the superego

c. the id

d. the inner child

## 54. What we fear, we hide in euphemism. Of the following, which one was not a management euphemism for firing people?

a. terminate with extreme prejudice

b. free agency

c. decruitment

d. rightsizing

e. coerced transition

f. redundancy elimination

## 55. Zyklon B was:

a. poison gas used to exterminate people in Nazi concentration camps

b. a pesticide now banned because it causes birth defects

c. the death ray used by Ming the Merciless in the Flash Gordon serials

d. an additive to Brylcreem that gave it more "hold"

56. Audit is a big fear word, but we did not have withholding tax in this country until:

a. the 1920s

b. the 1930s

c. the 1940s

d. the 1950s

57. *Who's Afraid of Virginia Woolf?* was a play by Edward Albee. Virginia Woolf was:

a. the first woman head of the Internal Revenue Service

b. an English novelist

c. Nancy Reagan's psychic advisor

d. a notorious New York landlady

58. Charles Manson claimed that his "family's" murder spree was intended to set off a race war. The words that were to trigger this race war were encoded in a Beatles song. That song was:

a. "Hey Jude"

b. "I Am the Walrus"

c. "Blackbird"

d. "Helter Skelter"

e. "Why Don't We Do It in the Road"

59. "Paranoia strikes deep;/into your heart it will creep."/These are lyrics found in the song "For What It's Worth." Speaking to the paranoia of its time, the song was a big hit for:

a. the Byrds

b. Country Joe and the Fish

c. Buffalo Springfield

d. Grand Funk Railroad

e. the Doobie Brothers

60. Anne Rice (*Interview With the Vampire*) was a dominant figure in the horror fiction genre during the century's last quarter. So prolific was she that she wrote some of her books under a pseudonym. Her occasional pen name was:

a. Mary Shelley

b. Joyce Carol Oates

c. Anne Sexton

d. Mary Mallon

e. Anne Rampling

61. He didn't invent the fear of intrusive totalitarian government, but he did invent the century's best metaphor for that fear. Big Brother was the literary creation of:

a. Aldous Huxley

b. Anthony Burgess

c. Evelyn Waugh

d. George Orwell

e. Bertrand Russell

**62.** The Black Muslims created fear among some white folks in the '50s and '60s before the black power phrase was heard in the land. The leader of the Black Muslims, and mentor to Muhammad Ali and Louis Farrakhan, was:

a. Elijah Muhammad

b. Malcolm X

c. Imamu Amiri Baraka

d. Kareem Abdul-Jabbar

**63.** In 1980, Love Canal was in the papers when:

a. police broke up a prostitution ring there led by the "Mayflower Madam"

b. Congressman Fred Grandy proposed that the Panama Canal change its name to Love Canal

c. homeowners had to give up their homes there because of chromosome-damaging toxic waste

d. scientists discovered a vessel in the human heart thought to be the locus of love

**64.** "If you see ten troubles coming down the road, you can be sure that nine will run into the ditch before they reach you." These were the words of president and noted deep thinker Calvin Coolidge. Of the following ten troubles, which (four) never happened?

a. An American river caught fire.

b. An American schoolteacher was blown up over Florida.

c. A Tennessee man was found guilty of teaching evolution.

d. A very annoying pop singer was elected to Congress.

e. On Mt. Rushmore, the left side of Theodore Roosevelt's nose fell away and had to be repaired with eight thousand tons of concrete.

f. A convicted crack smoker was elected mayor of the nation's capital city.

g. One of the smaller Hawaiian islands sank beneath the sea.

h. Radioactive lizards created a climate of fear in the suburbs of Las Vegas, Nevada.

i. In the early days of the women's movement, anxieties about aggressive women created impotence in 28 percent of American males.

j. A U.S. president had a White House affair with the mistress of a Mafia don.

**65.** "Fragging" was:

a. a banned fraternity initiation ritual of the 1950s in which pledges were made to crawl over broken glass

b. Strategic Air Command jargon for the moment when multiple-warhead missiles sought separate targets

c. the occasional practice of American soldiers lobbing grenades at their own officers in Vietnam

d. Wall Street jargon for the breakup of ATT and the creation of the "baby Bells"

**66.** If you had a teenage daughter during the last twenty-five years of the century, you probably feared the term "anorexia nervosa." Its most famous victim paid the price of the disease in 1983. She was:

a. Audrey Hepburn

b. Karen Carpenter

c. Twiggy

d. Dorothy Stratten

e. Courtney Love

f. Bette Davis

## 67. *The Hot Zone* was a 1990s bestseller that fueled fears of:

a. global warming

b. topsoil erosion

c. new viral strains

d. air pollution

e. accidental nuclear war

f. a worldwide depression

## 68. "Nips" and "Huns" were names for:

a. Hungarian freedom fighters in 1958

b. the Japanese and Germans in World War II

c. Soviet MIRV missiles

d. the two sides in the Falklands War of 1982

## 69. Shining Path was:

a. an apocalyptic Christian commune of the 1960s

b. a splinter group of the American Indian Movement

c. a Maoist guerrilla group in Peru

d. a group dedicated to deprogramming cult followers

## 70. Timothy McVeigh, the man charged with the 1995 bombing in Oklahoma City that killed nearly two hundred people, had earlier served in the:

a. Army

b. Navy

c. Air Force

d. Marines

## 71. A punji stick was:

a. a primitive pipe bomb made from sections of sugar cane, used by the Contras in Nicaragua

b. a potent (and sometimes lethal) dose of heroin sold to tourists in Morocco

c. a sharpened bamboo stake used by the Viet Cong to wound enemy soldiers in Vietnam

d. stick used to administer beatings in now-outlawed fraternity hazings in U.S. Ivy League colleges

## 72. "If it bleeds, it leads" is an axiomatic expression addressing:

a. the military truism that the first unit into battle is the one that suffers the most casualties

b. the idea that in sports, if you're going to win, you've got to exert yourself to the fullest—i.e., "no pain, no gain"

c. the journalistic philosophy that gives greater prominence and priority to violent stories

d. standard emergency-room policy for determining which patients get medical attention first

**73.** Black Thursday is the phrase by which we remember:

a. the penultimate day of the Cuban Missile Crisis in 1962

b. the Detroit race riot of 1943

c. the stock market collapse of October 24, 1929

d. The day in 1973 when the Organization of Petroleum Exporting Countries cut the flow of crude oil to the United States

**74.** Ground zero was:

a. the territory between enemy trenches in World War I, also known as "no man's land"

b. the exact point at which a nuclear device was detonated

c. land contaminated by nuclear plant accidents

d. hamburger thought to have been tainted with "mad cow" disease

**75.** The neutron bomb. Carter suspended its production; Reagan resumed its production. The special feature of the neutron bomb was that:

a. it killed people and vaporized their bodies, making burial and disposal unnecessary

b. it killed people with radiation, but left buildings and property largely intact

c. it could kill millions, but the bomb itself was only as big as a loaf of bread

d. it was cheap to produce, costing less than half as much as a conventional nuclear device

**76.** Franz Kafka drew the map of psychic fears in the first quarter of the century, and his legacy remains. Of the following, which was not a work by Franz Kafka?

a. *Amerika*

b. *The Day of the Locust*

c. "The Metamorphosis"

d. *The Trial*

e. *The Castle*

**77.** Though it seems almost quaint now, the domino theory struck such fear that it guided national policy, determined elections, and set the parameters of the way we thought for about forty years. The domino theory postulated that:

a. blacks and whites were entitled to separate but equal educational facilities

b. wage increases for blue-collar workers had a ripple effect, creating inflation as higher wages rippled upward

c. as one country fell to communism, another was sure to follow, like dominoes in a sequence

d. low culture (rock 'n' roll, etc.) would inevitably drive out high culture (opera, etc.)

**78.** Admit it: When you were a kid, she scared you. We're talking about the Wicked Witch of the West in *The Wizard of Oz*. That character was played by:

a. Margaret Sullivan

b. Billie Burke

c. Edna Mae Oliver

d. Butterfly McQueen

e. Margaret Hamilton

79. A major blow against disease—and fear—took place in 1928 when penicillin was discovered. The man who accidentally made one of the century's most important discoveries was:

a. Sir Alexander Fleming

b. Dr. Christiaan Barnhard

c. Dr. Jonas Salk

d. Dr. Richard Leakey

80. During the Reagan administration, the U.S. supported the Duarte regime in this Central American nation, a regime sustained by the terror of right-wing death squads. The country was:

a. Nicaragua

b. El Salvador

c. Honduras

d. Peru

e. Guatemala

81. It was the golden age of radio, and even if you weren't alive to hear it back then, you may know the answer to its weekly question. "Who knows what evil lurks in the hearts of men?"

a. the Phantom

b. the Shadow

c. the Fat Man

d. the Green Hornet

e. the Maltese Falcon

82. More than ninety years after it made headlines, the Triangle Shirt Waist Company is still remembered as:

a. the first successfully unionized garment factory

b. the place where New York City police fired on women striking for better working conditions

c. a sweatshop where over a hundred workers died in a fire

d. the fictional workplace in Upton Sinclair's novel *The Jungle*

83. Sharpville in 1960 and Soweto in 1976. In these times and places:

a. South African police killed scores of antiapartheid demonstrators

b. large diamond mines were discovered in Colorado

c. mass evacuations took place due to large-scale industrial pollution

d. antigrowth activists kept Wal-Mart from building stores

84. In the 1990s, a rumor swept the country that the Snapple beverage company:

a. produced a product that made black people sterile

b. was owned by the Ku Klux Klan

c. depicted a slave ship on its label

d. all of the above

85. Al Capone was brought down (and sent up) on charges of:

a. tax evasion

b. racketeering

c. extortion

d. bribery

e. murder

86. A Katyusha was:

a. a tribal faction in Nigeria

b. a kind of rocket fired at Israel from Lebanon

c. any Soviet woman who worked as a spy during the Cold War

d. a Polish tank

87. If you were an NBA coach in the waning 1990s, you might have had reason to fear a player suspended for choking his coach—twice. That player was . . .

a. Shaquille O'Neill

b. Dennis Rodman

c. Roberto Alomar

d. Lawrence Phillips

e. Latrell Sprewell

f. Lamont Sanford

88. Which of the following songs was not a hit song for British rock group Tears for Fears in their big year of 1985?

a. "Everybody Wants to Rule the World"

b. "Mother's Talk"

c. "Head Over Heels"

d. "Sultans of Swing"

89. The Selective Service system (or draft) was begun:

a. during the Wilson administration

b. during the Roosevelt administration

c. during the Truman administration

d. during the Kennedy administration

90. In the last decade of the century, the largest portion of the federal budget was in entitlements. Politicians routinely prey on our fear of losing entitlements. Only one of the following is an entitlement program. Which one is that?

a. the National Endowment for the Arts

b. Social Security

c. the Farm Subsidy Program

d. the Defense Department

91. As a measure of fear, it is interesting to note that for more than fifty years, the Strategic Air Command:

a. was a secret arm of the Air Force

b. was under the command of the CIA

c. answered only to the president

d. had a command plane in the air at all times

92. The hot line between the Kremlin and the White House was installed in:

a. 1948

b. 1953

c. 1958

d. 1963

**93.** Bela Lugosi (who acted under the name Ariztid Olt in the early days of his career) became a horror film immortal, but he is also remembered for his truly terrible last movie, which was:

a. *The Attack of the Killer Tomatoes*

b. *Plan 9 From Outer Space*

c. *Spooks Run Wild*

d. *The Mark of the Vampire*

**94.** Though it wasn't really about fear of flying, *Fear of Flying* was a best-selling and influential novel of the 1970s. Its author was:

a. John Updike

b. Erica Jong

c. Pearl Buck

d. Amy Tan

e. James Wong Howe

f. Jacqueline Susann

**95.** Newspapers said they'd gone "khaki wacky." Parents worried about it, and the newspapers fretted that it signaled a new decline in morality. That fear concerned:

a. young women wearing beige lipstick in the 1950s

b. young men wearing baggy beige pants in the 1920s

c. young women dating servicemen in the 1940s

d. a fad drink of the 1980s, concocted of Bailey's Irish Cream and Kahlua

**96.** Known as "the white plague," it was the most feared cause of death during the first decade of the century:

a. whooping cough

b. skin cancer

c. influenza

d. tuberculosis

e. heart disease

f. malnutrition

**97.** Of the following movies, which did not exploit our fear of bugs?

a. *Arachnophobia*

b. *Them*

c. *The Fly*

d. *The Hellstrom Chronicles*

e. *Kiss of the Spider Woman*

**98.** In 1992, he articulated the fears of many when he used the phrase "that giant sucking sound" to describe the loss of American jobs he predicted would come in the wake of NAFTA and GATT trade agreements. He was:

a. Pat Buchanan

b. Ross Perot

c. Bill Clinton

d. Alan Greenspan

99. Ronald Reagan played upon fears in the presidential campaign of 1980 when he talked about a "window of vulnerability." He was talking about our supposed vulnerability to:

a. high interest rates jeopardizing economic growth

b. losing the arms race with the Soviet Union

c. Japan's rise to dominance in the global economy

d. the breakdown of the environment

100. Of the following, which one is a form of cancer?

a. melatonin

b. melanin

c. melanoma

d. megalomania

## ANSWERS

1. Restrictive covenants were b. agreements between property owners not to sell to minorities.

2. "Duck and cover" was a jingle meant to teach schoolchildren c. what to do in case of a nuclear attack.

3. The word "banzai" means d. ten thousand years.

4. The word "ofay" is pig latin for b. foe.

Air Raid Drill, 1951

5. Rodan, Mothra, and Godzilla were all c. Japanese movie monsters.

6. The axe-iomatic Georgia governor was c. Lester Maddox.

7. Rumor had it that England's 11 million cow herd would be used to a. find the 11 million unexploded land mines left in Cambodia.

8. The scourge of 1918–19 was b. an influenza epidemic.

9. "Overkill" was an expression a. used in the Cold War to describe how many more

people would die in a nuclear exchange than were necessary to immobilize an enemy state.

10. Martha Mitchell's husband b. was attorney general of the United States

11. Many feared fluoridation because b. it was a process of putting an additive in municipal water supplies.

12. The handgun that killed Robert Kennedy was c. a .22-caliber revolver.

13. *Enola Gay* was c. the name of the plane that carried the first nuclear weapon to be used against human beings (named after the pilot's mother).

14. Duvall's character said napalm in the morning smelled like c. victory.

15. "Ring around the collar" was a commercial pushing a. the "New" Wisk.

16. "Often a bridesmaid, never a bride" was intended to sell b. Listerine.

17. It was erroneously feared that AIDS could be transmitted by b. mosquitoes.

18. Right-wing groups sought to have *Robin Hood* removed from school libraries because they feared the story glorified b. communistic values (specifically, they were troubled by that taking from the rich and giving to the poor business).

19. The song "Gloomy Sunday" was banned from airplay in the 1930s because it was feared that b. the song encouraged suicide.

20. *Birth of a Nation* was postponed after d. the O. J. Simpson verdict.

21. Ronald Reagan was talking about c. the Soviet Union.

22. Cruella de Ville was a villain in the Disney feature d. *One Hundred and One Dalmatians.*

23. Franklin Roosevelt said that we had "nothing to fear but fear itself" on the occasion of d. his first inaugural.

24. "Howl" was written by b. Allen Ginsberg.

25. The Mau Mau scared white folks in a. Kenya. (The noun Mau Mau became a verb when writer Tom Wolfe used it in a famous '60s essay entitled "Mau Mauing the Flak Catchers," about black militants intimidating fashionable white liberals.)

26. "Arbeit Macht Frei," German for "Work will make you free," were words found over the entrance to c. Auschwitz.

27. "Lions, and tigers, and bears. Oh my" were frightened words chanted by characters in c. *The Wizard of Oz.*

28. The '70s film and book about demonic possession was c. *The Exorcist.*

29. The man who led the team that killed Dillinger was d. Melvin Purvis.

30. Scientists have warned that cancer could be contracted by l. all of the above, except j (and k).

31. The only thing feared by Superman was c. Kryptonite.

32. The actress whose character was killed in *Scream* was c. Drew Barrymore.

33. Fed Chairman Alan Greenspan d. held the power to raise interest rates.

34. The author of *Unsafe At Any Speed* was b. Ralph Nader.

35. Backyard dwelling holes were known as c. fallout shelters.

36. Nosferatu was also known as c. Dracula.

37. The man who said "I licked the Big C" was c. John Wayne.

38. Fear of taking a shower swept the country after b. the movie *Psycho* gained popularity.

39. "Let us never negotiate out of fear . . ." were words from a. John Kennedy's inaugural address in 1961.

40. Ayn Rand, author of *The Fountainhead* and other popular books of midcentury, feared b. the erosion of individuality.

41. Jim Jones was the leader of d. the People's Temple.

42. If you were of draft age between World War II and the Vietnam war, you may remember that Lewis Hershey was b. the head of the Selective Service system.

43. Fellow travelers were c. people who were in sympathy with many of the ideals and goals of communism.

44. The original Phantom of the Opera was d. Lon Chaney.

45. "Three on a match" was considered bad luck because d. to light three cigarettes with one match gave WWI snipers time to draw a bead on trenchbound soldiers.

46. A "Gold Star Mother" was b. an American mother who had lost a son in World War II.

47. Hannibal Lecter was c. a character in *Silence of the Lambs.*

48. The Maginot Line was c. the fortified French line of defense against Germany in the days before World War II.

49. In 1970, none of those phrases yet existed to trouble our sleep.

50. Originally, a geek was b. one who bit the heads off chickens and snakes in sideshows.

51. The word Oreo was used metaphorically to describe b. someone who was black on the outside, but white on the inside (a '60s synonym for an Uncle Tom).

52. Paraquat was c. an herbicide used to spray South American marijuana fields in the 1970s.

53. According to Freudian theory, the part of our personalities we need to worry most about is c. the id.

54. The phrase that was not a euphemism for firing people is a. free agency—a term used in professional sports for players who are free to negotiate new contracts.

55. Zyklon B was a. poison gas used to exterminate people in Nazi concentration camps.

56. Withholding tax became a reality in the U.S. in c. the 1940s (1943, to be exact).

57. Virginia Woolf was b. an English novelist.

58. The Beatles's song Manson took as his sign to begin a race war was d. "Helter Skelter."

59. "For What It's Worth" was a '60s hit for: c. Buffalo Springfield.

60. Anne Rice occasionally writes under the name e. Anne Rampling.

61. Big Brother was the literary creation of d. George Orwell.

62. The leader of the Black Muslims, and mentor to Muhammad Ali and Louis Farrakhan was a. Elijah Muhammad.

63. In 1980, Love Canal was in the papers when c. homeowners had to give up their homes there because of chromosome-damaging toxic waste.

64. Of the ten troubles, the four that never happened were e. on Mt. Rushmore, the left side of Theodore Roosevelt's nose fell away and had to be repaired with eight thousand tons of concrete; g. one of the smaller Hawaiian islands sank beneath the sea; h. radioactive lizards created a climate of fear in the suburbs of Las Vegas, Nevada; i. in the early days of the women's movement, anxieties about aggressive women created impotence in 28 percent of American males.

65. "Fragging" was c. the occasional practice of American soldiers lobbing grenades at their own officers in Vietnam.

66. Anorexia nervosa's most famous victim was b. Karen Carpenter.

67. *The Hot Zone* fueled fears of c. new viral strains.

68. "Nips" and "Huns" were names for b. the Japanese and Germans in World War II.

69. Shining Path was c. a Maoist guerrilla group in Peru.

70. Timothy McVeigh had earlier served in the a. Army.

71. A punji stick was c. a sharpened bamboo stake used by the Viet Cong to wound soldiers in Vietnam.

72. "If it bleeds, it leads," is c. the journalistic philosophy that gives greater prominence and priority to violent stories.

73. Black Thursday is the phrase by which we remember c. the stock market collapse of October 24, 1929.

74. Ground zero was b. the exact point at which a nuclear device was detonated.

75. The special feature of the neutron bomb was that b. it killed people but left buildings intact.

76. The book Kafka didn't write was b. *The Day of the Locust.*

77. The domino theory postulated that c. as one country fell to communism, another was sure to follow, like dominoes in a sequence.

78. The Wicked Witch of the West was played by e. Margaret Hamilton.

79. Penicillin was discovered by a. Sir Alexander Fleming.

80. The Duarte regime held power in b. El Salvador.

81. "Who knows what evil lurks in the hearts of men?" b. the Shadow.

82. The Triangle Shirt Waist Company is still remembered as c. a sweatshop where over a hundred workers died in a fire.

83. Sharpville in 1960 and Soweto in 1976 were places where a. South African police killed scores of antiapartheid demonstrators.

84. Snapple was the target of a host of rumors in the 1990s, including d. all of the above.

85. Al Capone was brought down (and sent up) on charges of a. tax evasion.

86. A Katyusha was b. a kind of rocket fired at Israel from Lebanon.

87. The suspended coach-choker was: e. Latrell Sprewell.

88. The song that was not a hit song for Tears for Fears in 1985 was d. "Sultans of Swing."

89. The Selective Service system (or draft) was begun a. during the Wilson administration.

90. The entitlement program is b. Social Security.

91. For more than fifty years, the Strategic Air Command d. had a command plane in the air at all times.

92. The hot line between the Kremlin and the White House was installed in d. 1963.

93. Bela Lugosi's truly terrible last movie was b. *Plan 9 From Outer Space.*

94. *Fear of Flying* was written by b. Erica Jong.

95. "Khaki wacky" referred to c. young women dating servicemen during World War II.

96. The "white plague" was d. tuberculosis.

97. The movie that did not exploit our fear of bugs was e. *Kiss of the Spider Woman.*

98. That "giant sucking sound" phrase belonged to b. Ross Perot.

99. Ronald Reagan's "window of vulnerability" raised fears about b. losing the arms race with the Soviet Union.

100. The cancer answer is c. melanoma.

Scoring: This is "no-fear" scoring. Surely you scored more than 60 correct. If you didn't, you were an uncharacteristically untroubled person in your century. If you knew 90 or more, you were wired to the worry machine.

# 13

# Morbid Fascinations

*To bring the dead to life/Is no great magic./Few are wholly dead.*

—ROBERT GRAVES

Death was a constant companion in the twentieth century, as it always has been. It enlivened our days with anxiety, leavened our ease with worry, hastened our ambitions with the shadow it cast.

The material in this chapter might seem morbid to some readers. Among other things, it asks questions about when and how some famous people met their deaths, and that is, by definition, a morbid fascination.

But the cultural purpose of fame seems to be about instruction, and we tend to follow the course of that instruction into the graves of the famous. In fact, we tend to follow fame into the great beyond, sighting Elvis and waiting for Houdini long after their corporeal departures. The famous have implicitly taught the rest of us how to live, and how not to live, how to dress, and how not to dress. We sort our values based on how we judge their deeds and misdeeds. We often trace our own progress relative to theirs, counting their wrinkles as they teach us how to grow older. The powerful have often held our very lives in their hands. Famous generals commanded us to go where we didn't want to go, and politicians picked fights we didn't want with people we didn't know. So, though our interest in their deaths may seem morbid, it would be even stranger if we abandoned our interest in them at death's door. In a paradoxical way, by talking about their deaths, we bring them back to life.

In any event, to sort out history is to encompass chronology, and one way we mark the passage of time is by the milestone of death. As the British say, have a go, and be lively about it.

## MORBID FASCINATIONS

### Sequence 1: Alive, Dead, Not Yet Born

In the next sixty questions, your job is to ascertain if the people in question were alive, dead, or not yet born in the year that precedes each set of questions. You'll have to give some thought to these, but the answers can be deduced. The degree of difficulty is: 6.

**1905**

The year is 1905. Were the following people: a. alive, b. dead, c. not yet born?

1. Marshal/gunman Wyatt Earp ____

2. Revolutionary leader Mao Tse-tung

(Mao Zedong) ____

3. Madman Adolf Hitler ____

4. Queen Victoria ____

5. Chief Sitting Bull ____

6. President Franklin Roosevelt ____

7. Comedian George Burns ____

8. Actor/President Ronald Reagan ____

9. Actress Katherine Hepburn ____

10. Soviet leader Nikita

Khrushchev ____

**1955**

The year is 1955. Were the following people: a. alive, b. dead, c. not yet born?

11. Actress Meryl Streep ____

12. British prime minister Winston

Churchill ____

13. Trumpeter Wynton Marsalis ____

14. Comic Jerry Seinfeld ____

15. President Herbert Hoover ____

16. Quarterback Joe Montana ____

17. Tennis star Martina

Navratilova ____

18. First Lady Eleanor Roosevelt ____

19. Talk show hostess Oprah

Winfrey ____

20. *Late Night*'s David Letterman ____

## 1935

The year is 1935. Were the following people: a. alive, b. dead, c. not yet born?

21. Actor Marlon Brando ____

22. President Theodore Roosevelt ____

23. Novelist Jack London ____

24. Actress Jean Harlow ____

25. Actor James Dean ____

26. Actress Natalie Wood ____

27. President Calvin Coolidge ____

28. Religious zealot Ayatollah

Khomeini ____

29. Politician Pat Buchanan ____

30. Rolling Stone Keith Richards ____

## 1925

The year is 1925. Were the following people: a. alive, b. dead, c. not yet born?

31. Senator/presidential aspirant Bob

Dole ____

32. Aviation pioneer Orville Wright ____

33. Jazz giant Miles Davis ____

34. Singer Dinah Shore ____

35. Feminist/journalist Gloria

Steinem ____

36. Undersea explorer Jacques

Costeau ____

37. General Norman Schwarzkopf ____

38. Columnist Ann Landers ____

39. French artist Paul Gauguin ____

40. Singer Frank Sinatra ____

## 1968

The year is 1968. Were the following people: a. alive, b. dead, c. not yet born?

41. Baseball great Babe Ruth ____

42. Artist Jackson Pollock ____

43. Pop icon Michael Jackson ____

44. Multiple Academy Award winner

Tom Hanks ____

45. Actor Brad Pitt ____

46. Actress Drew Barrymore ____

47. Clinton advisor George

Stephanopoulous ____

48. Doors singer Jim Morrison ____

49. '90s singer Mariah Carey ____

50. Seinfeld's "Elaine," Julia Louis-

Dreyfus ____

**1915**

The year is 1915. Were the following people: a. alive, b. dead, c. not yet born?

51. Crusading attorney Clarence

Darrow ____

52. Welsh poet Dylan Thomas ____

53. Austrian novelist Franz Kafka ____

54. Writer/reformer Helen Keller ____

55. President George Bush ____

56. Painter Pablo Picasso ____

57. Opera diva Maria Callas ____

58. Nationalist leader Mahatma

Gandhi ____

59. Actor Gary Cooper ____

60. Actress Elizabeth Taylor ____

## MORBID FASCINATIONS
### Sequence 2: Causes of Death

We tend to be fascinated by the ways people take their leave of this temporal realm, and we are especially intrigued if those people are famous. The deaths we tended to remember were those that took us by surprise. The questions below are mostly made up of such deaths. Do you remember the people? Do you remember how they took their leave of us.

### CAUSES OF DEATH, SERIES 1

We all have to go sometime . . . and somehow. The following people all died through violence or accident. (The year of their demise is in parentheses.) Match each of the names with the fate that took that person. Choose from the following five categories: a. drowning, b. execution, c. aviation accident, d. assassination.

61. Singer Otis Redding (1967) ____

62. Political aide Mary Jo Kopechne (1969) ____

63. Humorist Will Rogers (1935) ____

64. War criminal Adolph Eichmann (1962) ____

65. Labor leader Walter Reuther (1970) ____

66. Murderer Gary Gilmore (1977) ____

67. Japanese war leader Hideki Tojo (1948) ____

68. Financier John Jacob Astor (1912) ____

69. Actress Natalie Wood (1981) ____

70. Actress Carole Lombard (1942) ____

71. Anarchist Nicola Sacco (1927) ____

72. Egyptian President Anwar Sadat (1981) ____

73. Singer Ricky Nelson (1985) ____

74. Archduke Franz Ferdinand (1914) ____

75. Singer/guitarist Stevie Ray Vaughn (1990) ____

76. Spy Ethel Rosenberg (1953) ____

77. Revolutionist Leon Trotsky (1940) ____

78. Revolutionary Emiliano Zapata (1919) ____

79. Rapist Caryl Chessman (1960) ____

80. War hero Audie Murphy (1971) ____

**CAUSES OF DEATH, SERIES 2**

Here are twenty more. The challenge is the same, but the categories are different. How did the following people pass from this sphere? Choose from the following categories: a. disappeared (cause of death uncertain), b. murder/shooting, c. auto/motorcycle accident, d. AIDS, e. cancer.

(Date of death or disappearance is in parentheses beside each name.)

81. Writer Ambrose Bierce (1913) ____

82. Actor Steve McQueen (1980) ____

83. Soul singer Marvin Gaye (1984) ____

84. Actress Jayne Mansfield (1967) ____

85. T. E. Lawrence (of Arabia) (1935) ____

86. Teamster boss Jimmy Hoffa (1975) ____

87. Father of psychoanalysis Sigmund Freud (1939) ____

88. Georgia rockers Duane Allman (1971) and Berry Oakley (1972) ____

89. Actor Yul Brynner (1985) ____

90. Argentinian leader Eva "Evita" Peron (1952) ____

91. Western film star Tom Mix (1940) ____

92. Writer/intellectual Albert Camus (1960) ____

93. Aviator Amelia Earhart (1937) ____

94. Judge Joseph Crater (1930) ____

95. Ryan White (1990) ____

96. Criminal Charles Arthur "Pretty Boy" Floyd (1934) ____

97. Actor John Wayne (1979) ____

98. Entertainer Liberace (1987) ____

99. Criminal Bonnie Parker (1934) ____

100. Actor Rock Hudson (1985) ____

**CAUSES OF DEATH, SERIES 3**

Here are some more, same as before, except the categories have again changed. This series has a category for suicide, and a separate category for drug- or alcohol-related deaths. For many people, that's a fine distinction to draw. People who abuse substances are often seen as suicidal, or their dependency can make them suicidal. Still, there's a difference, and the difference is in whether or not the deceased was seeking death. In some cases, we'll never know for sure, but in the list that follows, the answers follow the accepted general interpretations of these deaths. Do you know how the following people's lives ended? Choose from the following categories: a. suicide, b. drug/alcohol related, c. murdered, d. plane crash, e. sexually transmitted disease, f. automobile accident.

101. Poet Sylvia Plath (1963) ____

102. Actor William Holden (1981) ____

103. Actor Sal Mineo (1976) ____

104. Commerce Secretary Ron Brown (1996) ____

105. Writer Jack Kerouac (1969) ____

106. Senator Joseph McCarthy (1957) ____

107. Dictatorial consort Eva Braun (1945) ____

108. Bandleader Glenn Miller (1944) ____

109. Architect Stanford White (1906) ____

110. Notre Dame football coach Knute Rockne (1931) ____

111. Jazz pioneer Charlie Parker (1955) ____

112. Novelist Virginia Woolf (1941) ____

113. Russian mystic Grigory Rasputin (1916) ____

114. Revolutionary Pancho Villa (1923) ____

115. Diet doctor Herbert Tarnower (1980) ____

116. Grateful Dead keyboardist Ron "Pig Pen" McKernan (1973) ____

117. Blues pioneer Robert Johnson (1938) ____

118. Black Panther leader Huey P. Newton (1989) ____

119. Film icon Marilyn Monroe (1962) ____

120. Singer Sam Cooke (1964) ____

121. Poet Hart Crane (1932) ____

122. Gangster Alphonse Capone (1947) ____

123. Novelist F. Scott Fitzgerald (1940) ____

124. Mobster "Crazy" Joe Gallo (1972) ____

125. Air ace Baron Manfred Von Richtofen (1918) ____

126. Comedian Lenny Bruce (1966) ____

127. Comedian Freddie Prinze (1977) ____

128. Country legend Hank Williams (1953) ____

129. Original Rolling Stone Brian Jones (1969) ____

130. Italian dictator Benito Mussolini (1945) ____

131. Queen vocalist Freddy Mercury (1991) ____

132. Russian-American artist Mark Rothko (1970) ____

People should be taught what is, not what should be. All my humor is based on destruction and despair. If the whole world were tranquil, without disease and violence, I'd be standing in the bread-line—right back of J. Edgar Hoover.

—LENNY BRUCE

I met Lenny Bruce in 1965. A rumor had been circulated that he was dead. "I'm glad you're not dead," I said. "Me, too," he said. And then a year later, he was.

\* \* \*

133. Actor Leslie Howard (1943) ____

134. Political appointee Vince Foster (1993) ____

135. Gangster "Dutch" Schultz (1935) ____

136. Actress Sharon Tate (1969) ____

137. Irish playwright Brendan Behan (1964) ____

138. Presidential candidate's daughter Terry McGovern (1994) ____

139. Japanese nationalist and novelist Yukio Mishima (1970) ____

140. Punk girlfriend Nancy Spungen (1978) ____

141. General George Patton (1945) ____

142. Civil rights leader Medgar Evers (1963) ____

143. Nuclear plant employee Karen Silkwood (1974) ____

144. Princess Grace of Monaco (1982) ____

145. Blues legend Bessie Smith (1937) ____

146. TV innovator and funnyman Ernie Kovacs (1962) ____

147. Serial killer/cannibal Jeffrey Dahmer (1994) ____

148. Civil rights worker Viola Liuzzo (1965) ____

149. Fictional character Jay Gatsby (1920s) ____

150. Revolutionary Che Guevara (1967) ____

## ANSWERS

*Sequence 1: Alive, Dead, Not Yet Born*

**1905**

1. Wyatt Earp was a. alive (he was fifty-seven).

2. Mao Tse-tung (Mao Zedong) was a. alive (Mao was twelve).

3. Hitler was a. alive (he was sixteen years old).

4. Queen Victoria was b. dead (she died in 1901).

5. Sitting Bull was b. dead (shot to death in 1890).

6. FDR was a. alive (he was twenty-three in 1905).

7. Burns was a. alive (he was nine).

8. Reagan was c. not yet born (he would be born in six years).

9. Hepburn was c. not yet born (she would arrive in two years).

10. Khrushchev was a. alive (born in 1894).

**1955**

11. Meryl Streep was a. alive (she was four).

12. Churchill was a. alive (at eighty-one, he still had ten years to live).

13. Trumpeter Wynton Marsalis was c. not yet born (born in '61).

14. Jerry Seinfeld was a. alive (the comic was born in this year).

15. Herbert Hoover was a. alive (the ex-president was eighty-one).

16. Montana was c. not yet born (the quarterback arrives in '56).

17. Navratilova was c. not yet born (the tennis star also arrives in '56).

18. Eleanor Roosevelt was a. alive (at seventy-one, she was at or near the top of all lists of most admired women).

19. Oprah was a. alive (not yet talking, she is a one-year-old baby).

20. Letterman was a. alive (he was an eight-year-old Hoosier).

**1935**

21. Marlon Brando was a. alive (he was eleven years old).

22. Theodore Roosevelt was b. dead (and had been since 1919).

23. Jack London was b. dead (he died in 1916, at age forty).

24. Harlow was a. alive (but she would die of uremia in 1937).

25. Dean was a. alive (he was four).

26. Natalie Wood was c. not yet born (she will be born in three years).

27. Calvin Coolidge was a. dead (he died in 1933).

28. Ayatollah Khomeini was a. alive (he was a thirty-three-year-old scholar).

29. Pat Buchanan was c. not yet born (he will be in 1938).

30. Richards was c. not yet born (the Stone starts rolling in '43).

**1925**

31. Bob Dole is a. alive (he's two).

32. Orville Wright was a. alive (and has twenty-three years left to him).

33. Miles Davis is c. not yet born (he arrives in '26).

34. Dinah Shore is a. alive (she's an eight-year-old).

35. Gloria Steinem is c. not yet born (she will arrive in 1934).

36. Jacques Costeau is a. alive (he's fifteen).

37. Norman Schwarzkopf is c. not yet born (he's Steinem's age).

38. Ann Landers is a. alive (she's seven).

39. Paul Gauguin is b. dead (he died in 1903).

40. Frank Sinatra is a. alive (he's a ten-year-old in Hoboken).

**1968**

41. Babe Ruth is b. dead (and has been for twenty years).

42. Jackson Pollock is b. dead (and has been for twelve years).

43. Michael Jackson is a. alive (and has been for ten years).

44. Tom Hanks is a. alive (and has been for twelve years).

45. Brad Pitt is a. alive (he's five).

46. Drew Barrymore is c. not yet born (she will be, in seven years).

47. George Stephanopoulous is a. alive (he's seven).

48. Jim Morrison is a. alive (he will die in France in 1971).

49. Mariah Carey is c. not yet born (not until 1970).

50. Julia Louis-Dreyfus is a. alive (she's six years old).

**1915**

51. Clarence Darrow is a. alive (he's fifty-eight).

52. Dylan Thomas is a. alive (he's a one-year-old).

53. Franz Kafka is a. alive (he's thirty-two, with nine years to live).

54. Helen Keller is a. alive (she's thirty-five).

55. George Bush is c. not yet born (not for nine more years).

56. Pablo Picasso is a. alive (he's thirty-four).

57. Maria Callas is c. not yet born (not for another eight years).

58. Mahatma Gandhi is a. alive (he was born in 1869, and he will die in 1948).

59. Gary Cooper is a. alive (he's fourteen).

60. Elizabeth Taylor is c. not yet born (and won't be until 1932).

## MORBID FASCINATIONS, SEQUENCE 2

*Causes of Death, Series 1*

61. c. An aviation accident took Otis Redding.

"Great Soul," 1869–1948
    Interviewer: "What do you think of Western Civilization?"
    Gandhi: "I think it would be a good idea."

\*   \*   \*

62. a. Drowning took the life of Kennedy aide Mary Jo Kopechne.

63. c. An aviation accident killed Will Rogers.

64. b. Execution took Adolph Eichmann.

65. c. An aviation accident killed Walter Reuther.

66. b. Execution was the fate of Gary Gilmore.

67. b. Execution (for war crimes) took Hideki Tojo (he had tried to commit ritual suicide, but the attempt failed).

68. a. Drowning took Astor, who went down with the *Titanic*.

69. a. Drowning was also the fate of Natalie Wood, who drowned off Catalina Island. She had feared such a death her entire life.

70. c. An aviation accident took Carole Lombard.

71. b. Execution took the life of Nicola Sacco.

72. d. Assassination took the life of Anwar Sadat.

73. c. An aviation accident killed Ricky Nelson.

74. d. Assassination took Archduke Franz Ferdinand.

75. c. An aviation accident took the life of Stevie Ray Vaughn.

76. b. Execution took the life of Ethel Rosenberg.

77. d. Assassination took Leon Trotsky.

78. d. Assassination (and treachery) also took Emiliano Zapata.

79. b. Execution (at San Quentin) took the life of Chessman.

80. c. An aviation accident killed Audie Murphy.

*Causes of Death, Series 2*

81. Bierce a. disappeared in Mexico.

82. McQueen died of e. cancer.

83. Marvin Gaye was b. murdered by his father.

84. Jayne Mansfield died in an c. auto accident.

85. T. E. Lawrence died in a c. motorcycle accident.

86. Hoffa a. disappeared (but it is generally believed that he was murdered).

87. Freud died of e. cancer (it was an excruciating death, and Freud confronted it with stoicism and courage).

88. Allman and Oakley both died in c. motorcycle accidents.

89. Yul Brynner died of e. cancer.

90. Eva "Evita" Peron died of e. cancer (ovarian).

91. Tom Mix died in c. an auto accident.

92. Albert Camus also died in c. an auto accident.

93. Amelia Earhart a. disappeared.

94. Judge Crater a. disappeared.

95. Ryan White died of d. AIDS.

96. "Pretty Boy" Floyd was b. shot to death by FBI agents.

97. John Wayne died of e. cancer (or "the Big C," as he called it).

98. Liberace died of d. AIDS.

99. Bonnie Parker was b. shot to death.

100. Rock Hudson died of d. AIDS.

*Causes of Death, Series 3*

101. a. Suicide was the fate of Sylvia Plath.

102. b. Alcohol took the life of William Holden.

103. c. Murder was Sal Mineo's fate.

104. d. A plane crash killed Ron Brown.

105. b. Alcohol killed Kerouac.

106. b. Alcohol hastened the demise of Joseph McCarthy.

107. a. Suicide took the life of Eva Braun (in Hitler's Berlin bunker).

108. d. A plane crash killed Glenn Miller.

109. c. Murder took Stanford White.

110. d. A plane crash killed Knute Rockne.

111. b. Drugs hastened the end of Charlie Parker (at thirty-five).

112. a. Suicide was how Virginia Woolf made her exit.

113. c. Murder took Rasputin (and he was very hard to kill: He was poisoned, shot, stabbed, and thrown into a freezing river).

114. c. Murder was also the fate of Pancho Villa.

115. c. Murder befell Herbert Tarnower (he was shot to death by his longtime lover, Jean Harris).

116. b. Alcohol killed "Pig Pen" (he died of liver disease, hastened by legendary consumption of alcohol).

117. c. Murder took Robert Johnson.

118. c. Murder (on the streets of Oakland, California) took Huey P. Newton.

119. a. Suicide took Marilyn Monroe, though many suspect foul play.

120. c. Murder took Sam Cooke.

121. a. Suicide took Hart Crane (he jumped from a ship).

122. e. A sexually transmitted disease (syphilis) killed Capone.

123. b. Alcohol shortened the life of F. Scott Fitzgerald, though the cause of death was put down to a heart attack (at age forty-four).

124. c. Murder took "Crazy" Joe Gallo.

125. d. A plane crash killed Von Richtofen (the Red Baron). He was shot down just six months before the end of WWI.

126. b. Drugs killed Lenny Bruce.

127. a. Suicide took the life of Freddie Prinze.

128. b. Drugs and alcohol shortened the life of Hank Williams, who died of a heart attack at age twenty-nine. It was a tough year for drunks; Dylan Thomas succumbed to the effects of alcohol in this same year.

129. b. Drugs took Brian Jones.

130. c. Murder took Mussolini, though most would say he had it coming. He died with his mistress at the hands of antifascist partisans.

131. e. Sexually transmitted disease (AIDS) took the life of Freddy Mercury.

132. a. Suicide was how the life of Mark Rothko ended.

133. d. A plane crash killed Leslie Howard (who played Ashley Wilkes in *Gone With the Wind*). His plane was shot down by German fighters who thought Winston Churchill was on board.

134. a. Suicide ended the life of Vince Foster, though many on the right remain unconvinced.

135. c. Murder ended the life of "Dutch" Schultz. (Is this surprising to anyone?)

136. c. Murder (at the hands of the Manson family) took Sharon Tate.

137. b. Alcohol killed Brendan Behan at age forty-one.

138. b. Alcohol also killed Terry McGovern. The former senator wrote a book about her death, published in 1996.

139. a. Suicide (in the form of hari kari) took the life of Mishima.

140. c. Murder (at the hands of Sid Vicious) claimed Nancy Spungen.

141. f. An auto accident killed Patton.

142. c. Murder (by a racist) took Medgar Evers.

143. f. An auto accident killed Karen Silkwood, though there is reason to suspect foul play.

144. f. An auto accident killed Princess Grace.

145. f. An auto accident (and racism at the admitting hospital) killed Bessie Smith.

146. f. An auto accident also killed Ernie Kovacs.

147. c. Murder ended the life of Jeffrey Dahmer. He was killed by fellow inmates while in prison.

148. c. Murder took the life of Viola Liuzzo. (She died for the cause of civil rights, and her death should be remembered.)

149. c. Murder took the life of Jay Gatsby.

150. c. Murder took Guevara while he was in the custody of the Bolivian military. It is widely believed that the CIA ordered his death.

Scoring: If you knew more than 75 of these, you may have an unhealthy preoccupation with death. Or it just might be that you are possessed of a good bit of knowledge. You make the call.

Conversely, if you knew fewer than 75 of these, you may simply be too psychologically healthy to spend much time thinking about dead people. However, if you knew fewer than 40 of these, that would seem to indicate a paucity of knowledge about other things as well.

# 14

## A Visit to Outlandia

*What I claim is to live to the full the contradiction of my time,
which may well make sarcasm the condition of truth.*

—ROLAND BARTHES, 1957

*There is always something absurd about the past.*

—MAX BEERBOHM

In 1969, when men first walked upon the moon, CBS News broadcast an interview with a man who had been born in slavery. Walter Cronkite asked him what he thought of the scientific marvel before them on the enlarged television monitors in the studio where the interview was taking place. The wrinkled old gent paused as the men in space suits cavorted on the moon's surface, then he said: "Ain't no men on the moon. Them's just pictures." Neither the pictures nor Cronkite's attempts to change his mind could convince the former slave that men were walking on the moon.

And who could blame him for his skepticism? The arc of time from slavery to the National Aeronautics and Space Administration was too short to take a former slave's credibility on that ride.

We're all a bit like that former slave. The many incongruities of our world make the simple distinction between what is true and what is false a bit trickier than it might once have been.

The main reason for including true or false sequences in this book is that so much of what happened in the twentieth century hardly seems true. Much of what happened in our time barely seemed credible even as it transpired, and bizarre new events soon drove yesterday's anomalies out of mind. But before we lose track of how genuinely weird much of it was, see if you can tell the truth from the falsity in the hundred questions below.

As in the true/false tests we took in school, guessing is allowed, even encouraged. What is being exercised here isn't only memory, but a sense of what is real, what is plausible. We judge people's sanity by their ability to tell what is real. Perhaps that is why sanity has become so hard to define in the waning days of the often implausible twentieth century. It has been an outlandish period in human history.

Did your sanity survive the century? Can you tell the true from the false, the real from the contrived? One hundred chances to prove you can make these distinctions await your attention. (Hint: The things I was able to make up are usually not as bizarre as the things that actually happened.) Level of difficulty: 4.

## WOULD YOU BELIEVE?

1. In 1996, an alternate juror on the Whitewater trial in Arkansas wore a Star Trek outfit to court each day. She was dismissed, not for the costume, but for talking about it to the media.

TRUE or FALSE

2. While governor of California, Ronald Reagan reported seeing a fleet of flying saucers approaching Sacramento.

TRUE or FALSE

3. During the Carter administration, country music outlaw Willie Nelson smoked pot on the roof of the White House.

TRUE or FALSE

4. During World War II, it was proposed that the White House be painted black as a security measure.

TRUE or FALSE

5. When '60s media manipulator Jerry Rubin wrote, "I fell in love with [him] the first time I saw his cherub face and sparkling eyes on national TV," he was referring to Howdy Doody.

TRUE or FALSE

6. While president, it was not uncommon for Lyndon Johnson to receive visitors while he was on the toilet.

TRUE or FALSE

7. Before 1978, all tropical storms were named after women.

TRUE or FALSE

8. As Allied troops fought their way to the outskirts of Paris, Adolph Hitler ordered the city destroyed.

TRUE or FALSE

9. Evangelist Jimmy Swaggart and rocker Jerry Lee Lewis are cousins.

TRUE or FALSE

10. Country singer Dolly Parton was born Delbert Parton, and became Dolly only after a sex change operation in the late 1960s.

TRUE or FALSE

11. American Indians were not citizens of the United States until Congress recognized them as citizens in 1924.

TRUE or FALSE

12. Adolph Hitler was a vegetarian.

TRUE or FALSE

13. The FBI sent Martin Luther King, Jr., a copy of an audiotape that caught the civil rights leader in the act of adultery. Included with the tape was the suggestion that suicide would be a good way out of the embarrassment and pain of disclosure.

TRUE or FALSE

14. In the early 1990s, animals in the Sarajevo zoo starved to death. Their cries added to the horror, but city dwellers who tried to get food to the animals were shot by snipers.

TRUE or FALSE

15. In the late 1930s, a condemned black man being led to his execution cried out, "Save me, Joe Louis." Joe Louis was then the heavyweight champion of the world.

TRUE or FALSE

16. It took Charles Lindbergh 101 hours to fly across the Atlantic Ocean in 1927, something the Concorde does in about three hours.

TRUE or FALSE

17. Japanese women disfigured in the bombing of Hiroshima and brought to the U.S. for plastic surgery were known in the press as "Hiroshima Maidens."

TRUE or FALSE

18. President Ronald Reagan was of the opinion that trees caused more pollution than automobiles.

TRUE or FALSE

19. In 1955, John Wayne and a large cast assembled to make a movie in Utah, east of open-air nuclear tests being conducted in Nevada. Wayne and several other cast members would later die of cancer thought to be caused by radiation.

TRUE or FALSE

20. A customer approaches the desk clerk at a hotel and asks for a room on the top floor. "Would that be for sleeping or for jumping, sir?" asks the clerk. That was a commonly told joke following the stock market crash of 1929.

TRUE or FALSE

21. In the early days of television, censors did not permit use of the word "pregnant."

TRUE or FALSE

22. The breakfast cereal known as Post Toasties was originally called Elijah's Manna.

TRUE or FALSE

23. In 1970, Richard Nixon paid a late-night visit to a group of antiwar protesters at the Lincoln Memorial. As he was leaving, one of the protesters ran up to the presidential limo and gave Nixon the finger. Nixon replied in kind.

TRUE or FALSE

24. In the early 1950s, writer and pop hero William Burroughs killed his wife in Mexico City while attempting to shoot an apple off her head.

TRUE or FALSE

25. Paramount Pictures spent $25 million to make sixty movies in 1931, less than the cost of a single moderately expensive movie of the 1990s.

TRUE or FALSE

26. The daughter of the King of Rock 'n' Roll was briefly married to the King of Pop.

TRUE or FALSE

27. The real-life Betty Crocker was once arrested for shoplifting.

TRUE or FALSE

28. During World War II, over one million British children were evacuated from the cities to the countryside.

TRUE or FALSE

29. Country singer Merle Haggard was an inmate in San Quentin when Johnny Cash performed there.

TRUE or FALSE

30. "In politics, if you want something said, ask a man; if you want something done, ask a woman," was an observation made by Hillary Clinton.

TRUE or FALSE

31. Elvis Presley was made a special drug enforcement agent by President Richard Nixon.

TRUE or FALSE

32. Former Secretary of State Henry Kissinger's real first name was Heinz.

TRUE or FALSE

33. James Arness, better remembered as TV's Matt Dillon, got his start playing the part of alien vegetation in *The Thing*.

TRUE or FALSE

34. Right-wing political monologist Rush Limbaugh was never a registered voter.

TRUE or FALSE

35. Cigarette smoking didn't become widely popular until after soldiers in World War I were issued free cigarettes by the U.S. Army, thus addicting virtually an entire generation.

TRUE or FALSE

36. *National Review* publisher William Buckley proposed mandatory tattoos for AIDS sufferers—on the arms for IV drug users, and on the buttocks for homosexuals.

TRUE or FALSE

37. In 1970, Richard Nixon ordered the Army to deliver the mail in order to thwart a strike of postal workers.

TRUE or FALSE

38. In 1964, a best-selling book (*Calories Don't Count*) urged people to eat mass quantities of fat in order to stay thin.

TRUE or FALSE

39. When Elvis Presley played Little Rock, Arkansas, in the late 1950s, twelve-year-old Bill Clinton played the song "Kansas City" on his saxophone to open the show for the king of rock 'n' roll.

TRUE or FALSE

40. Five years after his confirmation hearings riveted national attention, fewer than one-third of Americans could identify Clarence Thomas.

TRUE or FALSE

41. In the late '80s, Stanford University students chanted, "Hey Hey, Ho Ho, Western Culture's got to go," as they sought to have a humanities course requirement eliminated.

TRUE or FALSE

42. Actress Ruth Gordon gave herself a Christmas present in 1920: She had both of her legs broken to correct a problem of bowleggedness.

TRUE or FALSE

43. Both Errol Flynn and Kevin Costner played corpses in their first movie parts.

TRUE or FALSE

44. In 1920, the Massachussetts Osteopathic Society sought legislation to ban the manufacture of high-heeled shoes.

TRUE or FALSE

45. In the early 1970s, the Pentagon proposed to turn the entire state of Wisconsin into a giant "Doomsday

transmitter." The plan was squashed by environmentalists.

TRUE or FALSE

46. Golda Meir, the prime minister of Israel from 1969 to 1974, grew up in Milwaukee, Wisconsin.

TRUE or FALSE

47. In 1972, the year of the Watergate break-in, 93 percent of American newspapers endorsed the reelection of Richard Nixon.

TRUE or FALSE

48. Conductor Leonard Bernstein had perfect pitch, but he could not read music.

TRUE or FALSE

49. In an attempt to change his image, Pauly Shore auditioned for the part of death-row convict Mathew Poncelet in *Dead Man Walking*, but was beaten out for the part by Sean Penn.

TRUE or FALSE

50. During the German occupation of France, the Nazi name for that country was Deutschland II.

TRUE or FALSE

51. A woman once said to "Silent" Cal Coolidge, "A friend bet me I couldn't get three words out of you." Coolidge replied: "You lose."

TRUE or FALSE

52. Johnny Cochran, attorney for O. J. Simpson, was retained by eighty-nine victims of the bombing of the federal building in Oklahoma City.

TRUE or FALSE

53. The first woman in country music to earn over a million dollars a year was Minnie Pearl.

TRUE or FALSE

54. In the 1920s, leading child psychologist John B. Watson gave this advice on child care: "Never hug them or kiss them. Never let them sit on your lap. If you must, kiss them once on the forehead when they say goodnight."

TRUE or FALSE

55. Fictional character Forrest Gump was based on a real Vietnam veteran named Nike Gump, famous for starting a successful running shoe company after the war.

TRUE or FALSE

56. The phrase "every day, in every way, I'm growing better and better" was originated by Tammy Fay Bakker on the PTL Club.

TRUE or FALSE

57. More American workers belonged to unions in 1953 than belonged to unions in 1995.

TRUE or FALSE

58. In the days before the first nuclear bomb was tested in New Mexico in 1945, some project scientists feared the explosion would set off a nuclear chain reaction and incinerate the entire planet. No one was entirely sure they were wrong, but the test was carried out, anyway.

TRUE or FALSE

59. During military service in World War II, Senator Joseph McCarthy was known as "Tailgunner Joe" because he was notorious for sneaking up on other servicemen in the showers.

TRUE or FALSE

60. In the first Tarzan book by Edgar Rice Burroughs, published in 1914, Tarzan didn't have a chimp named Cheetah; he had a dog named Pal.

TRUE or FALSE

61. FBI director J. Edgar Hoover had a box behind his desk, which he stood on to increase his stature when greeting visitors or his agents.

TRUE or FALSE

62. In 1939, a goldfish-swallowing fad swept the nation's colleges. A student at Clark University swallowed eighty-nine live goldfish, and a frat boy in Illinois swallowed five live baby mice.

TRUE or FALSE

63. During World War II, five brothers died aboard a single Navy ship.

TRUE or FALSE

64. In 1939, Adolph Hitler said: "As soon as I have carried out my program for Germany I shall take up my painting."

TRUE or FALSE

65. Humphrey Bogart was not the first choice for the role of Rick in *Casablanca*; Ronald Reagan was.

TRUE or FALSE

66. A head of state during the century's last decade spent twenty-seven years of his life in the prisons of the country he eventually governed.

TRUE or FALSE

67. Princess Diana's driver was legally drunk the night she (and he) were killed in a Paris car crash.

TRUE or FALSE

68. During the 1930s, a Capone syndicate mobster named Nicky "the Nuts" Nutella was on the FBI's ten-most-wanted list.

TRUE or FALSE

69. Decades after painting luminous watch dials with radioactive paint in the 1920s, scores of American factory workers died of cancer of the mouth and

jaw as a result of using their tongues to bring their brushes to a fine point.

TRUE or FALSE

70. President Franklin Roosevelt's daughter, Anna, helped to conceal her father's romantic interludes with paramour Lucy Mercer from her mother, Eleanor.

TRUE or FALSE

71. In a telephone conversation taped in the 1990s, Prince Charles, the man who will be king, told his lover Camilla Parker-Bowles that he wanted to be reincarnated as one of her Tampons.

TRUE or FALSE

72. In the 1960s, airline flight attendants were called stewardesses. Only women could be "stews," and their jobs were forfeited if the women got married, or if they exceeded strict weight guidelines.

TRUE or FALSE

73. In 1981, Walter Cronkite, America's most trusted man, did his farewell news broadcast wearing only boxer shorts below desk level.

TRUE or FALSE

74. Beehive, brioche, and artichoke were all names of hairstyles during the 1960s.

TRUE or FALSE

75. Women constituted 60 percent of the American workforce during World War II; 42 percent in the 1970s.

TRUE or FALSE

76. The reason PLO leader Yasir Arafat always appears to be in need of a shave is that he has a skin condition that does not allow him to shave. He uses barber's clippers, instead.

TRUE or FALSE

77. In 1959, *Life* magazine ran a feature piece about newlyweds who spent their honeymoon in a bomb shelter. "Fallout can be fun," said the article.

TRUE or FALSE

78. "Mickeyville," Walt Disney's first southern California amusement park, flopped in the late 1930s, but the lessons he learned from the failure paved the way for the success of Disneyland in 1955.

TRUE or FALSE

79. In the late 1930s, a German manufacturer marketed a board game called Juden Raus, German for "Jews Out."

TRUE or FALSE

80. During the Russian Revolution, movie mogul David O. Selznick cabled Czar Nicholas from Hollywood with the following offer: "Hear you are now out of work. . . . Can give you a fine position acting in pictures. Salary no object.

Reply my expense. Regards you and family." The czar and his family were executed soon after.

TRUE or FALSE

81. Songwriter Irving Berlin turned to writing rock 'n' roll songs in the 1950s. Most of those songs were unsuccessful, but he managed a big hit with "Love Letters in the Sand," recorded by Pat Boone.

TRUE or FALSE

82. Ads for a 1976 Rolling Stones album depicted a battered woman and the caption "I'm 'Black and Blue' from the Rolling Stones and I love it."

TRUE or FALSE

83. *The China Syndrome*, a film about a disastrous nuclear power plant accident, opened in American cities just three days before an actual nuke plant accident at Three Mile Island in Pennsylvania.

TRUE or FALSE

84. The Equal Rights Amendment was passed into law in 1978. In its entirety, the amendment guarantees that: "Equality of rights under the law shall not be denied or abridged by the United States or by any State on account of sex."

TRUE or FALSE

85. Apache shaman and war leader Geronimo rode a Ferris wheel at the St. Louis World's Fair in the century's first decade.

TRUE or FALSE

86. Ernest Hemingway said of F. Scott Fitzgerald that he was "90 percent Rotarian."

TRUE or FALSE

87. One night in the late 1940s, painter Jackson Pollock drunkenly kicked over several cans of paint in his studio. A few days later, an art dealer offered him a sizeable sum for the "painting," and the "action school" of painting was born. In 1988, one of Pollock's paintings sold for nearly $5 million.

TRUE or FALSE

88. In 1983, the Brown and Williamson Tobacco Company paid Sylvester Stallone five hundred thousand dollars to feature their products in his next five films.

TRUE or FALSE

89. One of the most popular American songs of 1915 was "I Didn't Raise My Boy to Be a Soldier." Two years later, one of the most popular songs was "Oh Johnny, Oh Johnny, O!" which featured lyrics like: "Oh, Johnny, Oh, Johnny! why do you lag? . . . Run to your flag. . . .

Don't stay behind while others do all the fighting."

TRUE or FALSE

90. During the war in Vietnam, the Viet Cong unleashed packs of rabid dogs in jungles where U.S. forces were thought to be.

TRUE or FALSE

91. During World War II, General George Patton slapped a soldier when he overheard the young private repeat the rumor that Patton wore women's underwear whenever he went into battle.

TRUE or FALSE

92. World War I flying ace Baron Munchausen was the inspiration for "The Red Baron," featured in Snoopy's fantasies more than thirty-five years later.

TRUE or FALSE

93. Auto industry pioneer Henry Ford would not hire anyone who smoked because he thought cigarettes caused mental degeneration.

TRUE or FALSE

94. In September 1956, Elvis Presley appeared on the *Ed Sullivan Show* for the first time. He wasn't introduced by Ed Sullivan, however; he was introduced by guest host Charles Laughton.

TRUE or FALSE

95. Shortly after Richard Nixon resigned the presidency, Francis Ford Coppola offered him a role in *Godfather II* as a mafia don. Nixon turned down the part.

TRUE or FALSE

96. The early 1990s dance fad known as the lambada faded from popularity when it became known that the dance was derived from human sacrifice rituals in Haiti.

TRUE or FALSE

97. When Ronald Reagan was shot in 1981, Secretary of State Alexander Haig quelled no one's anxieties when he presumptively bypassed constitutional succession procedures and announced, "I am in charge here."

TRUE or FALSE

98. Bobby Riggs's victory over Billy Jean King in a much-publicized battle of the sexes tennis match helped to defeat the Equal Rights Amendment in 1982.

TRUE or FALSE

99. During the Cuban Missile Crisis, John F. Kennedy squelched an argument between some of his generals by saying: "Gentlemen, you can't fight in here. This is the War Room."

TRUE or FALSE

100. The Chevrolet Nova didn't sell well in Latin America when it was introduced there in the 1960s. General Motors

executives were puzzled until it was pointed out that, in Spanish, "No va" translates to "doesn't go."

TRUE or FALSE

## ANSWERS

1. TRUE: an alternate juror on the Whitewater trial did wear a Star Trek outfit to court each day.

2. FALSE: Reagan did not report flying saucers.

3. TRUE: Willie Nelson did smoke pot on the roof of the White House.

4. TRUE: It was proposed that the White House be painted black, but the idea was rejected.

5. FALSE: Remarkably, and very much representative of the insanity of those times, Rubin was referring to Charles Manson.

6. TRUE: Johnson did receive visitors while he was on the toilet.

7. TRUE: Before 1978, all tropical storms were named after women.

8. TRUE: Adolph Hitler did order Paris destroyed. Fortunately, General von Cholitz ignored the order.

9. TRUE: Swaggart and Lewis are cousins.

10. FALSE: Dolly Parton was not born Delbert Parton.

11. TRUE: American Indians were not U.S. citizens until 1924.

12. TRUE: Adolph Hitler was a vegetarian.

13. TRUE: The FBI did send King a tape and the suggestion that suicide would be a good way out.

14. TRUE: Animals in the Sarajevo zoo did starve to death, and those who sought to help them were shot by snipers.

15. TRUE: In a poignant episode of black powerlessness in the 1930s, a condemned black man did call on Joe Louis for help.

16. FALSE: It took Lindbergh thirty-three and a half hours to fly across the Atlantic. (Did you think he could stay awake for 101 hours?)

17. TRUE: "Hiroshima Maidens" were brought to the U.S. for plastic surgery.

18. TRUE: Reagan was of the opinion that trees caused more pollution than automobiles, or so he said.

19. TRUE: The film was called *The Conqueror*, and John Wayne played Genghis Khan. Wayne and several other cast members did die of cancer, but the link between testing and their later cancers remains speculative.

20. TRUE: "Would that be for sleeping or for jumping, sir?" was the punch line of a joke common following the stock market crash.

21. TRUE: In the early days of television, censors did not permit use of the word "pregnant."

22. TRUE: Post Toasties were originally called Elijah's Manna, but protests by clergymen in 1904 led to the name change.

23. TRUE: Nixon did give the kid the finger, but what is interesting about the episode is Nixon's take on it. He was hugely amused, saying, "That SOB will go through the rest of his life telling everybody that the president of the United States gave him the finger, and nobody will believe him." More likely, the protester went through life telling everybody he flipped off the president of the United States . . . and nobody believed him.

24. TRUE: Burroughs did kill his wife in Mexico City.

25. TRUE: Paramount Pictures did spend $25 million to make sixty movies in 1931, and that is less than the cost of a single moderately expensive movie of the 1990s. In fact, it's less than the single-movie salary of some stars.

26. TRUE: You knew, of course, that Lisa Marie did marry (and divorce) Michael Jackson, or else where were you during the media blitz?

27. FALSE: There was no real-life Betty Crocker; she was a corporate concoction in 1921.

28. TRUE: In an enormous mass migration, over one million British children were evacuated during WWII.

29. TRUE: Haggard was in San Quentin when Cash performed there.

30. FALSE: " . . . if you want something done, ask a woman," was not an observation made by Hillary Clinton. It was made by Margaret Thatcher.

31. TRUE: In 1972, five years before he died of complications of massive drug abuse, Presley was made a special drug enforcement agent by President Nixon.

32. TRUE: Kissinger's real first name was Heinz.

33. TRUE: Arness did get his start playing alien vegetation in *The Thing*.

34. FALSE: Limbaugh did get around to registering to vote, but not until 1988.

35. TRUE: Cigarette smoking became a national addiction only after World War I exposed a generation to the addiction.

36. TRUE: Buckley did propose such tattoos.

37. TRUE: Nixon did turn soldiers into disgruntled postal workers.

38. TRUE: The book did urge people to eat mass quantities of fat, which might have helped it to become a best seller.

39. FALSE: Clinton never opened for Elvis Presley.

40. TRUE: In 1996, fewer than one-third of Americans knew who Supreme Court Justice Clarence Thomas was.

41. TRUE: "Hey Hey, Ho Ho, Western Culture's got to go," was the chant of Stanford protestors seeking to change course requirements.

42. TRUE: Actress Gordon did have both of her legs broken to correct bowleggedness.

43. TRUE: Flynn and Costner did play corpses in their first movies. Some critics thought it was a stretch for both actors.

44. TRUE: The Massachussetts Osteopathic Society did seek a ban on high-heeled shoes.

45. TRUE: Wisconsin was slated to become a "Doomsday transmitter," with grids buried under the entire state.

46. TRUE: Golda Meir did grow up in Milwaukee, Wisconsin.

47. TRUE: 93 percent of American newspapers did endorse Nixon in 1972 (so much for the myth of the liberal media).

48. FALSE: Of course Bernstein could read music.

49. FALSE: Pauly Shore did not audition for any part in *Dead Man Walking*.

50. FALSE: The name for France did not change during the occupation.

51. TRUE: Though the story sounds apocryphal, historians say that Coolidge did offer that reply.

52. TRUE: Johnny Cochran was retained by eighty-nine victims of the bombing of the federal building in Oklahoma City.

53. FALSE: The first woman in country music to earn over a million dollars a year was Loretta Lynn, the coal miner's daughter.

54. TRUE: Watson and many of his colleagues in the '20s did believe in withholding affection from children.

55. FALSE: Forrest Gump was the product of Winston Groom's imagination. There was no specific real-life counterpart.

56. FALSE: "Every day, in every way, I'm growing better and better" was originated by French positive-thinker Emile Coue in 1923.

57. TRUE: More workers did belong to unions in 1953 than in 1995.

58. TRUE: Some scientists did fear the explosion would incinerate the planet.

59. FALSE: McCarthy was known as "Tailgunner Joe," but not for that reason.

60. FALSE: Tarzan did not have a dog named Pal.

61. TRUE: Half-pint Hoover did stand on a box behind his desk.

62. TRUE: In 1939, a student did swallow eighty-nine live goldfish, and another swallowed five live baby mice.

63. TRUE: During World War II, all five Sullivan brothers did die aboard a single Navy ship.

64. TRUE: Hitler did plan to resume painting after the war.

65. TRUE: Reagan was considered for the *Casablanca* role first.

66. TRUE: The leader and country were, of course, Mandela and South Africa.

67. TRUE: The driver was drunk when Princess Diana was killed.

68. FALSE: There was no Nicky "the Nuts."

69. TRUE: Many workers did die of cancer thought to be from ingesting radioactive paint.

70. TRUE: Torn between love of both parents, Anna Roosevelt did help to conceal her father's romantic interludes from her mother.

71. TRUE: Prince Charles did tell Camilla Parker-Bowles that he wanted to be reincarnated as one of her Tampons.

72. TRUE: Stewardesses lost their jobs if they married or exceeded strict weight guidelines.

73. FALSE: So far as is known, Cronkite always kept his pants on during the news broadcasts.

74. TRUE: Beehive, brioche, and artichoke were hairstyles.

75. TRUE: Women did constitute 60 percent of the American workforce during

World War II, a number that shrank to 42 percent in the 1970s.

76. TRUE: Arafat does suffer a skin condition that does not allow him to shave.

77. TRUE: "Fallout can be fun," said the *Life* article.

78. FALSE: There never was a "Mickeyville."

79. TRUE: A German manufacturer did market such a board game.

80. TRUE: Selznick did offer Czar Nicholas a job.

81. FALSE: Berlin did not write rock 'n' roll of any kind.

82. TRUE: Promotion for *Black and Blue* inspired justified outrage from women's groups.

83. TRUE: *The China Syndrome* did open just three days before Three Mile Island.

84. FALSE: The Equal Rights Amendment was never passed into law.

85. TRUE: Geronimo did ride a Ferris wheel, and this is how he described the experience: "The guards took me into a little house that had four windows. When we were seated the little house started to move along the ground. Then the guards called my attention to some curious things they had in their pockets. Finally they told me to look out, and when I did so I was scared for our little house had gone high up in the air . . . I had never been so high . . . and I tried to look into the sky . . . After we were safe on the land I watched many of these little houses going up and coming down, but I cannot understand how they travel. They are very curious little houses" (from *Geronimo: His Own Story*).

86. FALSE: It was Ernest Hemingway who was "90 percent Rotarian," according to Gertrude Stein.

87. FALSE: Though one of Pollock's paintings did sell for almost $5 million, the "action school" was not begun in this way, though it is also true that Pollock was an alcoholic.

88. TRUE: The Brown and Williamson Tobacco Company did pay Stallone five hundred thousand dollars to feature their products in his films.

89. TRUE: The nation's shifting sentiments can be seen in the contrast between these two songs.

90. FALSE: The Viet Cong did not unleash rabid dogs.

91. FALSE: Patton did slap a battle-fatigued soldier, but not for this reason. Patton thought the soldier was malingering.

92. FALSE: Snoopy's inspiration wasn't Munchausen. The Red Baron was von Richtofen.

93. TRUE: Ford would not hire smokers because he did think cigarettes caused mental degeneration.

94. TRUE: The first time Presley appeared on the *Ed Sullivan Show* he was introduced by guest host Laughton.

95. FALSE: Nixon was not offered a role by Coppola.

96. FALSE: The lambada was not derived from sacrifice rituals.

97. TRUE: Haig did announce that he was in charge.

98. FALSE: Bobby Riggs did not beat Billy Jean King. King beat Riggs.

99. FALSE: Kennedy did not say the generals couldn't fight in the war room. The line is from Kubrick's *Dr. Strangelove*.

100. TRUE: The "No va" was an unfortunate goofup by Chevrolet.

Scoring: Every point away from 100 correct is a move in the direction of an even more bizarre century than the one that actually occurred. Miss more than 10 questions here and your world grows even stranger than the one we inhabited.

# 15

## Some Funny Things Happened on the Way to the Millennium

*Laughter . . . improves everything.*

—*JAMES THURBER*

In 1996, doctors amputated the left leg of a man named Willie King. It turned out, however, that Mr. King's right leg was the diseased limb. The doctors had amputated the wrong leg. Asked how he felt about this a few days after surgery, Mr. King said: "I've kind of taken it in stride."

Which is, after all, what we have to do. Though calamity may (and will) befall us, our task is to keep on striding, to "keep on keepin' on," as we said back in the '60s.

And the way people do that is with the consoling balm of laughter. Bless those who give it.

What follows are one hundred multiple-choice questions about people and things that made us laugh. Perhaps the questions will remind you of some of that laughter we shared. Perhaps they will evoke a few remembered chuckles from the past.

I wouldn't take these questions too seriously. If you're in your twenties, you're not likely to know many of these, and if you're over fifty, you've probably forgotten as much as you've remembered. Young or old, I hope you'll keep your sense of humor about my failure to include people and things you find far more amusing than the things I've included here.

## SOME FUNNY THINGS HAPPENED ON THE WAY TO THE MILLENNIUM

**1.** In 1995, ice skater Tonya Harding turned down a role in a Woody Allen movie because:

a. she didn't approve of Woody's morals

b. it didn't pay enough

c. she thought she looked ridiculous standing taller than her costar

d. Nancy Kerrigan, her skating competitor and victim, was also slated to be in the film

**2.** "This is another fine mess you've gotten me into" was a line often uttered by:

a. Oliver Hardy

b. Stan Laurel

c. Dick Van Dyke

d. Buster Keaton

**3.** Richard Nixon said "sock it to me" on the television show:

a. *That Was the Week That Was*

b. *Hee Haw*

c. *Laugh-In*

d. *The David Frost Show*

**4.** Garrison Keillor created the mythical Minnesota town of:

a. Lake Lakawanna

b. Bedford Falls

c. Lake Okeechobee

d. Lake Woebegon

e. Mount Idy

f. Chagrin Falls

**5.** When Lyndon Johnson said, "He's so dumb he couldn't pour piss out of a boot if the instructions were written on the heel," he was talking about:

a. Bobby Kennedy

b. Barry Goldwater

c. Gerald Ford

d. Ronald Reagan

**6.** Jack Paar gave the country a popular catchphrase that quickly became a cultural cliché in the late 1950s. That phrase was:

a. "Here come da judge"

b. "Would you believe . . ."

c. "The family that prays together, stays together"

d. "I kid you not"

e. "Why not?"

**7.** In the 1930s, ascerbic writer and social critic H. L. Mencken wrote an obituary for a former U.S. president in which he observed: "He had no ideas, and he was not a nuisance." He was talking about:

a. Warren Harding

b. Calvin Coolidge

c. Herbert Hoover

d. Woodrow Wilson

8. Of the following, which did not work as a writer for Sid Caesar in the early 1950s?

a. Mel Brooks

b. Neil Simon

c. Woody Allen

d. Lenny Bruce

e. Howard Morris

f. Carl Reiner

9. The character that made Charlie Chaplin famous was:

a. the Little Weasel

b. the Little Scamp

c. the Little Tramp

d. the Little Rascal

e. the Little Ragamuffin

10. David Letterman's production company was known as:

a. World Wide Antics

b. The Big L

c. Top Ten Productions

d. World Wide Pants

e. Carson Productions

f. World Wide Web

11. Begun in 1907, the first successful comic strip to run daily was called *Mutt and*:

a. *Pals*

b. *Artie*

c. *Friends*

d. *Fleas*

e. *Mary*

f. *Jeff*

12. Of the following, which never performed in one of Bob Hope's USO tours?

a. Joey Heatherton

b. Raquel Welch

c. Anita Bryant

d. Martha Raye

e. Debbie Harry

13. In 1941, *The Great Gildersleeve* was a successful spinoff from *Fibber McGee and Molly*, another successful radio show. On both shows, Throckmorton P. Gildersleeve was a small-town:

a. lawyer

b. politician

c. judge

d. dentist

e. pastor

f. businessman

**14.** Peter Sellers got his start in a British radio comedy called:

a. *The Goon Show*

b. *The Benny Hill Show*

c. *Only When We Larf Revue*

d. *The Loon Hour*

**15.** "What? Me Worry?" was a line associated with:

a. Edwin Newman

b. Edward R. Murrow

c. Arthur Murray

d. Alfred E. Newman

e. Bob Newhart

f. Anthony Newley

**16.** On *Seinfeld*, the first name of the Kramer character was:

a. Michael

b. Kinsley

c. Keister

d. Kozmo

e. George

f. Keebler

**17.** The abbreviation "T&A" can be traced to this satirist/comedian who once injured himself jumping out a window in San Francisco and calling himself "Super Jew." He was:

a. Sam Kinnison

b. Jonathan Winters

c. Dennis Miller

d. Mort Sahl

e. Lenny Bruce

f. Shelley Berman

**18.** "I'm Gumby, damn it," was a line associated with:

a. Dana Carvey

b. Arnold Stang

c. Redd Foxx

d. Bill Murray

e. Phil Silvers

f. Eddie Murphy

**19.** "We have met the enemy and he is us" is a famous line from Walt Kelly's comic strip:

a. *Dagwood*

b. *Tin-Tin*

c. *Maus*

d. *Spy vs. Spy*

e. *Pogo*

f. *Andy Capp*

**20.** A restricted country club turned him down for membership because he was Jewish. The club later accepted him, however, when they found out he was famous under a different name. He then turned them down, writing: "I would never belong to a club that would have me as a member." He was:

a. Jerry Lewis

b. Groucho Marx

c. George Jessel

d. Jerry Seinfeld

e. George Burns

f. Pat Boone

**21.** *Funny Girl* starred Barbra Streisand. It was based on the life of:

a. Fanny Brice

b. Gracie Allen

c. Flo Zeigfeld

d. Lucille Ball

e. Mae West

f. Ethel Merman

**22.** "The only trouble with capitalism is capitalists. They're too damn greedy." These words were uttered by the man who was president on Black Friday. He was:

a. Calvin Coolidge

b. Ronald Reagan

c. Franklin Roosevelt

d. Warren G. Harding

e. George Bush

f. Herbert Hoover

**23.** The kind of detective Ace Ventura was:

a. "cheap"

b. "lame"

c. "pet"

d. "clueless"

e. "bumbling"

f. "nutty"

**24.** Mark Twain's birth year (1835) and his death year (1910) were also, coincidentally, years when:

a. the planet was struck by earthquakes of great magnitude

b. Halley's comet streaked across the skies

c. American presidents were assassinated

d. the mighty Mississippi River flooded

**25.** *The General* was a silent comedy classic starring:

a. Fatty Arbuckle

b. Charlie Chaplin

c. Buster Keaton

d. Lloyd George

e. Harold Lloyd

f. Christopher Lloyd

**26.** Comedian Steve Martin expanded a comedy routine into a best-selling book of the early 1980s. The book was called:

a. *King Tut*

b. *Two Wild and Crazy Guys*

c. *My Point . . . And I Do Have One*

d. *Cruel Shoes*

e. *Dead Men Don't Wear Plaid*

27. Goulding and Elliott were better known as:

a. Cheech and Chong

b. Rowan and Martin

c. Bob and Ray

d. Abbott and Costello

e. Elliot Gould and Barbra Streisand

28. At his trial, a witness testified: "If you don't consider what happened in Oklahoma, [he] was a good person." Can you guess who the witness was talking about? Was it:

a. Clyde Barrow

b. Timothy McVeigh

c. Ted Bundy

d. Pretty Boy Floyd

29. Meathead, Lionel, and Stretch Cunningham could be found on:

a. *Duffy's Tavern*

b. *All in the Family*

c. *The Odd Couple*

d. *In Living Color*

e. *Sanford and Son*

30. The "Hippy Dippy Weatherman" was the creation of:

a. Redd Foxx

b. Richard Pryor

c. George Carlin

d. Carrot Top

e. the Smothers Brothers

f. Chevy Chase

31. In the mid-'60s, this group wrote a letter to the Defense Department, volunteering to serve as a "gorilla unit" in Vietnam, but only if they were not subject to military supervision. That group was:

a. the Veterans of Foreign Wars

b. the Young Americans for Freedom

c. the Hell's Angels

d. Alcoholics Anonymous

e. the Silent Majority

32. In 1995, in a political crusade for moral values in media, Bob Dole extolled the virtues of an Arnold Schwarzenegger movie that featured ninety-four killings. That movie praised by Dole was:

a. *Total Recall*

b. *True Lies*

c. *Last Action Hero*

d. *Terminator II*

e. *Kindergarten Cop*

33. In the early 1970s, segregationist and presidential wannabee George Wallace made campaign appearances supported by the entire cast of:

a. *Hair*

b. *Hee Haw*

c. *The Beverly Hillbillies*

d. 1776

e. *Petticoat Junction*

34. *National Lampoon* magazine was launched in:

a. 1960

b. 1970

c. 1980

35. Cheeky lad. "Those of you in the cheap seats—clap your hands. The rest of you just rattle your jewelry." These words were spoken at a Royal Command Performance in London in 1963. The speaker was:

a. Jerry Lewis

b. John Lennon

c. Mick Jagger

d. Monty Python

e. Anthony Newley

f. Tom Jones

36. Spanky, Alfalfa, and Buckwheat were characters in:

a. *The Dead End Kids*

b. *The Little Rascals*

c. *The Kids in the Hall*

d. *New Kids on the Block*

e. *The Katzenjammer Kids*

f. *KidnPlay*

37. "Transfusion," "Monster Mash," "Purple People Eater," and "Itsy Bitsy Teeny Weeny Yellow Polka Dot Bikini."

In the 1950s, such songs were known in the record business as:

a. race records

b. loony tunes

c. novelty records

d. laugh tracks

e. specialty records

f. chuckle numbers

38. Of the following, which was not one of the Bing Crosby/Bob Hope "Road" pictures?

a. *The Road to Mandalay*

b. *The Road to Rio*

c. *The Road to Bali*

d. *The Road to Zanzibar*

e. *The Road to Utopia*

f. *The Road to Singapore*

39. "People are dying these days who never died before," was an observation made by Ezzard Charles in the early 1950s. Mr. Charles is best remembered as:

a. a philosopher

b. an artist

c. a heavyweight boxing champ

d. a Supreme Court justice

e. president, Bank of America

f. Eisenhower cabinet member

**40.** "It's not my job, man," is the best-remembered line associated with meteoric comedian:

a. Stepin Fetchit

b. Sinbad

c. Freddie Prinze

d. Richard Belzer

e. Cheech Marin

f. Dick Gregory

**41.** "The Nazz" was a classic beatnik comedy routine by Lord Buckley, hipster royalty. The '50s routine was about:

a. hairstyles

b. Jesus Christ

c. Oreos

d. television evangelists

e. Marlon Brando

f. Tarzan

**42.** David Letterman made a very rare movie appearance in the film:

a. *Cabin Boy*

b. *Black Sheep*

c. *Dumb and Dumber*

d. *The Adventures of Ford Fairlane*

e. *Down Periscope*

**43.** For a time in 1996, the book *Rush Limbaugh Is a Big Fat Idiot* was number one on *The New York Times* best-seller list. Its author was:

a. Bill Maher

b. Al Franken

c. Mark Russell

d. Dennis Miller

e. Molly Ivins

**44.** "The Streak" was a '70s hit inspired by the fad of streaking. The song was written and performed by:

a. the Flamin' Groovies

b. Ray Stevens

c. the Village People

d. Duck's Breath Mystery Theater

e. Gary Muledeer

f. Jim Stafford

**45.** Minnie Pearl, comic star of the Grand Ol' Opry for half a century, hailed from the hick town known as:

a. Bug Tussle

b. Union Gap

c. Mount Idy

d. Grinder's Switch

e. Pea Holler

f. Dogpatch

**46.** Court jester to Ken Kesey's Merry Pranksters was quintessential hippie and ice cream flavor:

a. Mellow Yellow

b. Cherry Garcia

c. Wavy Gravy

d. Chubby Hubby

e. Raspberry Swirl

f. Suzy Creamcheese

**47. Lumpy Rutherford, Miss Landers, Whitey Whitney, and Mrs. Rayburn were all characters on:**

a. *Make Room for Daddy*

b. *That Girl*

c. *The Andy Griffith Show*

d. *Leave It to Beaver*

e. *Ozzie and Harriet*

f. *The Simpsons*

**48. During WWII, Sergeant Bill Mauldin's comic strip soldiers depicted the trials of the average G.I. Those two comic strip soldiers were:**

a. Willie and Joe

b. Arnie and Hap

c. Vinnie and Bill

d. Captain America and Billy

e. Dickens and Fenster

f. Mutt and Jeff

**49. That military equipment popularly known during World War II as a Mae West was:**

a. a torpedo

b. a Jeep bumper

c. a bazooka

d. a lifeboat

e. a life jacket

f. a depth charge

**50. "The Secret Life of Walter Mitty" is a famous short story classic by humorist:**

a. E. B. White

b. Walter Mitty

c. Hoagy Carmichael

d. James Thurber

e. Garrison Keillor

f. Ray Blount

**51. In Charlie Chaplin's 1940 film satire, *The Great Dictator*, the character based on Adolf Hitler was called:**

a. Arnold Ziffel

b. Adenoid Hynkel

c. Adolph Zukor

d. Arbuthnot Hackenfuss

e. Adolph Scheisskopf

**52. Take a guess. Jazz saxophone giant John Coltrane was known for his very long solos. Some of those solos lasted as long as three hours. Coltrane once complained that he just couldn't find a way to stop. Colleague Miles Davis replied:**

a. "Think of sleep."

b. "Give yourself four more bars."

c. "Take the horn out of your mouth."

d. "Think of the band, man."

53. "Mr. Natural" (the "Keep on truckin' " figure) is the emblematic '60s cartoon creation of:

a. Lynda Barry

b. Matt Groening

c. Robert Crumb

d. Peter Max

e. Virgil Partch

54. Comic Ellen DeGeneres wrote a best-selling book in the 1990s. Its title was:

a. *What I'm Going to Do, I Think*

b. *I'm Not a Nut. Elect Me*

c. *Men . . . and Other Annoyances*

d. *My Point, and I Do Have One*

55. It's usually quoted as, "You cannot govern a country with 265 varieties of cheese." It's a better quotation than what was actually said, which was: "You cannot ignore a country with 265 varieties of cheese." The man who said it was:

a. Mort Sahl

b. Charles DeGaulle

c. Maurice Chevalier

d. Papa Doc Duvalier

e. François Mitterand

56. His companions were White Fang and Black Tooth. He was:

a. Pee Wee Herman

b. Soupy Sales

c. Captain Kangaroo

d. Buffalo Bob

e. Henny Youngman

f. Winky Dink

57. It caused a bit of controversy in the mid-1990s when a sitcom star was asked to be a guest editor at *The New Yorker*. That guest editor was:

a. Harry Anderson

b. Candace Bergen

c. John Larroquette

d. Roseanne

e. Julia Louis-Dreyfus

f. Paula Poundstone

58. This comedian/social critic wrote a book in the 1960s entitled *Nigger*. His objective was to make the word so commonplace as to rob it of the power to hurt. It didn't work, apparently. The writer was:

a. Godfrey Cambridge

b. Redd Foxx

c. Mantan Moreland

d. Bill Cosby

e. Richard Pryor

f. Dick Gregory

59. The best-known and most loved Mexican funnyman of the century was:

a. Cantinflas

b. Canseco

c. Carreras

d. Carrillo

e. Castillo

f. Carranza

**60.** The British satirical novelist who wrote *Lucky Jim, Girl 20, The Green Man*, and *Jake's Thing*, among others. The father of Martin. His name was:

a. William Golding

b. Anthony Burgess

c. Kingsley Amis

d. Ben Kingsley

e. Salman Rushdie

f. P. G. Wodehouse

**61.** A popular radio character of the 1940s, created by "Funny Girl" Fanny Brice, was:

a. Baby Leroy

b. Baby Snooks

c. Baby Huey

d. Baby Bubbles

**62.** *You'll Never Get Rich* was a 1950s sitcom. It was recycled into a major motion picture in the 1990s. The lead character in the '50s and '90s versions was:

a. Richie Rich

b. Sergeant Bilko

c. Jed Clampett

d. Gomer Pyle

e. Sergeant Preston

f. Corporal Klinger

**63.** Writing in the 1930s, Nathanael West was one of the century's first literary practitioners of black comedy. Of the following, which is not one of his novels?

a. *Miss Lonelyhearts*

b. *The Day of the Locusts*

c. *A Confederacy of Dunces*

d. *A Cool Million*

**64.** Of the following people, which was better known in the 1970s as "the Galloping Gourmet"?

a. Martha Graham

b. Graham Greene

c. Graham Nash

d. Graham Kerr

e. Martha Stewart

f. Gram Parsons

**65.** Recipe for a midnight movie cult classic: Mix together one forbidding mansion, a young couple with car trouble, a dark and stormy night, a transvestite, and plenty of audience participation and you have:

a. *The Attack of the Killer Tomatoes*

b. *Eraserhead*

c. *The Rocky Horror Picture Show*

d. *The Texas Chainsaw Massacre*

e. *The Night of the Living Dead*

66. The year was 1952. When both she and the character she played on TV became "pregnant," CBS censors would not allow the word to be spoken on the air. The real child was a girl, but the television child was a boy. If I tell you any more, it will be too obvious that the mother was:

a. Gale Storm

b. Carole Burnett

c. Lucille Ball

d. Imogene Coca

e. Ann Sothern

67. "Smoking kills. If you're killed, you've lost a very important part of your life." It was a public service announcement, and the words were extemporized by an actress and Princeton graduate who made her controversial first film, *Pretty Baby*, when she was barely thirteen years old. Her name was:

a. Carol Baker

b. Drew Barrymore

c. Jody Foster

d. Susan Sarandon

e. Brooke Shields

f. Ally Sheedy

68. A quick study. In 1995, this rock star released an album called *HIStory*. Lyrics included the phrases "Jew me" and "kike me." A few days after the inevitable storm of protest came the equally inevitable press release that said, in part: "I have come to understand over the past days that these words are considered antisemitic." The quick study rock star was:

a. Cat Stevens

b. Michael Jackson

c. Courtney Love

d. Bruce Springsteen

e. Snoop Doggy Dog

69. Surely among the century's funniest men, he was born William Claude Dukenfield, but he is remembered as:

a. Bob Hope

b. George Burns

c. Milton Berle

d. W. C. Fields

e. Robin Williams

f. Red Skelton

70. Highbrow French film critics proclaimed him a genius and the French government gave him a medal, but most Americans thought that was a joke, though he was many people's guilty pleasure. He was born Joseph Levitch, but he is remembered as:

a. Steve Martin

b. Joe E. Lewis

c. Jerry Lewis

d. Jim Carrey

e. Charlie Chaplin

f. Woody Allen

71. "Fat Albert" and "Old Weird Harold" were the comic creations of:

a. Jonathan Winters

b. Red Skelton

c. Bill Cosby

d. Jon Lovitz

e. Huntz Hall

f. Richard Pryor

72. Before political correctness. In 1940, this radio humorist compared smoking and chewing tobacco: "When you smoke, you're likely to burn yourself to death; with chewing tobacco the worst you can do is drown a midget." He later had a famous radio feud with Jack Benny. He was:

a. George Burns

b. The Great Gildersleeve

c. Red Skelton

d. Groucho Marx

e. Fred Allen

f. Skinny Ennis

73. In 1942, his recording of "The Fuhrer's Face" was punctuated with a Bronx cheer. For a couple of decades, he made fun of popular songs with his band the City Slickers. He was:

a. Kay Kaiser

b. Spike Jones

c. Spike Milligan

d. Artie Shaw

e. Victor Borge

f. Spike Lee

74. She was most noted for her roles in "screwball" comedies of the 1930s, including *It Happened One Night*, for which she won an Academy Award. She was:

a. Jean Arthur

b. Lucille Ball

c. Claudette Colbert

d. Katharine Hepburn

e. Barbara Stanwyck

f. Joan Blondell

75. And it still holds true today. Speaking in favor of continuing Prohibition in 1929, this American industrial giant said, "Nobody wants to fly with a drunken aviator." Among other accomplishments, he developed the V-8 engine in 1932. He was:

a. Walter P. Chrysler

b. Henry Ford

c. Preston T. Tucker

d. Harley Earl

e. Igor Sikorsky

76. After a dinner party in 1964, Groucho Marx referred to his host as "the British poet from St. Louis." It's an accurate description of the poet named:

a. W. H. Auden

b. Ezra Pound

c. T. S. Eliot

d. Stephen Spender

e. e.e. cummings

f. A. E. Housman

**77.** Those Darn Poets, Part II. In 1955, the Ford Motor Company sought out an American poet for help in naming a new model. Among the names that poet submitted were the Ford "Utopian Turtletop," the Ford "Faberge," the Ford "Mongoose Civique," and the Ford "Pastelogram." Ultimately, the company ignored all the poet's suggestions and chose the name "Edsel," after Henry Ford's son. The poet, also from St. Louis, won a Pulitzer Prize for her *Collected Poems* in 1951, and she was a noted fan of the Brooklyn Dodgers. Her name was:

a. Marianne Moore

b. Amy Lowell

c. Sylvia Plath

d. Maya Angelou

e. Elizabeth Bishop

f. Louise Bogan

**78.** The Keystone Kops left an iconographic image of the silent movie period between 1912 and 1920. They were called "Keystone" Kops because:

a. the films were made in Pennsylvania, the Keystone State

b. the main "Kop" was played by an actor named Kent Keystone

c. the films were made at the Keystone Production Studio

**79.** Lanford, Illinois, and Wellman Plastics are details that might help you identify the television situation comedy known as:

a. *Moonlighting*

b. *Roseanne*

c. *Married . . . With Children*

d. *Moesha*

e. *Martin*

f. *Green Acres*

**80.** On stage in the late 1940s, and in the subsequent movie adaptation, Elwood P. Dowd's best friend was:

a. Irma

b. Flicka

c. Barney

d. Bill

e. Harvey

f. Mame

**81.** This comedian/impressionist had a hugely successful comedy album in 1963, but he was little heard of after the assassination of John Kennedy, his most successful impersonation. He was:

a. David Frye

b. Frank Gorshin

c. Fred Travalena

d. Vaughn Meader

e. Rich Little

f. Will Jordan

**82.** The writer who gave the century Jeeves and Bertie was:

a. P. G. Wodehouse

b. A. J. Liebling

c. J. R. R. Tolkien

d. A. L. Rouse

e. Evelyn Waugh

f. Agatha Christie

**83.** In 1943, Jimmy Durante had his nose insured for fifty thousand dollars. A gag line associated with Durante was:

a. "Damned if I know"

b. "Everybody wants to get into the act"

c. "Wanna buy a duck?"

d. "Mom liked you best"

e. "Get outta here, kid, ya bother me"

**84.** In 1957, she said of herself: "I'm as pure as the driven slush." On another occasion, a man said he hadn't seen her in over forty years. She said: "I thought I told you to wait in the car." In addition to her wit, she is remembered for a husky voice and roles in such films as *Lifeboat* and *My Sin*. She was:

a. Mae West

b. Tallulah Bankhead

c. Jean Harlow

d. Carole Lombard

e. Rita Hayworth

f. Susan Hayward

**85.** "Bean," "berry," "iron man," "plunk," "rock," and "kelp." In the 1920s, these were all slang words for:

a. baseballs

b. drugs

c. dollar bills

d. homosexuals

e. professional wrestlers

f. outhouses

**86.** Blondie and Dagwood have been around since 1933. It would have been difficult to avoid exposure to them if you lived in the last two-thirds of the twentieth century. If you were so exposed, you'll recall that the Bumsteads' neighbors are:

a. Fred and Wilma

b. Ed and Trixie

c. Herb and Tootsie

d. the Kramdens

e. the Flanders

f. the Bickersons

**87.** *Amos 'n' Andy* hit the radio airwaves in 1929, and it was never absent until the show moved to television in 1951. That's a big piece of cultural territory, even if many came to find it riddled with racist stereotyping. If you know your culture, you'll recall that Amos and Andy's last names were:

a. Brown and Jones

b. Jackson and Johnson

c. Riley and Rustin

d. King and Prince

e. Capulet and Montague

f. Ruby and Kingfish

88. He was one who helped make the 1990s such a tacky time. A radio talk show host, he made jokes about President Clinton's alleged sexual adventures at a 1996 press dinner—and the first lady was on the dais at the time. He was:

a. Howard Stern

b. Rush Limbaugh

c. Mark Russell

d. Don Imus

89. Harold Lloyd is not as well-remembered as some other screen comics of the silent era, but he kept the world laughing in the 1920s. In the following list, which film is the Harold Lloyd classic?

a. *Safety Last*

b. *The General*

c. *The Kid*

d. *The Life of the Party*

e. *Way Out West*

90. Will Rogers helped us keep our sanity in the '20s and '30s. Among his remembered lines: "My folks didn't come over on the *Mayflower*, but they were there to meet the boat." He was born in:

a. Wyoming

b. Texas

c. Indian Territory

d. Montana

e. Arkansas

f. Alabama

91. The first movie Mel Brooks directed was:

a. *History of the World, Part I*

b. *Blazing Saddles*

c. *Young Frankenstein*

d. *The Producers*

e. *Silent Movie*

92. Political satirist Mort Sahl is credited with asking a question that has stuck in the national consciousness. That question: "Would you buy a used car from this man?" What man?

a. Everett Dirksen

b. Joseph McCarthy

c. Barry Goldwater

d. Lyndon Johnson

e. Richard Nixon

f. Spiro Agnew

93. It's an oft-repeated observation made by playwright/producer George S. Kaufman. Fill in the blank.

"_____ is something that closes on Saturday night."

a. The bank

b. Satire

c. Musical comedy

d. Melodrama

e. Quality

f. Avant garde theater

94. Among other things, this novelist created the Tralfamadorians and the doomsday agent known as Ice Nine. He was:

a. Arthur C. Clarke

b. P. J. O'Rourke

c. Thomas Pynchon

d. Kurt Vonnegut

e. Ray Bradbury

f. Isaac Asimov

95. Peppermint Patty was a character in the comic strip called:

a. Calvin and Hobbes

b. Peanuts

c. Dilbert

d. Mutt and Jeff

e. Gasoline Alley

f. Dick Tracy

96. Lots of people know that Mickey Mouse first appeared in 1928, but fewer know that Donald Duck was first seen in:

a. 1934

b. 1944

c. 1954

d. 1964

97. Of the following, which was not one of the Marx Brothers?

a. Gummo

b. Zeppo

c. Jocko

d. Groucho

e. Harpo

f. Chico

98. Memory of her is slipping away, but she won acclaim on Broadway in 1946 and an Oscar in 1950 for her role as a dumb blonde in George S. Kaufman's *Born Yesterday*. She was:

a. Judy Canova

b. Judy Holliday

c. June Haver

d. Zazu Pitts

e. June Havoc

f. Imogene Coca

99. In 1925, W. C. Fields suggested that his tombstone should read:

a. "Dying's easy; comedy's hard."

b. "On the whole, I'd rather be in Philadelphia."

c. "It's not that I'm afraid to die. I just don't want to be there when it happens."

d. "Comedy is not pretty."

## 100. "Thanks for the Memories" was the theme song for:

a. Allen Funt's *Candid Camera*

b. Jack Benny

c. *The Colgate Comedy Hour*

d. Bob Hope

e. Milton Berle's *Texaco Star Theatre*

## ANSWERS

1. Harding turned down the role because: a. she didn't approve of Woody's morals.

2. "This is another fine mess" was uttered by: a. Oliver Hardy.

3. Nixon said "sock it to me" on: c. *Laugh-In.*

4. Keillor created the mythical town of: d. Lake Woebegon.

5. "He's so dumb . . ." was a Johnson reference to: c. Gerald Ford.

6. Paar's catchphrase was: d. "I kid you not."

Never Give a Sucker an Even Break
W. C. Fields, 1879–1946. Also known as: Otis J. Cribblecoblis, Mahatma Kane Jeeves, Larson E. Whipsnade, Egbert Souse, Cuthbert J. Twillie, and the Great McGonigle.

An oft-told tale has it that Fields was found reading the Bible shortly before his death in 1946.

"What in the world are you doing reading the Bible," asked the surprised friend.

"Looking for loopholes," Fields replied, "looking for loopholes."

\* \* \*

7. Mencken's "no ideas/not a nuisance" was about: b. Calvin Coolidge.

8. The one who didn't render unto Caesar was: d. Lenny Bruce.

9. The Chaplin character was: c. the Little Tramp.

10. Letterman's production company was: d. World Wide Pants.

11. First successful daily comic strip was: f. *Mutt and Jeff.*

12. The one who never toured with Bob Hope was: e. Debbie Harry.

13. Gildersleeve was a: b. politician.

14. Sellers started on: a. *The Goon Show.*

15. "What? Me Worry?" belongs to: d. Alfred E. Newman.

16. Kramer's first name was: d. Kozmo.

17. "T&A" was a comedy routine by: e. Lenny Bruce.

18. "I'm Gumby" was a line associated with: f. Eddie Murphy.

19. "We have met the enemy and he is us" is from: e. *Pogo.*

20. The man who said he "would never belong to a club that would have me as a member" was: b. Groucho Marx.

21. *Funny Girl* was based on the life of: a. Fanny Brice.

22. ". . . capitalists . . . too damn greedy." These words were uttered by: f. Herbert Hoover.

23. Easy one. Ace Ventura was a: c. "pet" detective.

24. Twain's birth and death years were also years when: b. Halley's comet streaked across the skies.

25. *The General* starred: c. Buster Keaton.

26. Martin's '80s bestseller was: d. *Cruel Shoes.*

27. Goulding and Elliott were: c. Bob and Ray.

28. The witness, Michael Fortier, was talking about: b. Timothy McVeigh, the perpetrator of the bloodiest act of terrorism ever committed on American soil.

29. Meathead et al. were to be found on: b. *All in the Family.*

30. "The Hippy Dippy Weatherman" was created by: c. George Carlin.

31. The "gorilla unit" volunteers were: c. the Hell's Angels.

32. Family values according to Dole: b. *True Lies.*

33. Wallace was accompanied by the cast of: b. *Hee Haw*.

34. *National Lampoon* was launched in: b. 1970.

35. "...just rattle your jewelry" was suggested by: b. John Lennon.

36. Spanky and the gang were in: b. *The Little Rascals*.

37. "Transfusion" et al. were known as: c. novelty records.

38. Bing and Bob did not make: a. *The Road to Mandalay*.

39. Ezzard Charles was: c. a heavyweight champ.

40. "It's not my job" belonged to '70s comedian: c. Freddie Prinze.

41. "The Nazz" referred to the Nazarene: b. Jesus Christ.

42. Letterman showed up for friend Chris Elliott in: a. *Cabin Boy*.

43. The Limbaugh book author was: b. Al Franken.

44. "The Streak" was written and performed by: b. Ray Stevens.

45. Minnie Pearl hailed from: d. Grinder's Switch.

46. Court jester to the Pranksters: c. Wavy Gravy, aka Hugh Romney.

47. Lumpy et al. were characters on: d. *Leave It to Beaver*.

48. Bill Mauldin created: a. Willie and Joe.

49. A Mae West was: e. a life jacket.

50. "Walter Mitty" was the creation of: d. James Thurber.

51. The character based on Hitler was called: b. Adenoid Hynkel.

52. Miles told Trane: c. "Take the horn out of your mouth."

53. "Mr. Natural" was the work of: c. Robert Crumb.

54. DeGeneres's book was: d. *My Point, and I Do Have One*.

55. The leader of a country "with 265 varieties of cheese" was: b. Charles DeGaulle.

56. The pal of White Fang and Black Tooth was: b. Soupy Sales.

57. The sitcom guest editor of *The New Yorker* was: d. Roseanne.

58. The author of *Nigger* was: f. Dick Gregory.

59. The Mexican funnyman was:
a. Cantinflas.

60. The British novelist who wrote *Lucky Jim* was: c. Kingsley Amis.

61. Funnywoman Brice created: b. Baby Snooks.

62. *You'll Never Get Rich* featured:
b. Sergeant Bilko.

63. The novel West didn't write was:
c. *A Confederacy of Dunces.*

64. "The Galloping Gourmet" was:
d. Graham Kerr.

65. The cult classic in question was:
c. *The Rocky Horror Picture Show.*

66. The TV star pregnant in '52 was:
c. Lucille Ball.

67. That antismoking Princeton grad was:
e. Brooke Shields.

68. "Jew me" and "kike me" were lyrics initially thought inoffensive by: b. Michael Jackson.

69. Dukenfield is, of course: d. W. C. Fields.

70. Joseph Levitch was: c. Jerry Lewis.

71. "Fat Albert" and "Old Weird Harold" were created by: c. Bill Cosby.

72. The man who feuded with Jack Benny was: e. Fred Allen.

73. "The Fuhrer's Face" was a contribution to the war effort by:
b. Spike Jones.

\*   \*   \*

Claudette Colbert
In a 1932 film, she was billed as "Poppea, the worst woman in Rome."

In a 1933 film, she was Mimi Benton, billed as the worst woman in New York.

In 1934, she played a sophisticated and emancipated woman and won an Academy Award for *It Happened One Night*, which film critic Pauline Kael later called "the *Annie Hall* of its day."

*Annie Hall* was the *Sleepless in Seattle* of its day. And so on . . .

74. The Oscar winner for *It Happened One Night* was: c. Claudette Colbert.

75. The V-8 was developed by: b. Henry Ford.

76. "The British poet from St. Louis" was: c. T. S. Eliot.

77. The poet who supplied the fanciful automobile names was: a. Marianne Moore.

78. The Keystone Kops were so called because: c. the films were made at the Keystone Production Studio.

79. Wellman Plastics in Lanford could be found on: b. *Roseanne*.

80. Elwood's friend was: e. Harvey.

81. When Kennedy was killed, it was over for: d. Vaughn Meader.

82. Jeeves and Bertie were created by: a. P. G. Wodehouse.

83. Durante's phrase was: b. "Everybody wants to get into the act."

84. The star of *Lifeboat*, was: b. Tallulah Bankhead.

85. "Bean," "berry," etc. were slang for: a. baseballs.

86. The Bumsteads' neighbors are: c. Herb and Tootsie.

87. Amos and Andy's last names were: a. Brown and Jones.

88. The raunchy radio show host was: d. Don Imus.

89. The Harold Lloyd classic was: a. *Safety Last*.

90. Rogers was born in what was then: c. Indian Territory (now Oklahoma).

91. First Mel Brooks movie: d. *The Producers* (1968).

92. Sahl asked if we'd buy a used car from: e. Richard Nixon.

93. What closed on Saturday night was: b. satire.

94. Tralfamadorians were thought up by: d. Kurt Vonnegut.

95. Peppermint Patty was a character in: b. *Peanuts*.

96. Donald Duck turned up in: a. 1934.

97. Not one of the Marx Brothers was: c. Jocko.

98. The Star of *Born Yesterday* was: b. Judy Holliday.

99. W. C. Fields's epitaph: b. "On the whole, I'd rather be in Philadelphia."

100. "Thanks for the Memories" was the theme song for: d. Bob Hope.

Scoring: Humor, it is said, is delicate, a matter of exquisite timing. It's also said that some things are funny only if you're present when they occurred. For many readers, some of these funny things and people happened long before you showed up. For those reasons, I've set the bar fairly low on this series of questions. If you knew more than half of these, count yourself a right jolly person who has had a goodly share of laughter as you've made your way through your portion of the century. If you scored below 30 correct, however, you've missed some of the compensatory laughter the century had to offer.

# 16

# The Bottom Line

*It is a very cynical century we find ourselves in.*

—*J A M E S   L E E   B U R K E ,   1 9 9 6*

"The bottom line." As a metaphor, it became a cliché in the 1980s, that decade of arbitragers, junk-bond jugglers, and tax evaders. Would we need an operation? Were we going to have to work over the weekend? Did we have relationship troubles? Whatever the problem at hand, we wanted "the bottom line." As is the case with all clichés, we lost the source of the comparison; we came to forget that we were talking about a balance sheet, an adding up of figures. It expressed our national impatience, our desire to get to the point, to convert complexity into simple addition.

Which, incidentally, is what this chapter asks you to do. In each of the tests that follow, you are to use your knowledge and your memory to produce answers in the form of numbers. If you've got those numbers right, they will lead you to the "bottom line," the correct number for each set of ten questions. If you don't know every number, the numbers you do know can help you deduce the numbers you don't know.

Do you know your century? It all adds up. You do the math, and proceed to the bottom line. (Degree of difficulty is 4 + 4.)

## SEQUENCE 1

If you have all answers correct in the following sequence, the bottom line will equal 61.

1. Number of thumps "Kato" Kaelin heard on the wall of his guest quarters on the night of the Brown/Goldman murders _____

2. Number of Oscars won by Tom Hanks (as of 1996) _____

3. Number of times Theodore Roosevelt was elected president _____

4. Number of U.S. presidents assassinated this century _____

5. Major league baseball seasons lost to strikes _____

6. Number of Oscars won by Spencer Tracy _____

7. Number of presidential terms served by Jimmy Carter _____

8. Number of times Franklin Roosevelt was elected president _____

9. Number of states in the Union when the century began _____

10. Number of Disney theme parks in 1950 _____

**Your bottom line is** _____

## SEQUENCE 2

This is an easy sequence, but only if you know your century. Add up the numbers you supply (don't include the "19" supplied in the first two slots), and if you arrive at the right answers, the bottom line will be 509.

11. The year Martin Luther King was assassinated was 19_____

12. The year Pearl Harbor was bombed was 19_____

13. The year Nixon resigned from office was 19_____

14. The year the Beatles first came to America was 19_____

15. The year Neil Armstrong stepped onto the moon was 19_____

16. The year of the armistice in World War I 19_____

17. The year Elvis Presley died was 19_____

18. The year Kennedy defeated Nixon was                    19____

19. The year Roosevelt defeated Hoover was                    19____

20. The year of San Francisco's first major quake was              19____

**Your bottom line is**            ____

## SEQUENCE 3

Know much about pop music? The following questions draw on a knowledge of numbers derived from music and musicians. If you get this set of answers right, your bottom line will total 180.

21. According to the song by Three Dog Night, it is the "loneliest number you will ever do"              ____

22. How old is the girl in the Beatles' song called "I Saw Her Standing There"              ____

23. One of Chuck Berry's hits, "Sweet Little ____ "

24. Before he was a solo act, Michael Jackson was in a group called the Jackson              ____

25. Freshmen, Seasons, Tops. How many people in all those groups combined              ____

26. Janis Joplin, Jimi Hendrix, and Jim Morrison all died at the same age. What age was that?              ____

27. Number of times Elvis Presley married              ____

28. The first hour mentioned in the lyrics to "Rock Around the Clock" is              ____

29. In 1966, ? (Question Mark) and the Mysterians had a hit song about crying. The title was specific about the number of tears. How many tears?              ____

30. Number of Nirvana albums released before the death of Kurt Cobain              ____

**Your bottom line is**              ____

## SEQUENCE 4

In the following set of ten, the correct numbers add up to 60.

31. Accused of being communists, called before the House Un-American Activities Committee in the early 1950s, they came to be known as the Hollywood              ____

32. Called to account for disturbances during the Democratic Convention in 1968, they came to be known as the Chicago ____

33. Chairman Mao's widow was sentenced to death for counterrevolutionary crimes. She was accused with others who came to be known as the Gang of ____

34. Sinatra and his "Rat Pack" starred together in a movie called *Ocean's* ____

35. He abdicated the throne of England in 1936. How many King Edwards came before him? ____

36. Total number of men who have played the Three Stooges ____

37. Number of brothers of John F. Kennedy ____

38. Number of Donald Duck's nephews ____

39. James Bond was Agent ____

40. Number of Bart Simpson's siblings (not counting Bart's evil twin brother) ____

**Your bottom line is** ____

## SEQUENCE 5

Try this series, unconnected by any discernible theme. The bottom line here adds up to 1,101.

41. D-Day took place on June ____

42. The day John Kennedy was shot was November ____

43. The "Day That Will Live in Infamy" was December ____

44. World War I ended on Armistice Day, November ____

45. Number of minutes missing during the mysterious gap on the Nixon Watergate tapes ____

46. George McGovern's 1972 VP choice Thomas Eagleton had undergone electroshock therapy. The percent McGovern said he would stand behind his choice was ____

47. Total number of daughters of presidents Ford, Kennedy, Nixon, Clinton, Carter, and Johnson ____

48. Total number of sons of presidents Ford, Kennedy, Nixon, Clinton, Carter, and Johnson ____

49. Lee Harvey Oswald was killed on November _____

50. Number of women Ronald Reagan married _____

**Your bottom line is** _____

## SEQUENCE 6

If you answer all ten correctly, your total will be 555.

J.F.K. Funeral Cortege

51. Number of new planets in our solar system discovered during the twentieth century _____

52. Number of poets who have read their work at twentieth-century presidential inaugurations _____

53. The French abortion pill, RU _____

54. Years Johnny Carson hosted *The Tonight Show* _____

55. Gangsters who died in Chicago's St. Valentine's Day Massacre of 1929 _____

56. Number of children in the Brady Bunch _____

57. Minutes of fame Andy Warhol said we'd all have _____

58. Kurt Vonnegut novel *Slaughterhouse* _____

59. Number of times Muhammad Ali won boxing's world heavyweight title _____

60. As of 1996, the number of Emmys won by soap opera veteran Susan Lucci (Erica on *All My Children*) _____

**Your bottom line** _____

## SEQUENCE 7

What follows is a little grab bag of questions about American politics. The correct answers add up to 59.

61. Percentage of votes cast that went to Bill Clinton in 1992 ____

62. Number of political parties to which Strom Thurmond and Ben Nighthorse Campbell have belonged, added together ____

63. Number of elective offices held by Colin Powell ____

64. Number of times Ross Perot entered the 1992 presidential race ____

65. Number of presidential elections won by Gerald Ford ____

66. Number of vice-presidential candidates who shared the ticket with McGovern in 1972 ____

67. Number of vice-presidents who served under FDR ____

68. Number of presidential elections won by Calvin Coolidge ____

69. Number of party affiliations under which Theodore Roosevelt sought the presidency ____

70. Number of times Newt Gingrich has been married ____

**Your bottom line is** ____

## SEQUENCE 8

You may not know all these, but it might be tempting to guess about the ones you don't know. You'll probably be close. The numbers you do know will help you make it all add up. Add only the numbers you supply. If it adds up correctly, the total will be 493.

71. Year American involvement in Vietnam ended 19____

72. Year Superman first appeared 19____

73. Year Mickey Mouse first appeared 19____

74. Year of the Gulf War 19____

75. Year of Lindbergh's solo transatlantic flight 19____

76. Year Jim Jones's followers committed mass suicide 19____

77. Year *Gone With the Wind* hit movie screens                    19____

78. Year *Wizard of Oz* hit movie screens                          19____

79. Year *Stagecoach* hit movie screens                            19____

80. Year *Citizen Kane* hit movie screens                          19____

**Your bottom line**                    ____

## SEQUENCE 9

Here are ten questions related only by the fact that they all concern twentieth-century people or events. If your answers add up correctly, that figure will total 83.

81. Rank of Babe Ruth in number of career home runs                ____

82. Number of African-American Supreme Court justices before Clarence Thomas                ____

83. The World War II heads of state who met at Yalta, Teheran, and Potsdam were known as the Big                ____

84. Number of Teenage Mutant Ninja Turtles                ____

85. Age of John Kennedy when he took office                ____

86. Number of Nixon vice-presidents                ____

87. Joseph Heller's first novel, *Catch*                ____

88. Chuck Yeager broke the sound barrier in a Bell X-                ____

89. Number of movies starring James Dean                ____

90. Number of twentieth-century wars that have resulted in more than fifty thousand American deaths                ____

**Your bottom line**                    ____

## SEQUENCE 10

Where necessary, round off your answers to the nearest (and higher) round number. If all goes well, your total will be 411.

91. Number of Mighty Morphin Power Rangers                ____

92. Years of Newt Gingrich's military service                ____

93. Years Rush Limbaugh served in the military ____

94. Years Bill Clinton served in the military (not counting time served as commander in chief) ____

95. Years of military service performed by John Wayne ____

96. Number of years the U.S. was engaged in WWII ____

97. Number of months the U.S. was engaged in WWI ____

98. Standard U.S. infantry weapon of World War II, The M- ____

99. Standard U.S. infantry weapon in Vietnam. The M- ____

100. Standard tour of duty in Vietnam, in days ____

**Your bottom line** ____

## ANSWERS

### SEQUENCE 1

1. Number of thumps "Kato" heard

2. Number of Oscars won by Tom Hanks

2

3. Number of times Theodore Roosevelt was elected president

1

4. Number of assassinated presidents

2

5. Number of seasons of major league baseball lost to strikes

1

6. Number of Oscars won by Spencer Tracy

2

7. Number of terms as president served by Jimmy Carter

1

8. Number of times FDR won the presidency

4

9. Number of states in the United States in 1900

45

10. Number of Disney theme parks in 1950

0

If you have all answers correct, the bottom line will equal

61.

3

## SEQUENCE 2

11. Martin Luther King assassinated

'68

12. Pearl Harbor bombed

'41

13. Year Nixon resigned

'74

14. The year the Beatles first came to America was

'64

15. The year Armstrong stepped onto the moon was

'69

16. The year World War I ended was

'18

17. The year Elvis Presley died was

'77

18. The year Kennedy defeated Nixon was

'60

19. The year Roosevelt defeated Hoover was

'32

20. San Francisco's first major quake was

'06

Add up the numbers you supplied. If you arrived at the right answers, the bottom line will be

509.

## SEQUENCE 3

21. The "loneliest number you will ever do"

1

22. In the Beatles song, "She was just

17

23. Chuck Berry's "Sweet Little

16

24. The Jackson

5

25. Freshmen plus Seasons plus Tops equals

12

26. Joplin, Hendrix, and Morrison all died at age

27

27. Presley marriages

1

28. The first hour in "Rock Around the Clock" is

1

29. How many tears?

96

30. Nirvana albums before the death of Cobain

4

If you've answered all questions correctly, the bottom line is

180

## SEQUENCE 4

31. The Hollywood

10

32. They came to be known as the Chicago

7

33. Chairman Mao's widow was part of the Gang of

4

34. Sinatra's "Rat Pack" movie was called *Ocean's*

11

35. Number of King Edwards before the one who abdicated

7

36. Number of men who have played Stooges

6

37. Number of brothers of John F. Kennedy

3

38. Number of Donald Duck's nephews

3

39. James Bond was, of course, Agent

007

40. Number of Bart Simpson's siblings

2

The correct answers will add up to

60

## SEQUENCE 5

41. D-Day took place on June

6

42. The day John Kennedy was shot was November

22

43. The "Day That Will Live in Infamy" was December

7

44. World War I ended on Armistice Day, November

11

45. Number of minutes missing during the mysterious gap on the Nixon Watergate tapes

18

46. George McGovern's 1972 VP choice Thomas Eagleton had undergone electroshock therapy. The percent McGovern said he would stand behind his choice was

1,000

47. Total number of daughters of presidents Ford, Kennedy, Nixon, Clinton, Carter, and Johnson

8

48. Total number of sons of presidents Ford, Kennedy, Nixon, Clinton, Carter, and Johnson

3

49. Lee Harvey Oswald was killed on November

24

50. Number of women Ronald Reagan married

2

The bottom line here adds up to

1,101

## SEQUENCE 6

51. New planets discovered in the twentieth century

1

52. Poets who have read at twentieth century inaugurations

3

53. The French abortion pill, RU

486

54. Years Johnny Carson hosted *The Tonight Show*

30

55. Gangsters who died on St. Valentine's Day

7

56. Number of children in the Brady Bunch

6

57. Minutes of fame Andy Warhol said we'd all have

15

58. Kurt Vonnegut novel *Slaughterhouse*

5

59. Times Ali won the world heavyweight title

3

60. Number of Emmys won by Susan Lucci

0

If you had these right, your answers totaled

556

## SEQUENCE 7

61. Percentage of votes for Clinton in 1992

43

62. Number of political parties to which Strom Thurmond and Ben Nighthorse Campbell have belonged, added together

4

63. Number of elective offices held by Colin Powell

0

64. Number of times Ross Perot entered the 1992 presidential race

2

65. Number of presidential elections won by Gerald Ford

0

66. Number of vice-presidential candidates who shared the ticket with McGovern in 1972

2

67. Number of vice-presidents who served under FDR

3

68. Number of presidential elections won by Calvin Coolidge

1

69. Number of party affiliations under which Theodore Roosevelt sought the presidency

2

70. Number of times Newt Gingrich has been married

2

If you had them all correct, your total should have been

59

## SEQUENCE 8

71. Year American involvement in Vietnam ended

'73

72. Year Superman first appeared

'38

73. Year Mickey Mouse first appeared

'28

74. Year of the Gulf War

'91

75. Year of Lindbergh's solo transatlantic flight

'27

76. Year Jim Jones's followers committed mass suicide

'78

77. Year *Gone With the Wind* hit movie screens

'39

78. Year *Wizard of Oz* hit movie screens

'39

79. Year *Stagecoach* hit movie screens

'39

80. Year *Citizen Kane* hit movie screens

'41

If you knew them all, the bottom line is

493.

**SEQUENCE 9**

81. Rank of Babe Ruth in career home runs

2

82. Number of African-American Supreme Court Justices before Clarence Thomas

1

83. The World War II heads of state who met at Yalta, Teheran, and Potsdam were know as the Big

3

84. Number of Teenage Mutant Ninja Turtles

3

85. Age of John Kennedy when he took office

43

86. Number of Nixon vice-presidents.

2

87. Joseph Heller's first novel, *Catch*

22

88. Chuck Yeager broke the sound barrier in a Bell X-

1

89. Number of movies starring James Dean

3

90. Number of twentieth-century wars that have resulted in more than fifty thousand American deaths.

3

If you figured all this out, the bottom line is

83.

**SEQUENCE 10**

91. Number of Mighty Morphin Power Rangers

6

92. Years of Newt Gingrich's military service

0

93. Years Rush Limbaugh served in the military

0

94. Years Bill Clinton served in the military

0

95. Years of military service performed by John Wayne

0

96. Number of years the U.S. was engaged in WWII

4

97. Number of months the U.S. was engaged in WWI

19

98. Standard U.S. infantry weapon of World War II, The M-

1

99. Standard U.S. infantry weapon in Vietnam. The M-

16

100. Standard tour of duty in Vietnam, in days

365

Your bottom line should total

411

Scoring: There are ten tests. If you made the numbers add up on half of them you're a mathematician of historical significance (and insignificance).

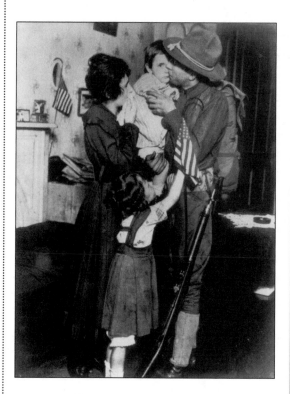

U.S. Recruit Leaves Family, World War I

# THE MORE THINGS CHANGED . . .

There is such a thing as a nation being so right that it does not need to convince others by force that it is right.

—Woodrow Wilson, 1915

I have said this before, but I shall say it again and again and again. Your boys are not going to be sent into any foreign wars.

—Franklin Roosevelt, 1940

We are not about to send American boys nine or ten thousand miles away from home to do what Asian boys ought to be doing for themselves.

—Lyndon Johnson, 1964

# 17

# The Best of Times/
# The Worst of Times

*Three ex-presidents: Carter, Ford, and Nixon—*
*See No Evil, Hear No Evil, and Evil.*

—BOB DOLE, 1980s

*The second half of the twentieth century will be known*
*as the age of Nixon.*

—BOB DOLE, 1990s

We have come to love "best/worst" lists. When the century closes, we will have had seventy-one years of Academy Awards and eighty years of Miss America pageants. The success of those cultural centerpieces—watched by billions all over the globe—has created dozens of imitations, and imitations of imitations. We are a score-keeping nation, and we love sizing things up. Best and worst lists either reaffirm our own opinions, or they prompt lively discussions.

Which is precisely what the next hundred questions are meant to do. The century bore witness to the best in us, and to the worst. Who decides what has been best and worst? Pardon the presumption, but in this book, the author does, not because I'm an expert, but because I've lived through a good chunk of this century, paid those particular dues, and have earned the right to an opinion (or a couple hundred opinions). But you needn't take these choices too seriously. After all, if the century has taught us anything it's that hardly anyone knows what the hell they're talking about anyway. And of course you are free to disagree with the

Miss America, 1921

best and worst selections I've made, but only if you can recall the best and worst people and things evoked in the questions that follow. Still, I have a feeling that most of you will agree with most of these choices.

We should do all we can to remember the best of our times, and to carry on discourse about what constitutes the best. And it is, perhaps, an even greater responsibility that we remember the worst. Though the concept of evil was not fashionable in our times, the reality of evil was plain to see. In Adolf Hitler, our century produced one of the worst men of all time, and there have been a raft of imitators in his wake, most

recently in the former Yugoslavia. It is difficult to think of a figure whose unqualified goodness serves as counterweight to Hitler's distinct evil, but the century has produced good people, and it may be that the goodness of our times was of the kind routinely ignored by history and derided by trends—the goodness of people who shouldered their responsibilities, loved their children, and lived their lives anonymously without bothering others. Lots of people did that, but they won't be chronicled in the questions below.

Each question is prefaced by a category that designates a superlative. Few readers will know all the answers. Of course, if you got them all right, that would be the best, and if you missed them all, that would be the worst. The task here is to avoid the latter extreme, and approach the former. (Level of difficulty: 6.)

## THE BEST AND THE WORST

1. Most idealistic, noble, and admirable mass act of voluntary courage:

In the Spanish Civil War, volunteers from all over the world formed a force to resist fascism in Spain. They were called _____ and the American contingent was called _____.

2. Most arrogant American military leader of the century:

In 1932, he ordered troops under his command to fire on former World War I comrades who'd marched to Washington to seek a speed-up on their pensions. He didn't die, he just faded away. He was _____.

## 3. Best rock 'n' roll album of the century:

It contains the songs "Honky Tonk Women" and "Midnight Rambler." The title of the album is _____.

## 4. Best jazz album of the century:

It features tracks entitled "So What?" and "Freddy the Freeloader." It was released in 1959. The title and the artist were _____.

## 5. Most stirring and memorable American oration of the century:

Martin Luther King delivered it in Washington. He said: "I have a dream," and he imparted that dream to the nation. He gave that speech while serving as the head of the SCLC, which was the
S _____ C _____
L _____ C _____.

## 6. Best song to come out of World War II:

Twenty years after it was a hit (for both Vera Lynn and Dinah Shore), Stanley Kubrick used it to close his film *Dr. Strangelove, Or How I Learned to Stop Worrying and Love the Bomb*. Name that tune. _____

## 7. Best adventure film of the century:

It was based on a novel by B. Traven. It starred

Humphrey Bogart as Fred C. Dobbs. It was directed by John Huston. That movie was _____.

## 8. Best comedy team of the century:

One was from England, and one was from Georgia. One of their films was *Babes in Toyland*. Name them. _____

## 9. Worst film director, by critical consensus:

He was himself the subject of a film. Johnny Depp played him in the title role of a 1994 film directed by Tim Burton. Among other really bad movies, he directed *Plan 9 From Outer Space*. Name him.

_____

## 10. Most acclaimed and influential American film of the century:

The key word is "Rosebud." The film was _____ and the director was _____.

## 11. Slimiest lawyer and all-around bad guy:

He prosecuted the Rosenbergs and served as counsel for Joe McCarthy during the period leading up to the Army/McCarthy hearings. Then he was a high-priced New York lawyer. His name? _____

## 12. Most enduring screen lovers:

"Of all the gin joints in all the world, why did she have to walk into mine?" Name the actor who says the line and the actress he is addressing.
_____ and _____

**13. Most self-aggrandizing, bigoted, and corrupt head of a federal agency (and that is a crowded contest):**

He was the czar of his agency from 1924 until 1972. When Lyndon Johnson was urged to force him to retire, Johnson declined, saying: "I'd rather have him on the inside of the tent pissing out than on the outside of the tent pissing in." Johnson was discussing _____.

**14. Most overblown trial of the century:**

Its jury was sequestered longer than any other in history. Do you really need a question in order to come up with the answer to this one? The man on trial was _____.

**15. Most notable American hero with Nazi sympathies:**

Think "Spirit of St. Louis," then name him. _____.

**16. Most overblown singer/songwriter of the second half of the century:**

"I Am . . . I Said" was one of his hits. "America" and "Cracklin' Rosie" were among dozens of others. He was _____.

**17. Worst American war crime of the Vietnam War, of those reported:**

It happened at My Lai. The lieutenant in command was _____.

**18. Most egregious example of justice publicly bought off:**

This pop singer paid hush money in the millions of dollars to the father of a boy he was accused of molesting. The singer? _____

**19. The most noble and dignified sports hero of the century:**

He beat Jimmy Connors at Wimbledon in 1975 and he later died of AIDS contracted from a blood transfusion. He courageously fought heart disease and racism. His name? _____

**20. Best-known American Indian athlete of the century:**

He won the Pentathlon in the 1912 Olympic Games, but he was forced to relinquish his medals after it was disclosed that he'd briefly played professional baseball and was therefore no longer an amateur athlete. He was _____.

**21. The meanest, nastiest SOB who ever played baseball:**

He was a bully, a racist, and a brawler. In 1912, he batted .420 for the Detroit Tigers. Tommy Lee Jones played him in a '90s movie. He was

_____.

**22. Greatest inspiration to nerds everywhere:**

The Seattle-based CEO of one of the most successful corporations of the century, in the 1990s he was reputed to be America's richest man. His name was _____.

**23. Best jazz composition of the century:**

Thelonious Monk wrote it, and nearly every jazz player since then has recorded it. Complete the first line of the lyrics written for it and you will have named that tune. "It begins to tell _____."

**24. Most annoying ego of the last quarter-century:**

His theme song was "Crazy," and he thought Republican operatives tried to mess up his daughter's wedding. _____

Stella!!!
 An actor's a guy who, if you ain't talking about him, ain't listening.

—MARLON BRANDO, 1974

**25. Most underrated western movie ever made:**

It was the only film Marlon Brando ever directed. _____

**26. The most powerful antiwar painting of the century:**

The painting is called *Guernica,* a place bombed by the Germans during the Spanish Civil War. Who was the painter? _____

**27. Best big-band song:**

Duke Ellington composed it, and its title tells how to get to Harlem. To get there, you " _____."

**28. Best novel to come out of World War II:**

It began Norman Mailer's career, and he drew upon his experience as an infantryman in the Pacific to write it. The title of that book was _____.

**29. Best novel to come out of World War I:**

It was written by Erich Maria Remarque and made into a memorable 1930 film starring Lew Ayres. It was _____.

**30. Best novel to come out of the war in Vietnam:**

It was Tim O'Brien's first novel. Name it. _____

**31. Best blues guitarist who wasn't B. B. King:**

He often teamed up with Jr. Wells. His '90s CD *Feels Like Rain* is a blues guitar showcase. He was _____.

**32. Best TV sitcom of the 1950s:**

Joyce Randolph played Trixie. _____

**33. Best TV sitcom of the 1960s:**

Otis the drunk was a recurring character. _____

**34. Best TV sitcom of the 1970s:**

The funeral of Chuckles the Clown was a classic episode. _____

**35. Best TV sitcom of the 1980s:**

Rhea Perlman played a recurring character. _____

**36. Best TV sitcom of the 1990s:**

It was a show "about nothing." _____

**37. Two comedians worthy of the term "genius":**

a. He was "the sick comedian" of the 1950s. _____

b. He set himself on fire while freebasing cocaine. _____

**38. Best visual record of the Depression years:**

Our memory of those times now is largely framed in her photographs. Name her. _____

**39. Movie actress whose beauty was most overrated by the media:**

Because she played in *Pretty Woman*, reporters decided she was one, though for all that, she was rather plain. _____

**40. Best gangster film of the century:**

James Caan played Sonny. _____

**41. Worst betrayal of the principle that no man is above the law:**

It was President Gerald Ford's first official act. _____

**42. Worst of the World War II war criminals:**

Though this is a fiercely competitive category, it is hard to think of anyone more evil than the chief SS physician at Auschwitz. His name? _____

**43. Actor of the '70s, '80s, and '90s most likely to shout his key lines:**

He won an Academy Award for *Scent of a Woman*, which, of course, featured high-decibel acting. _____

**44. Best display of dignified restraint in the face of relentless criticism:**

She wrote a book called *It Takes a Village*. _____

**45. Most principled and decent first lady:**

She resigned from the Daughters of the American Revolution when that group refused to let Marian

Anderson perform at Constitution Hall.

_____

### 46. Largest selling pop song written about both: a) a suicidal movie actress and b) a one-time princess.

Bernie Taupin was the co-writer. The song was

_____.

### 47. Most arrogant secretary of state and least-deserving recipient of the Nobel Peace Prize:

According to Bob Woodward, he prayed with Nixon in the final days of that administration.

_____

### 48. Best child actor of the century:

When he played Opie, he seemed like a real kid.

_____

### 49. Most handsome president, not counting JFK:

He died in office during one of the biggest political scandals in American history. His middle initial is "G." _____

### 50. Worst musical trend of the century:

Sugarhill Gang, Grandmaster Flash, and Run DMC were early exponents of the often numbing, misogynistic, repetitive, posturing music known as _____.

### 51. Most romantic revolutionary figure of the century:

In 1967, he was killed by the Bolivian army after he was captured, perhaps with the collusion of the CIA. _____

### 52. Most consistently inventive comic strip of the century:

It was drawn by Gary Larson, and it was called _____.

### 53. Best idea of the century which has yet to prove its value:

It was founded in San Francisco in October of 1945. _____

### 54. The "How Can We Miss You if You Won't Go Away" Award to dead celebrities whose careers keep going and going and going:

They each have their own postage stamp. He was born in Marion, Indiana; she was born in Los Angeles. You shouldn't need any more information to discern that he was _____ and she was _____.

### 55. The best novel about "the race issue" written in the last hundred years:

The year of publication was 1952. The author was Ralph Ellison. The novel was _____.

### 56. Lawyer with the worst "short-man complex":

In the O. J. Simpson trial, he questioned a witness "Marine to Marine." Robert Shapiro defended him in the longest drunk-driving trial in American history. He was _____.

## 57. Biggest jerk (East Coast, post-'50s division):

Think "Long Island Lolita," then name her boyfriend. _____

## 58. Biggest jerk (West Coast, post-'50s division):

In the '90s, he was elected to Congress from southern California . . . and the beat goes on. His name was _____.

## 59. Best example of a guy trying to impress a woman and getting in major trouble for his efforts:

The woman was an unsuccessful screenwriter, and she got him on tape using the "N" word ad nauseam. He was _____.

## 60. Most pathetic end of a war hero:

He was among the men who raised the flag on Mt. Surabachi. Tony Curtis played him in the movies; Johnny Cash sang a song about him. He died drunk on a Pima Indian reservation. He was

_____.

## 61. Best wakeup call, environmental division:

Rachel Carson wrote it. It was published in 1962. It helped popularize environmentalism. The book was _____.

## 62. Best American lawyer of the century:

He defended John Scopes, Eugene V. Debs, and Leopold and Loeb. He was _____.

## 63. The Hemingway "Grace Under Pressure" Award:

He was the man who integrated major league baseball, playing for the Brooklyn Dodgers despite intense hostility. _____.

## 64. The "Grace Under Pressure" Award, first runner-up:

He was the general manager of the Dodgers who hired the man who ended segregation in the major leagues. _____

## 65. Worst best-selling novel of the last quarter-century (deep and sensitive guy division):

It featured a photographer, a farm wife, and lots of overwrought prose. The title of that book was

_____.

## 66. Worst appeal for support by a U.S. president:

"I'm the only president you've got." Those were the words. Name the president. _____

## 67. Weakest qualifications for holding high office:

"I'm not a crook." Name the president who thus reassured the American people. _____

**68. Best ex-president of the century:**

His work with Habitat for Humanity and other philanthropic and humanitarian activities earned him more respect than he had while in office. He was _____.

**69. Our luckiest breaks.**

a. Had he not been elected, it is hard to imagine how badly things might have gone. His middle name was Delano. _____

b. Had he not backed down after Kennedy's ultimatum, the world might have been irradiated. That Soviet premier was _____.

**70. Happy Days:**

May 8, 1945, and August 14, 1945, were among the happiest days of the century. Why? _____

**71. Bad Stuff:**

Naphthenic and palmitic acids. Made by Dow Chemical. In combination the acids were more familiarly known as _____.

**72. Most influential noneconomic philosophy of the twentieth century:**

Sartre and Camus were among its best-known proponents. The philosophy was called _____.

**73. Worst poem read at a presidential inauguration:**

The poem was called "On the Pulse of Morning." The poet who wrote it and read it was _____.

**74. Most influential jazz pioneer:**

"Ornithology" was one of his tunes.

_____

**75. Best love poet of the century:**

He was sometimes a political exile from his Chilean homeland, and he was also the unlikely subject of a popular Italian movie of the 1990s.

_____

**76. Most obnoxious movie comedians since Jerry Lewis:**

a. He got his start on TV's *In Living Color,* before the movie biz took to paying him $20 million per picture. He was _____.

b. *A Thin Line Between Love and Hate* was as good an argument against movies as one could find. It starred _____.

**77. Best American conservationist of the first half-century:**

Ironically, he was an avid hunter. He founded the short-lived Bull Moose party. His name?

_____

**78. The "If At First You Don't Succeed" Award for the most indefatigable presidential candidate:**

He is all but forgotten now, but he was once the thirty-one-year-old Republican governor of Minnesota. Later, he would become something of a national joke as the "perennial candidate," running long-shot campaigns for the presidency from 1948 until 1987. Do you remember his name?

_____

## 79. Worst long-term legacies left by modern presidents:

a. (Erosion of public trust division.) He was born in Whittier, California _____

b. (Economic consequences division.) In eight years, he took us from being the world's largest creditor nation to being the world's largest debtor nation. After he left office, he took a $2 million fee from a Japanese company for an appearance there. _____

## 80. Profiles in courage. Among the century's best human beings (one question in twenty-five parts):

a. South African martyr, Steven _____

b. United Farm Worker leader, Cesar _____

c. Nicaraguan freedom fighter of the '30s, Augusto _____

d. Spanish Civil War heroine, known as La _____

e. He led a march to the sea for salt as part of his country's struggle for independence _____

f. Change agent author of *The Feminine Mystique* _____

g. The troubadour of the dustbowl, the slogan on his guitar read: "This machine kills fascists" _____

h. Often arrested, she led coal miners' strikes in the first decade of the century and was a courageous force for change until well into her nineties. Her slogan was, "Pray for the dead, but fight like hell for the living." Her first name was Mary, but she is remembered as _____.

i. "Don't mourn, organize" were the words left behind by this martyred troubadour of the IWW. His name? _____

j. It took rare courage for him to get the Pentagon Papers before the public. His name was _____.

k. He led an unsuccessful assassination attempt against Adolf Hitler in 1944. He (and more than two hundred others) paid the ultimate price. His name was Claus von _____.

l. This thirty-two-year-old Guatemalan woman won the Nobel Peace Prize in 1992 for her human rights work in that country. Her name was Rigoberta _____.

m. This truck driver was nearly killed in a thuggish beating during the riots following the Rodney King verdict in Los Angeles, but he didn't succumb to bitterness or race hate. His name was Reginald _____.

n. Her record of an adolescence spent hiding in an Amsterdam attic is a legacy of courage. Her name was _____.

Man and Tanks, 1989

o. Though his name is not generally known, the young Chinese man who stood in front of the tank in that peerless portrait of courage belongs in this list. He made his stand at _____ Square.

p. After her husband was assassinated, this woman took on the regime that killed him, and her courage prevailed. The name of this Philippine leader was _____.

q. Though few remember him, this Oregon senator was the earliest and most vigorous opponent of the war in Vietnam. That opposition got him vilified, and it cost him his Senate seat. His name was Wayne _____.

r. This British philosopher held to his pacifist convictions throughout a ninety-eight-year lifetime, and he was jailed for those convictions. He was also a leader in the movement for nuclear disarmament. His name was _____.

s. He was a Socialist party candidate for the presidency five times, and his opposition to American entry into World War I landed him in prison. While there, he garnered 1 million votes in the 1920 presidential election. His name?

_____

t. During the 1970s, this Australian pediatrician led a group called Physicians for Social Responsibility. She was a tireless speaker and advocate on behalf of the cause of nuclear disarmament. Her name was Helen _____

u. The decision to use atomic weapons against a civilian population had to have taken enormous courage. The man who made that decision was _____.

v. When this chain-smoking broadcaster took on Joseph McCarthy, it was a lonely act of courage. Later, at the end of his career, he served as head of the U.S. Information Agency. He was

_____.

w. This eloquent World War II leader inspired much courage through his own example and his soaring use of the English language, especially during the Battle of Britain. He was

_____.

x. Too little remembered now, she was the first woman elected to the U.S. Congress (from Montana). She took principled stands against U.S. entry into both world wars, and in 1968 at age eighty-seven, she led her antiwar brigade in a march against the war in Vietnam. She was Jeanette

_____.

y. Against fierce opposition, she established the first birth-control clinic in the U.S. (in Brooklyn in 1916). Her life is a model of courage, and her name was _____.

## 81. The paradigm for human dignity and character as exemplified in a single film role:

The character was Atticus Finch. The film was based on a novel by Harper Lee. The actor who played Atticus was _____.

## 82. Happy Days.

An event in Germany on November 10, 1989, sent ripples of happiness throughout the world. What happened? _____

## 83. Cheap Crooks in Expensive Suits:

a. Sleaze in High Places Award: As governor of Maryland, he took payoffs from contractors. As vice-president, he mouthed words written by

William Safire, railing against the "nattering nabobs of negativism." He was _____.

b. Filthy McNasty Award for Bilking Widows and Orphans. He was the key figure in the Savings and Loan debacle of the 1980s, a rip-off taxpayers will be paying off until well into the next century. The head of Lincoln Savings, his name was Charles _____.

## 84. Most significant problem we leave our twenty-first-century progeny:

Paul Erlich saw it coming in the 1960s, and Margaret Sanger was jailed for advocating a hedge against it in 1916. The problem is, of course _____.

## 85. Most Successful Hippie Entrepreneurs:

Think Vermont. Think Cherry Garcia. Then name the company. _____

## 86. Hitlerian Idea Most Popular With Americans:

It was introduced in 1936. We later called it a "bug." The idea behind it was prompted by Hitler. It was _____.

## 87. Best Fabian Socialist Irish vegetarian dramatist of the century:

He was, of course, George Bernard Shaw. *My Fair Lady*, the Broadway hit of the 1950s, was based on his 1913 play called _____.

## 88. Most Significant Mathematical Equation of the Century:

Einstein published it in 1905. It was _____.

## 89. Most Monstrous Chicken Farmer of the Century:

After that, he headed the SS. He was _____.

## 90. Best Poem of World War I:

"Dulce et Decorum Est" is the title. The poet was _____.

## 91. It Doesn't Take a Rocket Scientist . . .

a. "Outside of the killings, we have one of the lowest crime rates." The speaker was the mayor of the District of Columbia in 1989. He was _____.

b. "I stand by all the misstatements." The speaker was the vice-president in 1989. He was _____.

c. "Things are more the way they are now than they've ever been before." To his credit, the speaker of these lines also warned the nation of the growing "military-industrial" complex as he ended his presidency. He was _____.

d. "He is a casting director's ideal for a running mate." That was *The New York Times* describing McGovern's first running mate in 1972, the one who had undergone electroshock therapy for depression. Remember him? _____

## 92. Seven-Year Feast:

In 1996, he was awarded a contract of $120 million to throw rubber balls through hoops. This sum did not include fees paid for his endorsement of Pepsi, Reebok, and other products. His name? _____

## 93. The Best Twentieth-Century American Play:

It's about a man "way out in the blue, riding on a smile and a shoeshine." The playwright was _____ and the play is _____.

## 94. The Model for Wunderkinder Who Would Follow Him:

F. Scott Fitzgerald based his novel *The Last Tycoon* on him, and an award is given in his name each year at the Oscars. He became studio chief of Universal Pictures at twenty-one. He was _____.

## 95. Tackiest Cultural Phenomenon of the Last Quarter-Century:

Jenny Jones, Jerry Springer, and Ricky Lake are just some of the people who were part of it.

_____

## 96. Best President-to-Populace Communication:

When Franklin Roosevelt went on the radio, his talks were called _____

## 97. Most shamefully racist jury verdicts:

a. A Simi Valley jury vindicated Stacey Koon et al. in the case of the beating of _____.

b. Some jurors later attended a fund-raising soiree at the defendant's home in Brentwood, where he lived on _____ Drive.

c. Nine black men were convicted by an all-white jury in Alabama in 1931. Together, they are remembered by the name of the town where they were tried. They were called "the _____ Boys."

## 98. Best musical groups of the century.

a. (Rock category) The drummer's name was Starkey, and he originally dreamed of owning a beauty parlor. The group was _____.

b. (Jazz category/quartets) Heath, Kay, Jackson, and Lewis were collectively known as _____.

c. (Western Swing category) Bob Wills set the standard here. Can you name his backup band? _____

d. (Jazz category/quintets) In the 1920s, Louis Armstrong's band was called _____.

e. (Reggae category) The band was called the Wailers. The leader was the legendary _____.

## 99. Worst Urban Visual Pollution Aside from Billboards:

It's called graffiti, but the people who do it call themselves _____.

## 100. Technological Innovation That Has Prompted and Will Continue to Prompt the Most Change:

The microchip made it all possible. Steven Jobs was a midwife at its birth. It is the _____.

## BONUS SERIES: TEN NOVELS THAT MADE A DIFFERENCE

For about thirty years, it has been part of the conventional wisdom to say that the novel is dead, and it may be true that fiction does not command the power it once did (though more new novels are published each year than ever before). Dead or not, novels have left their stamp on this century, as they did in the nineteenth century. It may be that the power of novels has been even greater in this century. Surely they reached more people. And some of those novels prompted legislation, changed social attitudes, ushered in vast changes in cultural attitudes. They weren't necessarily always the best novels, but they had distinctive power to record or encourage changes in the ways we acted or thought.

The books below all cast long shades, influencing the way we thought and what we were to read in the decades that came after each of them.

Though their quality may vary, these are all novels that made a difference.

### 1. Novel that made a difference, 1900–10:

This Upton Sinclair novel created reform in the meat-packing industry. _____

### 2. Novel that made a difference, 1910–20:

Herman Hesse's novel spoke to young people in 1919, and even more loudly to the hippies of the 1960s. It concerns the coming of age of Emil Sinclair. Rock group Santana found the title of one of their albums in its pages. The name of the novel? _____

### 3. Novel that made a difference, 1920–30:

Sinclair Lewis's mythical Gopher Prairie still shapes how we think of small-town life, even if we haven't read it. _____

### 4. Novel that made a difference, 1930–40:

It was about the Joad family, _____

### 5. Novel that made a difference, 1940–50:

George Orwell's dystopia _____

### 6. Novel that made a difference, 1950–60:

Kerouac's Sal Paradise and Dean Moriarty drove the country into the 1960s. _____

### 7. Novel that made a difference, 1960–70:

The absurdity of Yossarian's struggles fueled the sentiments of the antiwar movement. Joseph Heller wrote it. _____

### 8. Novel that made a difference, 1970–80:

Erica Jong's first novel broke ground in portraying unbridled female sexuality. That best-selling novel was _____.

### 9. Novel that made a difference, 1980–90:

In his first novel, William Gibson helped create a style that came to be called "cyberpunk," a sci-fi,

techy, noirish futurism. The novel was called
_____.

**10.** Novel that made a difference, 1990–2000:

This Richard Ford novel won a Pulitzer Prize and helped instruct aging boomers in how to become adults. The novel was_____.

## ANSWERS

### THE BEST AND THE WORST

**1.** Most idealistic act of voluntary courage was: The International Brigades. The American contingent was called the Abraham Lincoln Brigade. They suffered stunning losses fighting a better-equipped foe, supplied by the Third Reich.

**2.** Most arrogant military leader was: General Douglas MacArthur.

**3.** Best rock 'n' roll album was: The Stones' *Let It Bleed*, 1969.

**4.** Best jazz album was: Miles Davis, *Kind of Blue.*

**5.** Most memorable oration: When King delivered the speech in 1963, he was the leader of the Southern Christian Leadership Conference.

**6.** Best World War II song was: "We'll Meet Again."

**7.** Best adventure film was: *Treasure of Sierra Madre*, 1948.

**8.** Best comedy team was: (See dedication page for visual answer.)

**9.** Worst film director was: Ed Wood.

**10.** Most acclaimed film was: *Citizen Kane*, Orson Welles, director.

**11.** Slimiest lawyer was: Roy Cohn. His list of perfidies is too lengthy to go into here, but as an opportunist without apparent ethics or character, he's hard to beat. Among other things, he was noted for gay-bashing, though he was, himself, a homosexual.

**12.** Most enduring screen lovers were: Humphrey Bogart and Ingrid Bergman.

**13.** Most corrupt head of a federal agency was: J. Edgar Hoover.

**14.** Most overblown trial was: O. J. Simpson's.

15. American hero with Nazi sympathies was: Charles Lindbergh. Lindbergh accepted an award from the Nazi government in Germany in 1938, and he was a leader of the pro-Nazi "America First" movement until the U.S. entered the war in 1941. During the war, he flew fifty combat missions against the Japanese in the Pacific.

16. Most overblown singer was: Neil Diamond.

17. Officer in command at My Lai was: Lieutenant William Calley.

18. Justice was bought off by: Michael Jackson.

19. Most dignified sports hero was: Arthur Ashe.

20. Best-known Native American athlete was: Jim Thorpe.

21. Meanest baseball player was: Ty Cobb, one of the first four men to be inducted into the Baseball Hall of Fame.

22. The nerd inspiration was: Bill Gates, multibillionaire.

23. Best jazz composition was: " 'Round Midnight.' "

24. Most annoying ego was: Ross Perot.

25. Most underrated western was: *One-Eyed Jacks*.

26. The man who painted *Guernica* was: Pablo Picasso.

27. Best big-band song was: "Take the A Train."

28. Best WWII novel was: *The Naked and the Dead*.

29. Best WWI novel was: *All Quiet on the Western Front*.

30. Best Vietnam War novel was: *Going After Cacciato*.

31. Best blues guitarist was: Buddy Guy.

32. Best '50s TV sitcom was: *The Honeymooners*.

33. Best '60s TV sitcom was: *The Andy Griffith Show* (but only until 1965, when Don Knotts left).

34. Best '70s TV sitcom was: *The Mary Tyler Moore Show*.

35. Best '80s TV sitcom was: *Cheers*.

36. Best '90s TV sitcom was: *Seinfeld*.

37. Genius comedians were: a. Lenny Bruce and b. Richard Pryor.

38. Best visual record of the Depression was that of: Dorthea Lange.

39. Most overrated movie beauty was: Julia Roberts.

40. Best gangster films were: *The Godfather I* and *II*, but definitely not *III*.

41. Worst betrayal of the principle that no man is above the law was: the pardon of Richard Nixon.

42. Worst war criminal of WWII was: Dr. Josef Mengele.

43. Actor most likely to shout his lines was: Al Pacino.

44. Restraint-in-the-Face-of-Criticism Award goes to: Hillary Clinton.

45. Most principled first lady was: Eleanor Roosevelt.

46. Largest selling pop song was "Candle in the Wind," sung by Elton John.

47. Most arrogant secretary of state was: Henry Kissinger.

48. Best child actor was: Ron Howard.

49. Handsomest president was: Warren Gamaliel Harding. (Though his administration was entirely undistinguished, except for the degree of corruption, it was said of him that he looked more like a president than any other. Theodore Roosevelt's grown daughter disagreed, however. She said he looked like a "debauched Roman emperor.")

50. Worst musical trend was: rap music, an oxymoron. (Note: I am aware that I risk looking stupid with each of these categorical absolutes. Though I'm quite committed to the opinion rendered in this particular question, my daughter—who did the illustrations for this book—assures me that there is some rap music that is not moronic and misogynistic, to which I say, "Ok, fine.")

51. Most romantic revolutionary figure was: Che Guevara

52. Most consistently inventive comic strip was: *The Far Side.*

53. Best not fully realized idea was: The United Nations.

54. Postage stamp icons were: James Dean and Marilyn Monroe.

55. Best "race issue" novel was: *Invisible Man.*

56. "Short-man complex" lawyer was: F. Lee Bailey. (Note: When Bailey went to jail in 1996, Patty Hearst, one of his former clients, said: "I enjoyed watching him taken off handcuffed and manacled. It seemed so properly humiliating.")

57. Biggest East Coast jerk was: Joey Buttafuco.

58. Biggest West Coast jerk was: Sonny Bono, political opportunist and bad singer.

59. Best example of guy trying to impress was: Mark Fuhrman.

60. Most pathetic end of a war hero was that of: Ira Hayes.

61. Best environment wakeup call was: *Silent Spring*.

62. Best American lawyer was: Clarence Darrow.

63. "Grace Under Pressure" Award goes to: Jackie Robinson.

64. "Grace Under Pressure" runner-up was: Branch Rickey.

65. Worst "sensitive guy" novel was: *Bridges of Madison County*.

66. Worst presidential appeal for support was from: Lyndon Johnson.

67. Weakest stated qualifications for high office is from: Richard Nixon.

68. Best ex-president was: Jimmy Carter.

69. Lucky Breaks.

a. Elected official who saved our bacon: Roosevelt

b. Soviet premier who saved our bacon: Nikita Khrushchev

70. The happy days were: May 8, 1945, was VE Day; August 14, 1945, was VJ Day.

71. The bad stuff was: Napalm.

72. Most influential philosophy was: existentialism.

73. The poet who wrote and read the worst inaugural poem was: Maya Angelou.

74. Most influential jazz pioneer was: Charlie Parker, bebop pathfinder.

75. Best love poet was: Pablo Neruda.

76. Most obnoxious comedians were: a. Jim Carrey and b. Martin Lawrence.

77. Best American conservationist 1900–50 was: Theodore Roosevelt.

78. "If At First You Don't Succeed" Award goes to: Harold Stassen.

79. Long-term presidential legacies were: a. erosion of public trust division, Richard Nixon; b. economic consequences division, Ronald Reagan.

## 80. Profiles in Courage.

a. South African martyr: Steven Biko

b. United Farm Worker leader: Cesar Chavez

c. Nicaraguan freedom fighter: Augusto Sandino

d. Spanish Civil War heroine: La Pasionara

e. Indian salt march leader: Mohandas Gandhi

f. Author of *The Feminine Mystique*: Betty Friedan

g. Dustbowl troubadour: Woody Guthrie

h. Coal strike organizer: Mother Jones

i. "Don't mourn, organize," the words of: Joe Hill

j. Pentagon Papers publicist: Daniel Ellsberg

k. Anti-Hitler coup leader: Claus von Stauffenberg

l. Guatemalan Nobel Peace Prize winner: Rigoberta Menchu

m. Courageous LA truck driver: Reginald Denny

n. Amsterdam diarist: Anne Frank

o. Chinese courage: Tiananmen Square

p. Philippine heroine: Corazon Aquino

q. The lonely Oregon antiwar senator: Wayne Morse

r. British pacifist philosopher: Bertrand Russell

s. Socialist party candidate; Eugene V. Debs

t. Australian pediatrician: Helen Caldicott

u. The man who made the decision to use atomic weapons against civilians: Harry S Truman (actually, this was not my choice; it was my father's. Since he was on a ship in the Pacific Theater of war at the time Truman made this decision, I defer to Dad's judgment on this matter.)

v. Chain-smoking broadcaster: Edward R. Murrow

w. Eloquent World War II leader: Winston Churchill

x. First woman elected to Congress: Jeannette Rankin

y. Birth-control pioneer: Margaret Sanger

81. **Film character exemplifying dignity was played by: Gregory Peck**

82. **Happy days. November 10, 1989: The fall of the Berlin Wall**

83. **Cheap crooks. a. Sleaze; Spiro Agnew; b. McNasty: Charles Keating**

84. **Biggest problem passed on to the next century: Overpopulation**

85. **Hippie entrepreneurs: Ben and Jerry's (begun in 1978 with a borrowed twelve thousand dollars by Ben Cohen and Jerry Greenfield)**

86. **Popular Hitlerian idea: the Volkswagen**

87. **Irish vegetarian playwright's 1913 play: *Pygmalion***

88. **Most significant equation: $E = MC^2$**

89. **Nastiest former chicken farmer: Heinrich Himmler**

90. **Best poem of WWI. The title, in its entirety, means "It is sweet and fitting to die for the fatherland." The poet who gave the lie to the words was Wilfred Owen.**

## 91. No rocket scientists.

a. DC Mayor in 1989: Marion Barry

b. VP in 1989: Dan Quayle

c. President who thought "things are more the way they are now than they've ever been before": Dwight Eisenhower

d. McGovern's first running mate: Thomas Eagleton

## 92. Seven-year feast. The $120 million dollar baby: Shaquille O'Neal

## 93. Best American play: Arthur Miller, *Death of a Salesman*

## 94. Mogul who became studio chief of Universal Pictures at twenty-one: Irving Thalberg

## 95. Tackiest cultural phenom: Daytime TV talk shows (Question: What do you get when you mate Jerry Springer and Jenny Jones? Answer: primordial ooze.)

## 96. Roosevelt on the radio: fireside chats

## 97. Racist verdicts:

a. Rodney King beating trial

b. O. J. Simpson lived on Rockingham Drive

c. "The Scottsboro Boys"

## 98. Best musical groups of the century

a. (Rock category) Starkey was Ringo Starr of the Beatles.

b. (Jazz category/quartets) Heath, Kay, Jackson, and Lewis were collectively known as the Modern Jazz Quartet.

c. (Western Swing category) Bob Wills and His Texas Playboys

d. (Jazz category/quintets) Satchmo's '20s band: the Hot 5

e. (Reggae category) Bob Marley and The Wailers

## 99. Visual pollution: graffiti, the work of taggers

## 100. Techno innovation that has prompted and will prompt the most change: the personal computer

## BONUS SERIES: TEN NOVELS THAT MADE A DIFFERENCE

1. 1900–10: Upton Sinclair's *The Jungle*

2. 1910–20: Herman Hesse's *Demian* (the Santana album was *Abraxas*)

3. 1920–30: Sinclair Lewis's *Main Street*

4. 1930–40: Steinbeck's *The Grapes of Wrath*

5. 1940–50: George Orwell's *1984*

6. 1950–60: Jack Kerouac's *On the Road*

7. 1960–70: Joseph Heller's *Catch-22*

8. 1970–80: Erica Jong's *Fear of Flying*

9. 1980–90: William Gibson's *Neuromancer*

10. 1990–2000: Richard Ford's *Independence Day*

Scoring: If you knew them all, then score yourself "very good." If you knew them all, and agreed with the selections in all the categories, then score yourself "the best."

If you knew 80 of these, your score was "good."

If you knew fewer than 60, score yourself poor. If you knew fewer than 60 of these, and disagreed with most of the categorizations, score yourself "the worst."

U.S. Vet, Vietnam Memorial, 1982

# THE MORE THINGS CHANGED . . .

Sensible and responsible women do not want to vote.

—Grover Cleveland, 1905

Direct thought is not an attribute of femininity. In this, woman is now centuries . . . behind man.

—Thomas Edison, 1912

The woman who doesn't want to make a home is undermining our nation.

—Mrs. Thomas A. Edison, 1930

A woman must accept herself as a woman and know she is dependent on a man. There is no fantasy in her mind about being an independent woman, a contradiction in terms.

—*Modern Woman*, Marynia Farnham and Ludwig Lundberg, 1947

Of all the accomplishments of the American woman, the one she brings off with the most spectacular success is having babies.

—*Life*, 1956

Let me make one thing perfectly clear. I wouldn't want to wake up next to a lady pipe fitter.

—Richard Nixon, 1972

If combat means living in a ditch, females have biological problems staying in a ditch for thirty days because they get infections. . . . Males are biologically driven to go out and hunt giraffes.

—Newt Gingrich, 1995

# Epilogue:
# We're History

One of my most distinct early memories is of looking down my street until it curved out of sight and I could see no farther. The limits of my experience and knowledge were marked by that bend in the road, and I remember the powerful curiosity I had about what lay beyond it, and beyond that.

But my grandparents knew, and I knew they knew. When they left after a visit, I would watch their car disappear into that mystery beyond the curve.

Each day I worked on this book, I have been haunted by my grandparents' people, a generation that came in with the century. When I was a kid, I hungered for their approval. After all, they had been to places I could never know, had lived in times I glimpsed only in movies.

Now I am the age they were when I was a kid, and all but a handful of them have gone around another bend, and I cannot see around this curve, either.

Their early times seem remote, in some ways impossibly remote. Most of what I know, most of what is knowable of their young time is now bookishly acquired, and books are resolute in their inability to render the whole truth, no matter the dedication and sincerity of writers. What it was like to be a young man or woman in an America without many bathtubs, cars, or telephones, without television or satellites overhead requires an act of determined imagination.

"In living memory." That was the first thought I had for this book's title. But the living memory is passing. The last survivors of the *Titanic* now number but a few. The last survivors of the 1906 San Francisco earthquake are dwindling in number. Those who remember the Stock Market Crash of 1929 are now getting quite elderly. Soon the living memory will be gone, and with that living memory we lose the mundane details that humanize the past. Though we can play a ragtime song on our CD players, we will never know the sense of what that music sounded like when it was new, when it sounded a threat to the status quo. Though we can look at a picture of a woman with bobbed hair in the 1920s, we cannot know the twinges of danger and excitement her defiance of the standards of the day elicited in those who saw her.

But the imagination can be stirred to re-create a sense of those times gone by. Once, more than a quarter-century ago, my friend Steve and I went to a small club in Berkeley for an evening of live jazz. The club, now defunct, was smoky and overheated, humming with the distracted energy and tension that seemed a part of the very air in that city and time. Even after the music started, the place was noisy with conversation, an excess of vitality confined in too-close quarters.

But, about ten minutes into their set, the musicians caught fire. The sax player and the guitar player began to trade solos with escalating intimacy, encouraging each other to genuine discoveries of music and feeling. The joint quieted. Even the most desperate pickup artists were put to silence. We all knew we were hearing something not often heard, something more than technique, more than mastery of instruments, more than craft. And we paid it the reverence such rare moments of honesty and heart deserve.

The musicians were inspired that night; their powers of invention seemed limitless. I looked around the room for recording equipment. This had to be caught on tape, I thought. It was magical, unlikely to ever come together quite like this again, and too good to be expended on this Friday night Berkeley crowd. But there was no recording equipment.

Those players took it as far as it could go, nearly a half-hour of improvisation, and when they found their way back to the main melody and brought it to a close, the house exploded in applause. The musicians were bathed in sweat, but they were beaming, surprised themselves at what had just happened.

Now, all these years later, with the century passing and me grown older with it, I know that the special music of that evening was recorded. It recorded itself on me, and I pass it on. Though it felt as though the music was being lost, evaporating into the smoky air of that club, it lives in me. And, in some indefinable way, it lives apart from me, too.

We're history, all of us who lived these times. Our lives are the sum total of what we recorded, all we took in, all we pass along. The past has registered itself on us. Though much may be lost, more is left than we tend to think. This book was made in hopes of revivifying the past, of putting the needle down on the grooves of recordings we made long ago.

# Index